МАТЧ НА ЗВАНИЕ ЧЕМПИОНА МИРА
FIDE
КАРПОВ-КАСПАРОВ
МОСКВА'85

This book belongs to:-
Yashowanto N. Ghosh
Yashowanto N. Ghosh
March 10, 1987

CHESS LIBRARY (VOL. 4)
(Not for glory,
Not for fame,
But for safety
I write my name.
—Yashowanto N. Ghosh.)

Yuri AVERBAKH
Mark TAIMANOV

KARPOV

The World Chess Championship

KASPAROV

Moscow 85

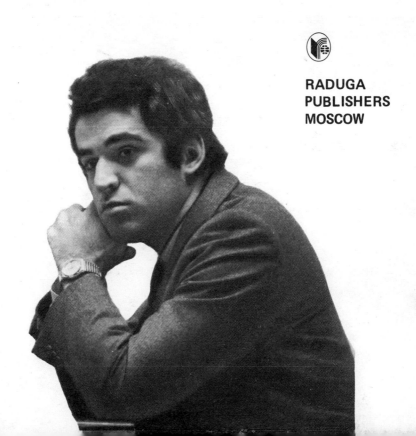

RADUGA
PUBLISHERS
MOSCOW

Translated from the Russian
Edited by Graham Whittaker and Yevgeny Kopytkin

Юрий Авербах, Марк Тайманов
Матч на звание чемпиона мира по шахматам:
Карпов — Каспаров. Москва — 85
На английском языке
© Издательство "Физкультура и спорт", 1986
Редакция литературы по спорту и туризму

Editor of the Russian text *Valeri Yefremov*
Designed by *Vladimir Miroshnichenko*
Photographs by *Dmitri Donskoy* and *Yuri Rost*
Art Editor *Liubov Cheltsova*

A $\dfrac{4202000000-347}{031(05)-86}$ 056—86

ISBN 5-05-000553-1

CONTENTS

Mark Taimanov

THE DUEL FOR OLYMPUS

A Trip into the Past

> How splendid to be king, ruling
> not by right of succession or by
> chance plebiscite, but by the
> power of one's own mind.
>
> *Alexander Kuprin*

It is not surprising that the title of world chess champion has always had an aura of exclusiveness about it. History tells us the names of a whole legion of exceptional chess maestros, but the honour of wearing the crown has been given to very few, the few outstanding personalities who have had not only great talent, but also powerful intellect, originality and explosive energy. A champion is not only admired, he is also a teacher, and he is imitated.

There have only been twelve such idols, only twelve from among the countless multitudes of chess devotees throughout the world.

But the title itself is not yet a hundred years old. It was officially established in 1886, and was conferred on the great German chess master Wilhelm Steinitz after his defeat of Johann Zukertort in a match of twenty games.

Before Steinitz, of course, there were famous names in the world of chess, masters of the game who overcame all opposition. Pedantic historians even tell us the date of the first match of "international significance", a match played in Rome in 1560 between the Italian Giovanni Leonardo and the Spaniard Ruy López. And the fame of such outstanding chess virtuosos of the eighteenth and nineteenth centuries as Francois André Danican Philidor, Paul Morphy and Adolf Anderssen has not faded even to this day. They are still referred to as "the uncrowned kings of chess"; and Steinitz himself was for a long time considered the strongest player in the world, without him being given an official title. But fate decided that he was the man, in the words of Grandmaster Alexander Kotov, "to bring to a close one epoch, and to open another". When Steinitz was proclaimed world champion, so began the "genealogy" of a chess "dynasty".

The man who became world champion immediately acquired great authority. Interest in chess contests "at the highest level" was almost as singular in those distant times as it is today. For example, the *International Chess Magazine* in 1886 described the events surrounding the first match for the world title in the following words: "A special committee of the Manhattan Chess Club was formed to work out all the details of the contest. Several thousand programmes, including the rules under which the match was to be played, were printed. Each move was reproduced on a wall-board measuring four square feet. The moves were immediately transmitted not only to clubs in various American towns but also to London. The table on which the match was played had once belonged to the legendary Paul Morphy."

Such was the way of things in days long passed, almost a century ago. In those days, incidentally, it was decided that henceforth the title of world champion would be decided between the current champion and one challenger, in a match with a mutually agreed number of games. Unfortunately this was the only rule concerning the match for the world title, and it was clearly inadequate; but the chess world was not yet ready for more.

The first chess kings were given many rights, without being bound by any obligations. They chose their own opponents from among the potential challengers, they were allowed to name the time and place to play and, perhaps most importantly, they set the financial terms on which they would play. This sometimes led to people playing for the world title who had little or no right to it, while such great players as Akiba Rubinstein, Richard Réti, Aron Nimzowitsch and many others never had the opportunity to challenge the champion.

Unfortunately the chess kings did not always have regard to the principles of fair play; they were subject to human weaknesses just as much as other mortals, and at times they looked after their own interests to the detriment of world chess as a whole. Even such chess genii as José Raúl Capablanca and Alexander Alekhine...

The turning point came only after the Second World War, and was brought about by two important events. Firstly the powerful chess organisation of the Soviet Union joined FIDE; and secondly the world title was won by the acknowledged champion of Soviet chess, Mikhail Botvinnik.

I remember that happy day, the 9th of May, 1948. It was in Moscow, the Hall of Columns in the House of Trade Unions, the contest between the five strongest Grandmasters in the world was coming to its climax. After the death of the reigning champion, Alexander Alekhine, FIDE was forced to amend the traditional form of a two-way contest and to organise a tournament-match to find the new world champion. Botvinnik, who was leading the tournament, was to play the ex-champion Max Euwe from Holland. Botvinnik needed only to draw the game to win the world title. The hall was full to overflowing, everyone held their breath, waiting for the denouement. Then Botvinnik played b2-b4, the players exchanged a few words, shook hands, and the hall broke into a tumult. The match referee, an old chess and scientific colleague of Botvinnik, the highly respected Yugoslav professor Milan Vidmar, had difficulty making himself heard above the noise of the crowd as he proclaimed Botvinnik the world champion. Everyone jumped out of their seats in a single burst of enthusiasm, complete strangers embraced one another and rejoiced together.

A new era had begun in the history of chess, the era of the Soviet chess masters. For almost a quarter of a century the Soviet hold on the world title was unquestioned; all the champions and all the challengers were pupils of the Soviet chess school.

When Botvinnik "came to power", the problem of the rules surrounding the contest for the world title was resolved. At the suggestion of the new champion, FIDE drew up a new code which provided for fair play and democracy in choosing challengers. A strict multi-stage system of selection opened the way to the chess throne to any player from any corner of the world, and guaranteed impartiality. Obligations were now imposed on the champion; he was no longer allowed to dictate the terms under which he would defend his title, a defence, which he now had to make at least once every three years, with the challenger being the person who showed his superiority over all the other "potential" challengers.

The objectivity of this system has been firmly corroborated in practice. In the twelve world-title matches played under the new rules, the struggle has always been exceptionally tough, and the challengers have proved themselves worthy opponents for the champions. Suffice it to say that the champions have won only three times, there have been two matches drawn and the challengers have won the remaining seven!

In the 24 years of the Soviet monopoly of the world title, the crown changed heads more than once. Apart from Botvinnik, the title has been held by Vasili Smyslov, Mikhail Tal, Tigran Petrosyan and Boris Spasski. But Botvinnik reigned longest of all. With two intervals of a year each, when he—as it were—merely "loaned" the title, he was the world champion for a total of fifteen years! This was a veritable triumph. Only Emanuel Lasker had held the title longer, but in those days,

9

around the beginning of the present century, the opposition was incomparably weaker and there were really only three or four serious claimants to the title, whereas between the late 1940s and the early 1960s the number of such claimants had increased nearly tenfold. And the nature of the struggle for the title had become immeasurably sharper. Botvinnik himself once said: "Playing for the world title takes a whole year off your life". And he played seven times!

A monopoly in anything cannot last for ever, and the early 1970s saw the beginning of a period of disappointment even among the Soviet chess players. In the West there appeared a Grandmaster capable of rocking the accustomed alignment of forces: the brilliant American Robert Fischer (when I write about him it is unfortunately in the past tense, for such was his tragic fate: he left the world of chess while still in his prime).

Bobby Fischer's career was as transient as it was glittering. He drew the attention of the chess world at an early age, and by the age of sixteen he was already considered to be a challenger for the world title. After a series of brilliant tournament wins, he played against Boris Spasski in 1972 and became world champion; it seemed then that "Fischer's era" was going to be a prolonged reign. It was beyond the strength of the older generation to keep up with him, and no one of the younger generation had showed themselves seriously capable of challenging him. And Fischer himself was convinced that his crown was secure: when Max Euwe expressed the opinion that Fischer would remain champion for 9 years, the champion took offence, and commented: "Surely Mr. Euwe does not expect me to die so soon?"

But fate had something else in store.

The first, dramatic surprise was Fischer's spiritual crisis, when he saw the world title as his absolutely, and refused point-blank to take part in any matches.

The other, happier surprise was the mercurial rise of the young Anatoly Karpov.

When he first began his ascent towards the chess Olympus, he did not set himself to aim for the world title; "I'm not in that class yet", he remarked modestly in 1973. But the improbable happened, and like a fairy-tale knight he gathered strength "not day by day, but hour by hour", and within two years he had grown to be a Grandmaster in a class of his own, and to be the main challenger for the chess king's crown. It was probably the very fairy-tale nature of Karpov's successes which undermined the American champion's usual confidence, and which finally led to him refusing to meet Karpov in defence of his title.

The president of FIDE, Dr. Euwe, tried in vain to persuade Fischer to meet his challenger across the chess board, and the match, which the chess world awaited with such interest, was not destined to take place. In accordance with the rules of FIDE, therefore, Anatoly Karpov was proclaimed world champion in the spring of 1975. After a break of three years the crown returned to Moscow.

But public opinion suffers from inertia, and the aura of the deposed champion did not fade immediately. Although Karpov's achievements were unquestioned, the world expected new proofs of his right to the title. And Karpov, despite his relatively young years, fully understood this. Many years later, when at the height of his fame, he commented: "When I became world champion without having played Fischer, I vowed that I would prove that the title was not a gift of fate, that I was worthy of it. And I entered, and won, the vast majority of tournaments open to me, although the world champion is by no means obliged to win every competition."

Anatoly Karpov can indeed say with a clear conscience that he fulfilled the promise he made when he took the world title, the promise to be an active chess player, and to play matches in every corner of the world, so that masters and Grandmasters could try their strength against him, learn from him and perhaps, in their turn, teach him something.

During the years of his reign Anatoly Karpov was a continual participant in all the most difficult, responsible and prestigious competitions. His achievements are quite staggering: in his ten years as champion he won more than thirty tournaments, as well as defending his throne twice! And not one of his eleven predecessors can really claim such an impressive record as that.

But the life of a champion is not easy, and there is no time to rest on his laurels. He must show his supremacy again and again. As Vasili Smyslov once said: "Reaching the throne requires titanic strength and colossal effort, but wearing the crown imposes even greater obligations."

Let the Battle Commence!

The World Champion, besides his well-deserved and unquestioned priveleges, has many obligations, the most important of which is that he defends his title once every three (but henceforth, every two!) years. Thus we have the tradition of world-title matches, the high points in the chess calendar.

The duels between the strongest Grandmasters arouse world-wide interest not only for their sporting significance. They further the development of the game, they form styles, they resolve many theoretical problems and they stimulate new ideas. Every world-title match is a unique landmark in the evolution of chess.

But these matches in the past, for all their importance, have not all been equal in stature. The contests reached a peak of creative sharpness only when the two sides were equally strong and in the necessary state of inspirational élan. And history provides us with but few such contests.

In days of old the credentials of the challenger did not always match the high class of play required of him. At other times either the champion or the challenger would not be at the peak of his ability. And a frequent upset of the creative balance between the players would be the "age factor", so inexorable in such a stiff ordeal.

Let us take, for example, Karpov's last two defences of his title (Baguio-City-78 and Merano-81) which were dramatic and, in their way, quite rich in content: nevertheless, the final outcome was never in serious doubt. The gripping finale in Baguio was more an intriguing episode than the result of a natural development of events. At the decisive moment Karpov gave his opponent no chance.

But it was a different matter altogether when the young Garri Kasparov appeared on the chess scene. It soon became apparent that we were looking at a Grandmaster of exceptional talent, capable of posing a serious threat to the Champion. Kasparov's rise was very reminiscent of Karpov's own earlier career: each had begun playing chess at an early age, each became a chess master at fifteen and—a little later—world youth champion and a Grandmaster, and hardly had each turned twenty when he began his ascent of the chess Olympus.

When Karpov first took the Champion's laurels, Garri Kasparov was only just twelve; and less than a decade later the two men's achievements were equally brilliant. Kasparov had played a total of 88 matches against the élite of the chess world (apart from the World Champion), and had won 41 matches, drawn 44, and lost only three! Like Karpov before him, Kasparov overcame the selection hurdle at the first attempt, with victories over Belyavsky, Korchnoi and Smyslov, and earned himself the right to throw out a challenge to the Champion.

It would seem that history itself predetermined their rivalry, and when the match between Karpov and Kasparov was to become a reality the chess world was gripped by a foretaste of extraordinary impressions. Stepping into the ring were Grandmasters with auras of recognition and fame, full of energy and creative power, capable of striking with new and hitherto unseen facets of their talents.

The duel was often compared to the unforgettable, titanic match in 1927 between Capablanca and Alekhine in Buenos Aires. With all the conventions of comparison, the characteristic styles of the players were automatically seen to have common features. The clear, classical method of Karpov's play and his crystalline technique are akin to the creative credo of Capablanca, while Kasparov's energetic thrust for the initiative, his audacity and strategic depth are closer to the principles of Alekhine's play.

But it is interesting to note that other associations appeared in chess commentaries. One commentator noticed that the strict mental discipline of Karpov was a feature of Botvinnik's game, and that Lasker provided a model for Karpov's finesse of psychological nuances. Kasparov was often compared with Fischer in his younger years. The journal *Deutsche Schachzeitung*, for example, noted that Kasparov's exceptional combinational capabilities, his originality of design and enterprise, and his determination at crucial moments are very reminiscent of Fischer.

And this variety of parallels bears witness not only to the conventionality of such comparisons, but also to the breadth of these remarkable players' creative range. As Petrosyan once said: "Every Grandmaster (and especially an outstanding one) is an extremely complex personality, and the public conception of this personality does not always correspond to reality. Tal was not only 'sacrifice', Fischer—not only 'computer', and Petrosyan—not only 'caution'."

Chess today is such that a person can only become world champion if he holds the full arsenal of modern chess competition. Both Karpov and Kasparov, despite the differences in their approach, have a universal style.

Recently, Karpov admitted: "Gambling in the style of a chess musketeer ... is not to my liking." But if we look, for instance, at his game against Timman in the London-84 tournament, what expression, excitement and fantasy we see!

On the other hand, how courageously Kasparov curbs his sometimes lashing temperament. He not only masters the clear, classical manner of play, but he has managed to make its charm a part of his very nature. And the two games with Smyslov which he won in such a delicate style, à la Smyslov, how well he wove them into the garland of his best performances which are generally so steeped in sharp tactical content. In his book *Ordeal by Time* (Baku, 1985), he writes modestly of these two games that they "merely illustrate the supremacy of two Bishops in the open".

In fact, these games showed new creative horizons in a dynamic Grandmaster.

Great chess players are by no means deprived of their individuality by the universal nature of their play. Being in possession of the whole range of the chess armoury, they each use this armoury in a completely different way. Both in theory and on the chess board each great player's approach to the game of chess is totally original.

Karpov comments: "I always play against a specific opponent. I learn about his strengths and weaknesses, and I always keep them in mind. The age of 'romantic' chess is gone. To win today, you have to know the psychology of your opponent."

Kasparov's programme reads somewhat differently: "I try to find the strongest move in every game, and for me it does not matter who my opponent is."

They are also different in character. Karpov is restrained, self-disciplined and composed. His energy and temperament are subjected to his will. He has the amazing ability to bring about the full mobilisation of his inner resources at the crucial moment.

Kasparov is dynamic, impulsive and adventurous. But his southern temperament does not hinder him at the chess board. He is wholly consumed by his passion for the process of creative struggle, by his love for the game, and he plays each game with the maximum concentration of his powers.

When two such highly individual and contradictory natures come together, the sharpness of competition reaches fever point, and the final outcome is totally unpredictable.

And this is why the world of chess, on the eve of the Karpov-Kasparov encounter, was in a state of unrest.

159 Days in Battle

> All records of duration have been broken. Even in terms of emotion.
>
> *Florencio Campomanes*

Interest in the struggle between Karpov and Kasparov was exceptional. Almost 500 journalists from 27 countries came together in Moscow to report on the match. It need hardly be said that the Hall of Columns was unable to accommodate all those wishing to see the struggle, and crowds of chess devotees daily besieged the House of Trade Unions in the hope of penetrating the "inner shrine" of the chess kingdom.

Before the match began Florencio Campomanes, president of FIDE, called it an historic contest. He told the two players: "The world expects you to produce diamonds on the chess board! " And to realise that these expectations were not in vain, one need only take a look at the games played; as the saying goes, it is better to see something once than to hear about it a hundred times.

This unforgettable duel broke all records of duration, persistence, physical and psychological strain. For almost half a year—from September 1984 to February 1985—it held the whole chess world in continual suspense. Its denouement, too, was without precedent: with 48 games played, and neither player having the requisite six victories, the match was stopped on the decision of Florencio Campomanes.

But one thing at a time. It is wrong of some critics to complain of the excessive number of draws and the outward monotony of play at various stages of the match. To judge the match from the bare statistics is as fruitless an exercise as, for instance, trying to appreciate an opera by reading the libretto, but not hearing the music or seeing the action on the stage. The Karpov-Kasparov duel was full of psychological tension and had a deep hidden meaning.

Let us recall the match's stunning opening. Without warning the contestants threw themselves into hand-to-hand combat with the adventure and temperament of Kasparov, who was striving to inflict a "preventive blow" on the Champion, being met by a cool and confident rebuff from Karpov. After nine games the score was already 4:0 in favour of Karpov, which gave the impression that his victory was just around the corner.

Foreign journalists were upset at having come so far only to witness what would be almost the shortest world-title match in the history of chess, and at having so little to write about. Who could have known at that stage that there were still several months of struggle ahead and that the final result of the Karpov-Kasparov duel would be delayed for a whole year!

Only later did the contestants themselves explain the riddle of the opening sessions. "I did not take into account," Kasparov admitted, "that a world-title match would have a special psychological intensity." And he added that he felt he had had a lack of match experience in comparison to his opponent. "In terms of the play I actually had more opportunities, but I made many serious errors."

Karpov was more categorical, saying that Kasparov had been affected by his excessive self-confidence before the match, and by the overly optimistic estimates of his chances by some commentators and journalists.

The next stage of the match, seventeen consecutive draws, was outwardly the most monotonous and sluggish; it was marked by Karpov having the upper hand. Kasparov was simply gaining time, settling down, renewing his strength and gaining match experience. But what of Karpov? Afterwards he justifiably complained that in this period of relative calm he had allowed himself to be drawn into lulling rhythm: "I had four wins in hand, and I wasn't looking to intensify the pace. Perhaps that was my mistake, I should have been prepared to 'strike while the iron was hot'."

It would seem that Karpov had set himself the task not merely of winning the match, but of winning it by the greatest possible score, 6:0. The World Champion considered that he had a rare opportunity of securing a psychological advantage for his future meetings with his main rival, and for this reason he allowed his creative talent to take a short rest.

But Karpov underestimated the character of his opponent. Although Kasparov found himself in a shaky position, he had sufficient courage and determination to continue the fight. Playing Black he managed to hold off the rather uninspired attacks of the World Champion, and as White he had little difficulty each time in reaching the salutary haven of a draw. This lasted for 50 days, a record run of barren results which became for Kasparov the best reassurance he could wish for.

But then Karpov won the twenty-seventh game in truly classical style to stretch his lead to 5:0, and no one doubted that the match was now close to its end. In this critical situation, however, Kasparov not only refused to give up, but, as though leaving all his illusions behind him, he threw off his psychological depression and began to play freely, with passion and flair. "I felt light and free," he commented afterwards, "and I only had to show the world that I could play chess and, perhaps, to convince myself as well."

Kasparov seemed to "get his second wind", he now had more energy and his creative imagination began to work. And even fortune smiled on him at last. After his lucky escape in the thirty-first game, the initiative in the match began to slowly but surely move over to the Challenger, and in the following game he won his first victory. And although the next fourteen games made no difference to the score, they did represent a change in the pattern of the match. Those watching clearly felt that Kasparov's energy and optimism were growing day by day, and Karpov's taste for the fight was slowly draining.

And after nearly fifty (!) games came the turning point. With two wins in a row Kasparov significantly reduced his deficit, and the situation in the match became perceptibly sharper. It was apparent that the duel had taken on a more dogged and unrelenting character. Everyone wondered how much more time, and how many more games, it would take to decide the winner. But we were not kept guessing for long, because the plot of this record-breaking match had one last twist in store.

On the 15th of February, 1985, Florencio Campomanes took the decision to stop the match, and to set a new date for September 1985. "The physical, and possibly also the psychological resources," he commented, "both of the participants themselves and of everyone connected with the match, are exhausted. A match of this calibre should not be turned into an endurance test."

Despite the representations made to him (a letter from Karpov in particular), the president stood by his decision, and a meeting of FIDE's executive committee, held in Tunis in May 1985, confirmed that Campomanes was empowered to make his decision of 15th February. The committee therefore agreed a series of measures concerning the rules for the forthcoming re-play.

Offers to stage the new match were made by Moscow, Marseilles and London, but after weighing the arguments carefully, FIDE decided to keep the duel in Moscow.

Not everyone agreed with the president's decision to stop the first match, least of all the two contestants. Both Karpov and Kasparov had reason to wish the match to continue: the World Champion had the score in his favour, while the Challenger could hope to continue his run of recent performances.

Nevertheless, despite the complexity of the president's position ("I cannot hope to please everyone," he commented), there is no denying that his motives were well-founded. The idea that the marathon contest had become unreasonable and inhuman, had been voiced by public opinion after four months of the titanic struggle. Letters, expressing concern for the health of the participants, had begun flooding into the offices of the match's organising committee, onto the desks of newspaper editors, and into the studios of Soviet television. One typical line: "We must not let this noble game turn into a trial of endurance. It is not a gladiatorial combat." The more partial supporters affirmed: "To heck with a sixth win! Karpov's won five, and that's enough. Have some pity on the two of them, they've got enough matches still to come! " Many doctors were worried: "A strain of this sort can lead to a severe nervous breakdown."

There could be only one decision: such an exhausting fight

went beyond the bounds of art, beyond the bounds of sport. Why do we need an endless test of nerves if we can have another match with a different, more reasonable set of rules? Chess can only win by it.

Now that we have witnessed the magnificent second match, all these arguments sound particularly convincing.

As for the inevitable disappointment arising from the uncompleted 159-day contest, to which so much time, energy and emotion was devoted, we should perhaps remember Schubert's "Unfinished Symphony": is it really any less of a masterpiece than his other, finished works? Thus, the creative legacy of the first match is truly invaluable. The games between these two remarkable players justify all the effort involved, despite the indeterminate result of the long and bitter struggle.

Long Live the Victor!

The whole chess world awaited the new match with particular interest and impatience; its memorable predecessor had left too many intriguing questions unanswered.

When the players took their places at the chess board as usual, all the outward signs were as before, the same friendly ritual of greetings, the same characteristic (though hardly perceptible) initial nerves. But there was a feeling that this was not simply a continuation of the previous battle. Everything was beginning afresh—new rules which would leave no time to "wait and see", new creative wares on both sides, and the two opponents made wiser by the experience of their last encounter.

Preparation for the new match acquired a special significance, and we should have this in mind before we look at the match itself. Judging by the comments of the two players, they had very similar approaches to their preparation.

"First and foremost," Karpov was already planning by the end of February, "I shall take a rest. Then I shall think through the course of this match and carefully analyse anew all 48 games; from this I shall draw my conclusions for the future, both in terms of my chess and from the psychological point of view. I shall probably take part in one tournament in the summer."

Kasparov set himself a similar programme: "Before our new match we have just half a year. In that time I shall not only have to rest and renew my energies, but I also need to prepare myself properly for September. At the end of May or beginning of June I want to take part in a major international tournament or to have a match against a Grandmaster. Then the preparation

proper will begin, the run-up to the world-title match."
There is no reason to doubt that these plans were fulfilled.
But for the most part they were like icebergs, hidden from
outside eyes. On the surface we saw only the public appearances.
Such appearances on the eve of important contests can have
more than one function. Does one play deliberately restricting
one's choice of openings and preserving one's creative energies?
Mikhail Botvinnik, for example, avoided this kind of preparation,
preferring private training sessions in matches against a sparring
partner with a particular style of play. On the other hand, taking
part in official competitions has its undoubted advantages, both
practically and psychologically. This singular "flexing of muscles"
is at one and the same time a demonstration of power, while
keeping one's new arsenal strictly secret, a confidence booster,
and a means of providing one's opponent with misinformation.
But this approach requires resolution and a strong belief in one's
abilities.

They achieved their aims with great assurance. Kasparov won
convincingly in Hamburg against Robert Huebner ($4\frac{1}{2}:1\frac{1}{2}$)
and in Belgrade against Ulf Andersson (4:2). Karpov took
first prize with consummate ease in a tournament of Grandmasters in Amsterdam.

In short, the practical preparations for September went quite
according to plan. And the hidden part of the iceberg? Let us
remind ourselves of the tasks before the players. They needed to
take into account the changed rules and to reconsider their
match strategy, to find more active strategical devices (in the
previous match, of course, the "shield" proved to be more
reliable than the "sword"); they had to make corrective
adjustments to their openings, to develop new ideas and, most
importantly, to use the experience gained in order to find the
key to their opponent's game.

In this respect we can say, with hindsight, that Kasparov was
more successful. Karpov himself admitted this after the match:
"Kasparov was particularly well-prepared. If we compare the
current match with the last one, we can see that he raised himself
up one step (or half a step), and I fell accordingly. Therefore the
difference between us was now greater."

Kasparov, too, was quite definite about this: "To a great
extent, my success was predetermined by the better quality of
my preparation, not so much in the opening play but in the
game in general."

In the match itself, however, this was not immediately
apparent. Let us look at the development of events, not at the
outward signs which the bare statistics show us, nor even at the

creative side of things, which an analysis of the games could give; let us look rather at the psychological plot of this dramatic duel.

The match began with an impressive win for Kasparov, the importance of which it would be difficult to overestimate. The first game, as we know, has particular implications: the mood and creativity of the players, in the initial stages of the match at least, usually depend on the result of the first game and on the way it was played. As Karpov commented: "The first to win a game in a world-title match has a serious psychological advantage." And this is confirmed by the statistics: in the history of world-title matches, those who have won the first game have gone on to win the match thirteen times, and only seven times have they lost the match as a whole.

Kasparov's success was even more significant because it was the first time during the whole contest that he had taken the lead. The win, which he had waited months for in the first match, had now come at the first time of trying. The game was a pointer to success; it was clear that Kasparov's star was in the ascendancy.

The next game confirmed this. Kasparov played brilliantly, with great intensity, boldness and imagination. And although Karpov showed marvellous ingenuity in a difficult defensive situation, the game was adjourned in a position which boded well for the Challenger. No one could have expected such a start to the match. Not even the optimistic Kasparov. Later he admitted: "When I won the first game, I was quite taken aback: it was so unexpected. I had been losing in the match which was stopped in February, and here I was in front. Then I was in a good position at the adjournment of the second game. I was in a state of euphoria and didn't know what to do with myself. We had not predicted anything like that."

Could this be why Kasparov took his failure after the resumption in the second game so much to heart? However that may be, his game showed a sharp deterioration after the disappointing draw. In the third game he soon showed reluctance to fight for the initiative, in the fourth he was losing concentration and failed to take his opportunity at the critical moment, and in the fifth he seemed to be in utter confusion.

The other side of the coin was that saving the second game allowed Karpov to survive the crisis of the opening period of the match and to adopt his more usual creative stance. It was as though there had been a redistribution of optimism, and this was reflected directly in the results.

Karpov convincingly won two games in a row; all commentators consider the fourth game to be his best creative achievement in the match, and the fifth game, most of all, was to the liking of Karpov himself.

A turning point had come. Karpov took up his usual position—in the lead. Kasparov, on the other hand, had anxious days ahead. In his book *Ordeal by Time* he describes this sort of situation: "Two defeats in a row can unsettle any player, even the most experienced of fighters."

To give him his due, Kasparov retained his self-possession and his courage, although—by his own admission—he had begun to doubt his ability to win, particularly between the sixth and tenth games. It was no easy task: "Not only to hold Anatoli Karpov in check when he was playing very strongly, but also to force a change in the match, to begin to dictate the game." But Kasparov accomplished just this. It was not simply a matter of him standing his ground and achieving "reassuring" draws five games in a row; far more important was the nature of the struggle in these games. Kasparov was by no means prepared to withdraw all his forces into defence in an attempt to gain time for an inner re-organisation, as was the case in the first match. Rather, he used every opportunity to draw the game boldly into the melee of irrational complications which he so wanted. In almost every game in this period he sacrificed pawns, and at the end of the ninth game he created a chess masterpiece. It may well be that this "unremarkable" episode (unremarkable since, as a draw, it did not affect the status quo) provided the psychological impetus for yet another turning point in the match. And perhaps for the first time Karpov was surpassed in the art of analysis, because on only the third move after the resumption of play he required more than thirty minutes thought. Although Karpov managed to take himself in hand and find the solution to the problem set before him, his inevitable frustration at the sudden turn of events was reflected in the following games. In the tenth game Karpov got caught up in Kasparov's whirlpool of tactical complications, he failed to take the chances which came his way, and at the end he even had one or two anxious moments to live through before he reached the safety of a draw. In the eleventh game he suffered what was probably the most catastrophic oversight of his whole chess career, losing a basically even contest in just two moves. And in the twelfth game Kasparov added to his opponent's misery in the shape of an entirely new opening combination. Within a relatively short space of time the World Champion experienced appreciable difficulties in all stages of his game. At the half-way point of the match the score was level, although the psychological advantage was firmly in Kasparov's favour.

By sheer will-power Karpov managed to hold the match in balance for a short time, the thirteenth, fourteenth and fifteenth games being drawn; but the crisis was fast approaching. It is interesting to note that after the outwardly rather unremarkable fifteenth game Kasparov, as he later admitted, thought he would eventually win: "It was after this game that I started to believe fairly confidently that I could win the match. Perhaps that was why I won the sixteenth game."

This was to be the day that the comparatively calm, even plot of the duel suddenly took a sharp turn. In the sixteenth game there was a change not only in the balance of the match, but also in the very nature of the fight. This was Kasparov's hour: he won one of the best games of his life!

Winning the sixteenth game was of exceptional importance: firstly, Kasparov won playing Black; secondly, he won convincingly and in fine style; thirdly, he vindicated his theoretical innovation; and finally, in the run-up to the finish line, he regained the lead.

But even then no one was predicting the outcome of the match. There were eight games still to play, and Kasparov's lead was only by one point—no guarantee of victory, especially as the World Champion would retain his title if the final result was a 12:12 draw.

Although the nature of the struggle witnessed the creative ascendancy of Kasparov, it would be wrong to ignore the enviable determination and composure of his opponent. It was now obvious that the next game won by either player would be of major significance at the finish.

The decisive moment came after two "customary" draws: the nineteenth game reflected not so much the alignment of forces between the two players (there can be no doubt that they were worthy opponents for one another), as the relative activity of their creative temperaments. Kasparov's game was filled with attacking adventure and optimism, while Karpov's game showed unusual sluggishness. The Challenger won confidently, and with the score now $10^1/_2:8^1/_2$ in his favour it seemed that the match could have no more new twists.

But subsequent events came to be directed not by logic, but by the characters of the players. The twentieth game was characterised by the determination of Karpov, who was not willing to meekly accept what fate chose to throw at him: in eighty-five moves and two evenings he tried to "squeeze" victory from the longest and most stubborn game of the match. But "he had met his match": Kasparov, with the care and diligence of a sapper, defused all the onslaughts of the Champion, and preserved not only half a point, but also his belief in his eventual victory.

That victory was now so near. After drawing the twenty-first game Kasparov required only one further point, while Karpov required a minimum of two-and-a-half. The Challenger's supporters had reason to celebrate. But the Champion's followers did not lose heart: "Karpov needs to win not two games, but one—the next one; then he can think of winning the one after that—which is all quite possible."

And there were the philosophical evaluations: "If Kasparov cannot take one point from three games, then it's too soon for him to be World Champion. On the other hand, if Karpov manages to carry out the gargantuan task before him, then he deserves to remain champion for some years yet! "

In the twenty-second game Karpov was playing White, which gave him his last real chance to change the course of the match. Looking through the text of this game, the reader will clearly see how the weight of responsibility had fettered both players. It was a nervous contest in which the scales tipped first one way then the other. The crisis point came at the very end. Kasparov needed only to make a few careful moves to achieve the requisite draw, but he faltered and committed a serious error, giving Karpov the game on a silver platter.

Capricious fate had been pleased to give yet another twist to the match when it seemed to be settling down. Again everything was in the balance. Especially so, when the Challenger set up the twenty-third game so well but then let the victory, which he so richly deserved, out of his grasp. This was becoming disastrous: for three games in a row Kasparov had given in to the tension, and between the thirty-fifth and fortieth moves he had once lost the chance of a draw (in the 22nd game), and twice lost the chance of winning (in the 21st and 23rd games).

And now everything would be settled in the final encounter. Two hundred and twenty-eight days they had already played, spending three hundred and twenty hours at the chess board, and they had seventy-one games behind them! And the title was to be decided in one day, five hours of play and a single game, the twenty-fourth of the current match, the most important and a truly historic game.

The game progressed in such a way that to the very end, literally up to the last minutes, the outcome was unpredictable. This decisive encounter required immense self-control! Karpov, for whom only victory would suffice, played with the courage of a pilot preparing for a dog-fight. Kasparov played with the inspiration and devotion of an artist completing the masterpiece of a lifetime. The game had everything, a clash of characters, creative self-assertion, and the excitement of battle.

If you follow through the game move by move, you will realise its extraordinary and thrilling dimensions.

The crisis point came in the last hour. Karpov found himself with a terrible choice: to submit to the logic of the events unfolding on the board and to offer a draw, which would of course mean losing the match, or to ignore the objective analysis and throw himself into a desperate fight, where his chances of success were practically nil and where blind fate could be his only hope. He made his choice, but no miracle occurred. Kasparov faultlessly repulsed the spirited onslaught of his opponent, answered him with a dynamic counter-attack and drove him up a blind alley.

The dramatic denouement had come. Karpov knew better than anyone that his hope was gone, but he was unable to accept this. He could be clearly seen on the monitor in the press-centre gathering every last ounce of his will-power, silently moving his lips and considering all the now hopeless possibilities. And Kasparov, as though drained to the depths, was leaning back, tired, in his chair and awaiting with suppressed impatience the longed-for capitulation.

And everything happened suddenly. Karpov could no longer bear to see his broken forces and he shook his successful opponent by the hand, the first to congratulate him on his deserved victory.

The clock showed 21:56 on the 9th of November, 1985. It was an historic moment, and the birth of a new world champion.

Garri Kasparov is a worthy successor to the chess throne. His victory is the more significant for having been won against a most powerful opponent, still in his prime and unbeaten in the last ten years!

And although Karpov was, of course, "dissatisfied with himself, both from a creative and a sporting point of view", Kasparov still thought very highly indeed of his formidable opponent's game. The new World Champion said in one interview: "In the second match Karpov made it a true fight, he played open chess and did everything he could to win. His play was quite amazing, even when everyone thought his position in a game was beyond help. I must give him his due for his defensive efforts towards the end of the match when he was playing Black, and for his attacking power playing White."

Kasparov sees the basis of his victory in his more thorough and more accurate analysis of the previous match. But this, no doubt, was only one of the many components of his success.

No less important was the fact that Kasparov was able to fight the duel as he himself wanted it, to impose on the majority of games his "own play", using complex double-edged strategy and dynamic development. In this second match, where perhaps more than ever before we have seen the polarity of the two players' styles, Kasparov's creative self-assertion played an important psychological role.

Looking at the games in this match, it is easy to see that it was Kasparov who set the tone in the majority of them, his game had an improvisation very like—in the words of Alexei Suetin—"an acrobat walking a tightrope". And besides, his play was steeped in the strategy of risk, in the spirit of experimentation. The English Grandmaster, Raymond Keene, remarked that Kasparov, as it were, brought a new dimension into our understanding of chess. His ideas were first and foremost directed towards seizing the initiative, and to this end he did not hesitate at making a sacrifice.

Only on rare occasions did Karpov manage to employ his favourite, razor-sharp positional armoury, which he generally uses so impeccably. How did Kasparov entice Karpov, a man who believes so strongly in the right of classical concepts, into his "romantic" territory? The answer is given by an analysis of the games: Kasparov was better equipped theoretically, his choice of opening was far richer, and he therefore more easily laid his roads into battle.

It is worth noting that the new Champion has paid great attention to the study of openings from his earliest years. In his book *Ordeal by Time* he asserts: "Matches between two high-class players often become testing grounds for certain types of opening. In a number of consecutive games the players first and foremost try to vindicate their creative conceptions. Obviously, success in this theoretical duel, by its very nature, has a great bearing on one's success in the whole match."

Kasparov's shrewd assessment was fully corroborated in this match. Kasparov was superior to his opponent in the openings, and this automatically gave him the initiative in each ensuing battle, as well as making a significant contribution to his overall success. Suffice it to say that by his exhaustive study of the Sicilian and Nimzowitsch defences he was able to destroy those very weapons which had brought Karpov so much success in the past. Using these openings he gained five victories without suffering a single defeat—a most decisive achievement!

Of course, the outcome of each game was not firmly decided in the opening stages, but the whole character of the struggle was formed according to the creative aspirations of Kasparov. He explains his victory in the following way: "We managed to work through a whole mass of information and we evaluated it correctly. We took a great deal into consideration. Our choice of new openings was based on all this work. Let us take, for example, the Nimzowitsch defence, which was so successful for us. It is, incidentally, one of the cornerstones of Karpov's openings which we had not until now tested in our games. And using this opening he got, as we say, 'minus three', he lost three games. That is the advantage of preparatory theoretical study! And I am convinced that it is possible to impose one's own play on a game only if one has had the best possible preparation and can create a sufficient number of surprises for one's opponent."

The question remains unanswered as to why Karpov, with such a wide range of openings in his repertoire, so stubbornly kept to a routine which was only bringing him disappointment. We may find the explanation in the psychology of the duel, where subjective considerations often take precedence over the objective evidence. All in all, the psychological factors in this contest proved to be most important. With so many games behind them, the players had come to understand one another so well that both in the choice of openings and in the individual strategic and tactical decisions they were often guided not so much by normal chess criteria as by their personal perception of their opponent's playing credo. And even all the Grandmasters, gathered in the press-centre, were seldom able to decipher the intriguing plans and particular moves of the two combatants.

Inasmuch as psychology determined both the creative and the fighting qualities of the players, we should stress that both Karpov and Kasparov demonstrated great courage, self-possession and will-power. Little need be said about Karpov: he is famous for his fighting spirit, and even in this particularly difficult match he fought doggedly to the very end. In an interview after the match he stressed that he was pleased with one thing: that even after the unbelievable happenings of the eleventh game he kept up the fight and was able to take it to the last hurdle.

By this second match Kasparov had become a markedly stronger player. In the previous match he had sometimes (and particularly at the start) lacked steadfastness, but now everything was different. It should be no surprise that the reporting journalists noticed grey streaks in his hair. In this duel Kasparov had days of joy and days of disappointment, days of creative genius and days of regress, and if after all this he could play the last and most arduous game, and conclude his grandiose fight with a flourish, then in the short time since the first match he had steeled his character enormously.

Garri Kasparov is at the height of his fame. He is young and talented, and he has the widest of horizons before him. The new chess king does not intend to rest on his laurels. "Like my predecessor, I intend to be an active world champion," he has declared. "Being the champion does not mean that I have reached the ceiling and can go no further. I shall strive to perfect my game, and to raise chess to new heights."

And his devotion to the game is a guarantee of that.

PARTICIPANTS

ANATOLY KARPOV

was born in Zlatoust, a city in the Chelyabinsk Region of the Soviet Union, on the 23rd of May, 1951.

He graduated from the Economics Faculty of Leningrad University.

Karpov plays for the Soviet Army Central Sports Club (Moscow).

Karpov's career record

Soviet Chess Master—1966;
International Master—1969;
International Grandmaster—1970;
Merited Master of Sport of the USSR—1974;
World Junior Champion—1969;
Winner of the Students' Olympiad in 1971 and 1972;
Member of the Soviet team which won the Olympic Team Championships in 1972, 1974, 1980, and 1982;
Member of the Soviet team which won the European Team Championship in 1973, 1977, 1980, and 1983;
Member of the Soviet team which won the World Team Championship in 1985;
World Champion from 1975, and USSR Champion in 1976 and 1983;
Winner of nine "Chess Oscars" (1973—77, 1979—81, 1984).

Member of the Komsomol Central Committee, Chairman of the Board of the Soviet Peace Fund and Editor-in-Chief of "Soviet Chess Review-64".

He has been awarded the Order of Lenin and the Order of the Red Banner of Labour.

WINNING RECORD
Tournaments

1967	Trshinets
1967/68	Groningen
1970	Russian Federation Championship, Kuibyshev
1971	Alekhine Memorial, Moscow
1971/72	Hastings
1972	San Antonio, Texas
1973	Leningrad Interzonal
	Madrid
1975	Portoroz, Ljubljana
	Milan

1976	Skoplje
	Amsterdam
	Montilla
	USSR Championship, Moscow
1977	Bad Lauterberg .
	Las Palmas
	London
	Tilburg
1978	Bugojno
1979	Montreal
	Waddinxveen
	Amsterdam
	Tilburg
1980	Bad Kissingen
	Bugojno
	Amsterdam
	Tilburg
1981	Linares
	Moscow
1982	London
	Turin
	Hamburg
1983	USSR Championship, Moscow
	Hanover
	Tilburg
1984	Oslo
	London
1985	Amsterdam

Matches

1974	against L. Polugayevsky, Moscow
	against B. Spassky, Leningrad
	against V. Korchnoi, Moscow
1978	against V. Korchnoi, Baguio City
1981	against V. Korchnoi, Merano

GARRI KASPAROV

was born in Baku on the 13th of April, 1963. He is currently
a student at the Institute of Foreign Languages in Baku.
Kasparov plays for the Spartak Sports Society (Baku).

Kasparov's career record
Soviet Chess Master—1978;
International Master—1979;
International Grandmaster—1980;
Merited Master of Sport of the USSR—1985;
USSR Junior Champion—1976 and 1977;
World Junior Champion—1980;
Member of the Soviet team which won the Olympic
Team Championships in 1980 and 1982;
USSR Champion—1981;
Member of the Soviet team which won the European Team
Championship in 1980;
Member of the Soviet team which won the World Junior
Team Championship in 1981;
Winner of three "Chess Oscars" (1982, 1983, 1985).
Member of the Azerbaidjan Komsomol Central Committee.
Holder of a Diploma of Merit from the Presidium of the
Azerbaidjan Supreme Soviet.

WINNING RECORD
Tournaments

1978	Sokolski Memorial, Minsk
	USSR Championship Preliminary, Daugavpils
1979	Banya-Luka
1980	Baku
1981	USSR Championship, Frunze
1982	Bugojno
	Moscow Interzonal
1983	Niksic

Matches

1983	against A. Belyavsky, Moscow
	against V. Korchnoi, London
1984	against V. Smyslov, Vilnius
1985	against R. Huebner, Hamburg
	against U. Andersson, Belgrad

Chairman—*Pyotr Demichev*
Deputy Chairman—*Marat Gramov*

Officials

President of FIDE, **Florencio Campomanes** (Philippines), International Master, International Referee.

Chief Arbiters: **Andrei Malchev** (Bulgaria), International Referee (even-numbered games); **Vladas Mikenas**, International Master, International Referee (odd-numbered games).

Arbiters: **Lembit Vakhesaár** (USSR), International Referee; **Lodewijk Prins** (Netherlands), International Grandmaster, International Referee.

Chairmen of the Appeals Committee: Vice-President of FIDE, **Roman Toran** (Spain), International Master, International Referee; **Alfred Kinzel** (West Berlin), International Referee, Member of the FIDE Executive Council.

Members of the Appeals Committee: **Vitali Sevastyanov** (USSR), President of the Soviet Chess Federation; **Yevgeny Pitovranov** (USSR), Member of the Presidium of the Soviet Chess Federation.

Director of the press room—**Mikhail Arkhangelsky**, USSR Master of Sport.

The Participants' Seconds

Karpov's Seconds: **Igor Zaitsev** (USSR), International Grandmaster; **Sergei Makarychev** (USSR), International Grandmaster.

Kasparov's seconds: **Alexander Nikitin** (USSR), USSR Master of Sport and Merited Coach, **Iosiph Dorfman** (USSR), International Grandmaster.

EXTRACTS FROM REGULATIONS FOR THE MEN'S INDIVIDUAL WORLD CHAMPIONSHIP MATCH 1985

The match shall consist of twenty-four games. The competitor who scores 12.5 or 13 points is the winner. If a player scores 12.5 or 13 points in less than 24 games, the remaining games shall not be played. If one of the players wins six games, he is the winner irrespective of the number of games played.

If the score of the match is even (12:12), the World Champion retains his title. If the title holder scores 12 points in less than 24 games, the match shall be continued until he gains at least half a point more (i.e. 12.5) or until the score becomes 12:12.

Three games shall be played each week (on Tuesdays, Thursdays and Saturdays). Each main playing session shall be followed by a day for adjourned games (Wednesdays, Fridays and Sundays). The seventh day (Monday) shall be free.

Each player may, for reasons of his own, postpone any three playing sessions (other than the first session of the match), provided that in each case he notifies the Chief Arbiter at least five hours before the session is due to start. The postponement of an adjournment session is regarded as a time-out.

Play shall be conducted in conformity with FIDE rules. The control will be 40 moves in the first $2^1/_2$ hours and 16 moves per hour thereafter, with unused time carried forward.

Sessions for adjournment games will last for up to 6 hours. A game that remains unfinished after its first adjournment session shall be continued on the next adjournment-session day. If two games are to be completed on a day for adjournments, the earlier game shall be continued first. After a pause of 30 minutes, the later game will be continued, provided that at least 2 hours' playing time remains.

Moscow 1985

FIDE

Explanation of Symbols

For the benefit of those readers who may be unfamiliar
with some of the symbols and abbreviations used in the Games
Section, the following explanation is appended:

K	—King
Q	—Queen
R	—Rook
B	—Bishop
N	—Knight
+	—check
++	—discovered check
0-0	—King-side castling
0-0-0	—Queen-side castling
!	—good move
!!	—outstanding move
?	—bad move
??	—blunder
!?	—interesting move
?!	—dubious move

GAME ONE

Nimzo-Indian Defence

G. Kasparov   A. Karpov

The first game of a World Championship match has an importance all its own. Someone once aptly compared the victory in such a game to a fair wind in a winner's sails. It inspires the winner and affects the mood of both players in the early stages of the match.

In contrast to the drawing of lots in the previous match, it was now Kasparov who was to play White in the opening game. Undoubtedly, the advantage of the first move has some significance: White takes the initiative and Black has to defend himself. But this advantage is far from decisive, and it can be neutralised by accurate defensive play. Perhaps more importantly, the lucky draw may influence the players' mood, a factor that should not be underestimated. One can recall that in the previous encounters between Karpov and Kasparov the colour of the pieces did play a part. Indeed, White won six games, whereas Black—only two.

To close this introduction, let us compare a first game to a dress-rehearsal, when the Grandmasters, the actors of this particular performance, are getting into the way of things, adapting themselves to the new surroundings, the auditorium, the tempo of play. They are also trying to calm down, but they do not always succeed at once.

1. d2-d4 (1)*   Ng8-f6 (0)

*The number in parentheses indicates the time the player took on the move.

2. c2-c4 (1)   e7-e6 (0)
3. Nb1-c3 (1)   . . .

The first surprise for the first game! In none of his many previous encounters with the World Champion did Kasparov move his Queen's Knight to c3. Now he invites Karpov to a dispute over the Nimzo-Indian Defence.

3. . . .   Bf8-b4 (2)

Very significantly, Karpov feels obliged to accept the challenge. Thus one more opening becomes the subject of the creative polemic between the world's two strongest players.

4. Ng1-f3 (0)   c7-c5 (16)
5. g2-g3 (0)   . . .

Kasparov adopts a system used by Alexander Alekhine in the thirties and reintroduced into modern tournament play by Oleg Romanishin. White fianchettoes his King's Bishop to exert pressure on the centre and on Black's Q-side.

To our knowledge, this variation has never before occurred in Karpov's games. Understandably, the World Champion took almost half an hour to respond.

5. . . .   Nf6-e4 (29)
6. Qd1-d3 (1)   Qd8-a5 (0)
7. Qd3xe4 (1)   Bb4xc3+ (0)
8. Bc1-d2 (0)   Bc3xd2+ (0)
9. Nf3xd2 (0)   . . .
(No. 1)

The diagrammed position has been seen more than once in master play. Theory contends that although Black makes certain concessions in the centre and temporarily delays the deployment of his forces, he has a good basis for solving

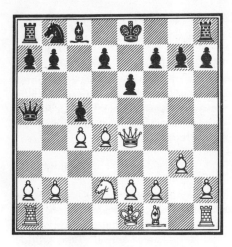

No. 1

his opening problems in a satisfactory way. Black's main trump is the pin on the White Knight on d2, which prevents, for the time being, any active operations White might undertake.

9. ...   Qa5-b6 (7)

It is this experimental move that seems to be the primary source of Black's further difficulties. The well-tested and "approved" lines are 9. ... 0-0 10. dxc Na6, and 9. ... Nc6 10. d5 Nd4.

10. d4xc5 (4)	Qb6xb2 (0)
11. Ra1-b1 (0)	Qb2xc3(3)

The capture 11. ... Qxa2 looks very risky, yet the move is worth considering. For instance, 12. Bg2 0-0 13. Qe3 Na6 14. 0-0 Nxc5! 15. Qd4 e5! , and though he seems to be in danger, Black holds his own; or 12. Qd4 0-0 13. Qc3 Qa4! 14. Bg2 Nc6 15. 0-0 Qa5. Also interesting is 13. Ra1 (after 12. Qd4 0-0) 13. ... Qc2 14. Bg2 Nc6 15. Qd6 b6, and 16. cxb? is met by 16. ... axb! . However,

who would be happy to obtain such a position voluntarily? Obviously, White has an initiative that more than compensates him for the sacrificed Pawn.

Another possibility is 11. ... Qa3, as was played in the Ubilava-Lerner game (51st USSR Championship, Semifinal, 1983): in this game, White continued 12. Bg2, thus sacrificing a pawn, which seems quite unnecessary. For example, 12. Qd4 0-0 13. Bg2 looks rather attractive, and 13. ... Nc6 14. Qd6 b6 can be answered with 15. 0-0! Qxc5 16. Qxc5 bxc. Now White should not play 17. Bxc6 dxc 18. Ne4, because of 18. ... e5! 19. Nxc5 Bf5 20. e4 Bg6 21. Rb7 f6, with counterplay. He should continue simply 17. Nb3! . And now after the better move 17. ... Ba6 18. Rfc1, Black has to sacrifice the Exchange by 18. ... Nd4, because 18. ... Rab8 19. Nxc5 Rxb1 20. Rxb1 Bxc4 loses in view of 21. Nxd7 Rc8 22. Bxc6.

Bearing in mind that Kasparov spent very little time on his previous moves, one can hardly doubt that he had been well prepared to meet 11. ... Qa3. It was probably this consideration that made Karpov reject the well-known line. However, as future events in the game will show, the retreat to c3 is no better.

12. Qe4-d3 (5)   ...

A venomed move. White offers to exchange the Queens on d3, whereupon the Pawn at c5 will be supported by its colleague which goes over from the e-file.

12. ...   Qc3xd3 (18)

On 12. ... Qa5, White would have a wide choice of good lines; for example 13. Rb5, or 13. Qd4. White could even continue 13. Bg2 Qxc5 14. 0-0 0-0 15. Ne4, and his Knight would be very strong on d6.

13. e2xd3 (0)   . . .

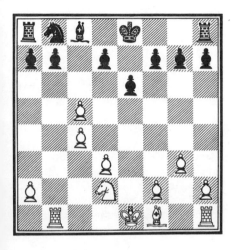

No. 2

A glance is enough to see that the outcome of the opening is unfavourable for Black. First, he is far behind with the development of his pieces; second, it is hard to see how his Q-side forces, especially the Bishop on c8, might be mobilized. Finally, the hole in his camp on d6 is gaping, inviting White's Knight to head for this square. And should one formally count the number of useful moves made by both sides, one would obtain a very unusual ratio of seven to one in favour of White! Clearly, Black has failed to solve his opening problems. If the World Champion is unsuccessful with this line, one has to admit that the whole plan with 9. ... Qb6 is unpromising. This is confirmed by the further course of events.

13. . . .   Nb8-a6 (0)

Here 13. ... Nc6 14. Bg2 Ke7 suggests itself to meet 15. Ne4 by 15. ... b6, striving for counterplay. In this case, the plan suggested by E. Gufeld is rather good, viz. 16. cxb axb 17. Nc3! , followed by 18. Kd2 and doubling the Rooks along the b-file.

14. d3-d4 (17)   Ra8-b8 (0)

Could Black have gained counter-chances by playing 14. ... e5, to get rid of the highly unpleasant White Pawn on c5? Gufeld answers in the affirmative, backing up his opinion by the variation 15. dxe Nxc5 16. Bg2! (16. f4 b6 17. Bg2 Bb7). 16. ... Nd3+ 17. Kf1 0-0 18. f4 f6. However, let us take it a little further: 19. Bd5+ Kh8 20. Ne4! , and one can see that, with the threat of 21. Ke2, Black's position has become critical.

15. Bf1-g2 (4)   Ke8-e7 (19)

In the event of the immediate 15. ... b6 16. cxb axb (16. ... Rxb6 17. Ke2! ?) 17. Ke2, the Pawn on b6 becomes a source of worry to Black. For instance, 17. ... Bb7 18. Bxb7 Rxb7 19. c5 b5 20. Nc4.

16. Ke1-e2 (15)   Rh8-d8 (13)

Here 16. ... b6 does not solve Black's problems either. After 17. cxb axb 18. Rb3 Bb7 19. Bxb7 Rxb7 20. Rhb1, it would be hard for Black to repulse White's onslaught. 16. ... d6 would be little better, because of 17. cxd+ Kxd6 18. c5+, followed by 19. Nc4.

17. Nd2-e4 (15)   b7-b6 (0)

Black cannot wait any longer, and Karpov makes an attempt to break through the encircling blockade, even at the cost of inevitable material sacrifices.

18. Ne4-d6! (0)   Na6-c7 (4)

At this point, Black had at his disposal an interesting possibility of gaining counterplay, viz., 18. ... bxc. After 19. Rxb8 Nxb8 20. dxc, he could offer a piece by playing 20. ... Na6! 21. Nxc8+ Rxc8 22. Bb7 Rxc5 23. Bxa6 Ra5, for example, 24. Bb7 (or 24. Bb5 a6) 24. ... Rxa2+ 25. Ke3 Rc2 26. Ra1 Rxc4 27. Rxa7 Rc7, and White may only lose. The stronger line is 24. Bc8 Rxa2+ 25. Ke3 Rc2 26. Rd1 d5 27. Ra1, but here, too, Black has a good chance of a draw.

However, White does not have to play as above. The correct continuation is 19. Nxc8+! Rdxc8, and only now 20. Bb7. After 20. ... Rxb7 21. Rxb7 cxd 22. Rxa7 Nc5 23. Rb1, White's passed a-Pawn will decide the issue. Hardly better would be 20. ... Nb4 21. Bxc8 Rxc8 22. dxc Nc6 23. Rb7 Kd8 24. Rd1 Rc7 25. Rxc7 Kxc7 26. Rd6, and White should gradually win the game.

19. Rb1-b4 (8)   ...

Taking advantage of his lead in development and his greater command of space, White increases the pressure on the Q-side. Doubling his Rooks along the b-file is White's unanswerable trump.

19. ...   Nc7-e8 (11)
20. Nd6xe8 (5)   Ke7xe8 (4)

At last Black has rid himself of the White Knight on d6, but even this achievement does not lessen his diffi-

culties, such are the consequences of Karpov's unhappy choice of opening line.

21. Rh1-b1 (0)   Bc8-a6 (0)

Black's Bishop has finally come into play, but its position is highly unstable. Still, White should be on the alert. Thus, the tempting 22. Ra4 could be met by 22. ... Bb7! 23. Bxb7 (not, of course, 23. Bf1 bxc! 24. Rxa7?? Bf3+) 23. ... Rxb7, and Black has a good chance to save himself.

22. Ke2-e3 (2)   d7-d5 (8)

Karpov defends his position very resourcefully. By sacrificing a Pawn he does his best to hinder the exploitation of White's advantage. 22. ... Rdc8 would not help, because of 23. Bf1, threatening 24. Ra4.

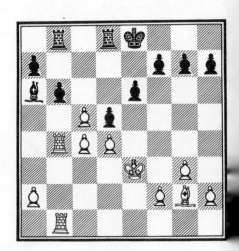

No. 3

23. c5xd6 (8)   ...

That's the way! If 23. cxd5 exd 24. cxb Rxb6 25. Rxb6 axb 26. Rxb6 Bc4, then Black's pieces would at long last come to life.

23. . . .   Rb8-c8 (6)

After 23. . . . Rxd6, there would certainly follow 24. c5.

24. Ke3-d3 (4)   . . .

Also playable is 24. Bf1 Rxd6 25. Ra4, but the most convincing is 24. Ra4! Bxc4 25. Bb7 b5 26. d7+! , forcing a winning endgame.

24. . . .   Rd8xd6 (0)
25. Rb4-a4 (2)   b6-b5 (2)
26. c4xb5 (0)   Rc8-b8 (1)
27. Ra4-b4 (4)   . . .

Here 27. Ke3 is also worth considering. Black then cannot play 27. . . . Rxb5, in view of 28. Rxa6, while after 27. . . . Bxb5, the line 28. Rab4 Rdb6. 29. Rxb5 is decisive.

27. . . .   Ba6-b7 (0)
28. Bg2xb7 (0)   Rb8xb7 (0)
29. a2-a4 (2)   Ke8-e7 (1)

In the two-Rook ending that has resulted White has an extra pawn, and Black has no real counterplay. His fate is sealed.

30. h2-h4 (9)   h7-h6 (0)
31. f2-f3 (6)   . . .

Under time pressure, Kasparov is not in a hurry to force matters.

31. . . .   Rd6-d5 (1)
32. Rb1-c1 (0)   Rb7-d7 (0)
33. a4-a5 (3)   g7-g5 (1)

34. h4xg5 (3)   Rd5xg5 (0)
35. g3-g4 (0)   h7-h5 (1)
36. b5-b6 (1)   a7xb6 (0)
37. a5xb6 (2)   Rd7-b7 (0)
38. Rc1-c5 (1)   f7-f5 (0)

Karpov desperately defends himself, but there is no escape.

39. g4xh5 (2)   Rg5xh5 (0)
40. Kd3-c4 (0)   . . .

This is the right method—the King marches to escort his passed Pawn.

40. . . .   Rh5-h8 (1)
41. Kc4-b5 (4)   Rh8-a8 (0)

Here the game is adjourned. White seals the move 42. Rb4-c4 (21). However, Black resigns without resumption.
     Time: 2.32—2.28.

5 and 6 September 1985

GAME TWO

Sicilian Defence

A. Karpov   G. Kasparov

After the dramatic start of the match, one would naturally expect that the players should want to take a respite. As is known, Karpov always keeps his cool and, on losing a game, he is never in a hurry to take immediate revenge. As for Kasparov, why should he, now with the black pieces and leading in the match, try to sow the wind? Yet, the struggle in a world-title match has a logic of its own, whose unpredictable character is one of the reasons why it is so attractive.
     Unexpectedly, the second game turned

out to be an exceptionally fierce fight, requiring from the players the utmost exertion of their will and creative power.

1. e2-e4 (1)	c7-c5 (0)
2. Ng1-f3 (0)	d7-d6 (1)
3. d2-d4 (0)	c5xd4 (0)
4. Nf3xd4 (0)	Ng8-f6 (0)
5. Nb1-c3 (0)	a7-a6 (1)
6. Bf1-e2 (0)	e7-e6 (0)
7. 0-0 (0)	Bf8-e7 (1)
8. f2-f4 (3)	0-0 (0)
9. Kg1-h1 (0)	Qd8-c7 (1)
10. a2-a4 (8)	Nb8-c6 (1)
11. Bc1-e3 (0)	Rf8-e8 (1)
12. Be2-f3 (1)	Ra8-b8 (6)

Those who have closely followed the games played in the previous match between Karpov and Kasparov will find this position familiar. Indeed, it occurred twice in that match. In the fifth game, Karpov tried 13. Re1, but after 13. ... Bd7 14. Qd3 Nxd4 15. Bxd4 e5 16. Ba7 Rbc8 17. Be3 Qc4, he gained nothing out of the opening. In the forty-fifth game, the World Champion came up with an improvement: 13. Qd2, extracting some positional advantage after 13. ... Nxd4 14. Bxd4 e5 15. Ba7 Ra8 16. Be3 Bd7 17. a5. It is not surprising then that, renewing their theoretical dispute, Karpov adopts the better line.

13. Qd1-d2 (2)	Bc8-d7 (3)

On the other hand, Kasparov, remembering the past, searches for new paths. To move the Queen's Bishop, he spent three minutes in the game and perhaps many hours before the game. Without a doubt, this move was carefully analysed before the match.

14. Qd2-f2 (31)	...

Karpov pondered for over half an hour to decide on the above manoeuvre. Now the B-Q tandem takes aim at the weakened b6-square.

14. ...	Nc6xd4 (9)

A typical discharging manoeuvre in this scheme. The move 14. ... e5 would be less expedient here, because of 15. Nf5, and after 15. ... Bxf5 16. exf exf 17. Bxf4 Ne5 there can follow 18. Nd5 Nxd5 19. Bxd5 Bf6 20. Rad1, with a clear positional advantage for White. An attempt at counterplay by the impulsive 14. ... b5 would be equally unjustifiable, because after 15. axb Nxd4 16. Bxd4 axb 17. Ra7 White's activity becomes menacing.

15. Be3xd4 (0)	e6-e5 (1)

Not very long ago, such a weakening of the central square d5 would be judged as a mistake. Nowadays, with the greatly increased importance attached to dynamic factors, such static considerations are no longer dominant and the whole evaluation has drastically changed.

16. Bd4-e3 (10)	...
(No. 4)	
16. ...	Bd7-e6!? (32)

An unexpected and bold decision. In accordance with all strategic principles, Kasparov could release the tension in the centre by 16. ... exf 17. Bxf4 Rbc8 (or 17. ... Be6), and look serenely to the future. But, as his last move indicates, it was precisely serenity that he did not want at that moment. The Bishop's manoeuvre is a daring challenge for a relentless tactical fight.

No. 4

17. f4-f5 (19)   . . .

Anatoly Karpov is not the one to disregard the gauntlet thrown down to him. Should he want a quiet game, the solid 17. Rfd1 would suffice.

17. . . .   Be6-c4 (13)

The Black Bishop's position here is active, but vulnerable. One can readily see that the Bishop cannot retreat from its present post. To foresee the advantages resulting from its temporarily wider range is far more difficult.

18. Be3-b6 (3)   . . .

An important interposition, which precludes the possibility of Black's counterplay associated with b7-b5.

18. . . .   Qc7-c8 (19)

Evidently Kasparov sets his most optimistic hopes on the undermining d6-d5; accordingly, the Black Queen's place is on c8, and not on c6!

19. Rf1-c1 (22)   . . .

It is exactly this manoeuvre that emphasises the instability of the Black Bishop on c4. The unavoidable threat of 20. b3 brings about a tactical crisis. Obviously, White will now gain a material advantage, while Black will have yet to demonstrate that he has sufficient compensation for the inevitable loss of material. In spite of all these considerations, and giving due to the consistency of Karpov's commitment to refute his opponent's daring plan, one can still find the World Champion's decision debatable. The simple 19. Rfd1 would stress all the advantages of White's position, while questioning the validity of Kasparov's attempt to violate the natural course of the game by a tactical skirmish. Now a storm breaks out.

19. . . .   d6-d5 (7)
20. b2-b3 (5)   . . .

Needless to say, it would be pointless to depart from the course already taken. After 20. exd, there would follow the unpleasant 20. . . . Bb4.

20. . . .   Be7-b4 (1)

Black has no choice, either. In the event of 20. . . . dxe? 21. Nxe4, he would lose a piece.

21. Nc3-a2 (1)   . . .

This is the only move. After 21. Nxd5?! Bxd5 22. exd e4, White would throw away everything.

21. . . .   Bb4-a3 (1)
22. b3xc4 (4)   Ba3xc1 (1)
23. Na2xc1 (5)   Qc8xc4 (1)

24. e4xd5 (0) e5-e4!? (1)

This move is more vigorous than 24. ... Nxd5, although the latter also has its advantages.

25. Bf3-e2 (1) Qc4xc2 (3)
26. Qf2-d4!? (5) ...

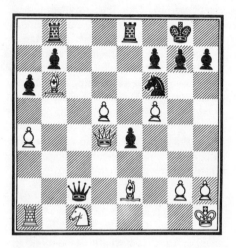

No. 5

The time has come to evaluate the consequences of the first phase of the tactical complications. Even with fore-knowledge, the position is hard to assess because of its irrational character, and general reasoning has to give way to intuitive estimates.

What should be preferred—White's slight material advantage or Black's indisputable initiative? What is the relative strength of the passed pawns on the d- and e-files? Well, we can only refer the reader to the events that follow.

26. ... Rb8-c8!? (18)
27. h2-h3!?(1) ...

This seems to be a practical decision, because an outlet for the White King may help White in surmounting many tactical barriers. That the preventive move in the text is useful is confirmed by the following variations: 27. d6! Qxc1+!! 28. Rxc1 Rxc1+ 29. Bd1 e3 30. d7 e2! 31. deQ+ Nxe8, and in spite of his overwhelming material superiority, White has to resign. After 27. Bd1 Qxc1! 28. Rxc1 Rxc1 29. Qd2 (of course, the line 29. h3 e3 30. Kh2 e2 31. Bxe2 Rxe2 is to Black's advantage) 29. ... Rb1 30. Be3 Ng4! 31. Qc2 Rxd1 32. Qxd1 Nxe3 33. Qd2 Nc4 34. Qe2 e3!, White will find it hard to defend himself. Very likely, White could encounter other dangers lurking in this highly intricate position.

However, White has an excellent possibility of cutting the Gordian knot. Let us come back to the last-mentioned variation and closely inspect the position that would arise after Black's 29th move.

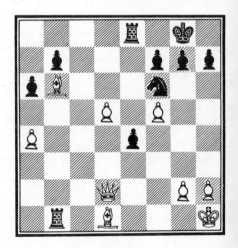

No. 6

42

It turns out that White need not blockade Black's dangerous passed Pawn. Instead of the obvious 30. Be3, he may respond with the paradoxical 30. Bg1! . At first glance this seems a dangerous thing to do, because of 30. ... e3 31. Qd3 Rxd1! 32. Qxd1 e2 33. Qe1 Nxd5 34. Bf2 Nf4 35. Qd2 Nd3! , and in the event of 36. Be1 Nxe1 37. Qxe1 b5, White would be almost helpless (although there is still the hope that he can scrape along somehow). Yet White has at his disposal an ingenious counter-chance: after 36. Be1 Nxe1, he should, instead of the routine 37. Qxe1, answer with the resolute 37. Qd7! , forcing a draw (37. ... Kf8 38. Qd6+ Kg8 39. Qd7).

Thus by playing 27. Bd1 Karpov could happily overcome all his difficulties. This would be a logical, though not quite evident, outcome of the events that began many moves ago. But a true lover of chess would hardly complain, because the game, as it will actually be played, will be no less interesting and exciting. Besides, Karpov does not seem to have broken the balance as yet.

27. ...   e4-e3! (6)

This vigorous move poses yet more complicated problems for White to solve: Black threatens 28. ... Qd2. We note, in passing, that it would be pointless for Black to depart from the main course of his initiative by playing 27. ... Nxd5 28. Qxd5 Qb2, in view of 29. Bd4 Rxc1+ 30. Kh2.

28. d5-d6! (14)   ...

The World Champion is up to the task. The move he played is probably the only one. Bronstein's recommendation of 28. Bf3 is refuted by 28. ... Rc4 29. Qd3 e2! 30. Bxe2 Qxd3 31. Bxd3 Re1+.

28. ...   Qc2-d2! (3)
29. Nc1-d3! (2) Qd2xe2 (2)

In the heat of the moment, many commentators criticised this move, believing that here Kasparov had let his winning chances slip. This is hardly so, because the suggested 29. ... Nd7 is unconvincing. True, the line 30. Nf4 Rc6 31. Nh5, as suggested by the analysts, will indeed lead White, after 31. ... Qxd4 32. Bxd4 g6, into difficulties, but instead of 30. Nf4 White may simply play 30. Re1, whereupon neither 30. ... Rc6 31. Bc7, nor 30. ... Rc3 31. Ba5 Rxd3 32. Bxd3 Qxa5 33. Rxe3, nor the Exchange at b6 would be dangerous for him.

As it is, Kasparov liquidates the menacing d-Pawn.

30. d6-d7 (1)   Nf6xd7 (0)
31. Qd4xd7 (0)   Qe2-d2 (2)
32. Ra1-e1 (2)   e3-e2 (1)

As a result of all preceding complications, Black has some advantage, both because he has more fighting units and because he has a far advanced passed Pawn. Still, the importance of these factors should not be overestimated, for the White pieces have begun co-ordinating. In particular, the White Queen, which has penetrated deep into the enemy territory, keeps vigilant guard over the movement of Black's heavy pieces, thereby restraining their freedom. Without them, obviously, any active operations Black might launch will be unpromising.

33. Kh1-g1! (0)   ...

It is not easy to decide on such a move, especially under time pressure, but Karpov's faultless intuition suggests the most rational defensive plan. The White King should defuse the main danger—Black's e-Pawn.

33. ...   a6-a5 (4)

Making use of the fact that, in the event of 34. Kf2 Black may strike the tactical blow 34. ... Rcd8! (35. Bxd8 Qe3 mate!), Kasparov attempts to prevent White from blockading the Q-side and deprives him of an important resource, a4-a5. True, the Challenger achieves this at the cost of some weakening of his Pawn configuration. But how otherwise could he dynamize the struggle? The tempting 33. ... Rf8, which would set the other Black Rook free, gives White nothing, because of 34. Kf2! Rc3 35. Ne5 Qf4+ 36. Nf3.

34. g2-g3 (5)   ...

Perhaps it is here that the World Champion goes astray. In his persistent attempts to complete the intended transfer of the White King to the centre, Karpov allows a noticeable weakening of its Pawn shelter. He had at his disposal the strong 34. Qb5, which would solve all his problems at once.

34. ...   Qd2-h6! (4)

Under time pressure one may easily overlook such a long move. Now White is burdened with new cares.

35. Bb6-f2 (1)   ...

Hastening to help his King. Fortunately, White can meet 35. ... Rcd8, or 35. ...

Qxh3, by the tactical blow 36. Rxe2! , while the attack 35. ... Red8 can be repulsed by the convenient retreat 36. Qb5.

35. ...   Qh6-c6! (0)

A profound treatment of the position. Kasparov foresees that in the endgame his Rooks will be much more active, which will ensure him an enduring initiative.

36. Qd7xc6 (0)	Rc8xc6 (0)
37. Re1-b1 (1)	Rc6-c4 (1)
38. Rb1xb7 (1)	Rc4xa4 (1)
39. Bf2-e1 (0)	Ra4-a3 (0)
40. Rb7-d7 (0)	a5-a4 (2)
41. Kg1-f2 (0)	...

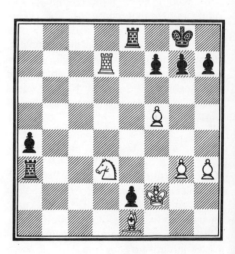

No. 7

With the control moves made, the players were at last able to get their breath. The game was adjourned. The preliminary diagnosis stated that Black had the advantage, but it would be more difficult for him to exploit his advantage

44

than for White to draw. A thorough analysis made at a later time has introduced a substantial correction into the initial evaluation: White will have to overcome many difficulties before he can reach a draw.

$$41. \ldots \qquad Ra3-b3 \ (8)$$

The sealed move. Other possibilities are 41. ... h6, or 41. ... h5, to determine the plan of further play by analysis in private.

$$42. Nd3-c1 \ (0) \qquad \ldots$$

After 42. Nc5 Rb5 43. Nxa4 Rxf5 44. Kg2 Rf1, White loses.

$$42. \ldots \qquad Rb3-b1 \ (5)$$

Now 42. ... Rb5 can be met by 43. Ra7! Rxf5+ 44. Kg2 Kf1 45. Nd3. Black will lose his Pawn on a4, and after 45. ... Rd8 46. Rxa4 h5 47. Ra3 Rxd3 48. Rxd3 Rxe1 49. Re3, the game reduces to a drawable Rook and Pawn ending.

$$43. Nc1-a2 \ (0) \qquad Re8-a8 \ (5)$$

The most consistent line is 43. ... Ra1 44. Nc3 h5, and here 45. Nxe2 will lose the game, because after 45. ... a3 46. Bc3 Ra2 47. Rd2 Rxd2 48. Bxd2 a2 49. Bc3 Ra8 50. Ba1 Rb8, White has to give up his Bishop.

$$44. Rd7-e7 \ (15) \qquad \ldots$$

It is possible that Kasparov underestimated the strength of this move. The line 44. Rd2 Rb5 45. g4 Rb3 would be much worse for White, as the Rook would prevent the Bishop from reaching c3.

$$44. \ldots \qquad Rb1-b2 \ (5)$$
$$45. Re7xe2 \ (0) \qquad Rb2xe2+ \ (0)$$

Black makes an important decision and trades one of his Rooks. Without a detailed analysis one can hardly maintain that 45. ... a3 46. Bc3 Rb3 would be better than the text.

$$46. Kf2xe2 \ (0) \qquad Ra8-e8+ \ (0)$$
$$47. Ke2-f2 \ (1) \qquad \ldots$$

The King has to retreat to its former place, because after 47. Kd2 h5 it would be very difficult for White to defend his K-side Pawns.

$$47. \ldots \qquad h7-h5 \ (0)$$

Threatening 48. ... Re5 49. g4 hxg 50. hxg Re4, to win a Pawn.

$$48. Be1-c3 \ (0) \qquad Re8-b8 \ (3)$$
$$49. Bc3-b4 \ (5) \qquad Rb8-d8 \ (1)$$
$$50. Kf2-e2 \ (5) \qquad \ldots$$

White's main task is to prevent the Black Rook from penetrating to his rear lines, whence it could threaten both wings.

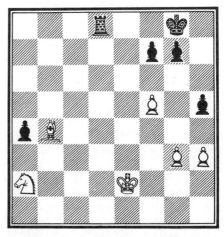

No. 8

50. ...   a4-a3 (20)

A very committing decision. The Pawn
has advanced to a dark square, where it
will be subject to attack. But it seems
that Kasparov wants to divert the White
pieces to the Q-side, thus giving him the
possibility of attacking his opponent's
Pawns on the K-side. Of course the
Pawn on a3 is immune, because of the
threat of Ra8.

51. Bb4-c3 (5)   f7-f6 (1)
52. Bc3-b4 (10)   Kg8-f7 (0)
53. Na2-c3 (4)   Rd8-b8 (1)
54. Nc3-a2 (0)   ...

Here 54. Bxa3 would be decisively met
by 54. ... Rb3.

54. ...   Rb8-b5 (4)
55. g3-g4 (0)   Rb5-b8 (0)

The line 55. ... Re5+ 56. Kd3 Rd5+ 57.
Kc4 Rd1 58. Bxa3 would lead to the
same position as in the actual game.

56. Ke2-d3 (11)   Rb8-d8+ (4)
57. Kd3-c4 (0)   Rd8-d1 (0)

At the price of a Pawn Black has finally
penetrated with his Rook to the enemy
camp, but White's defensive resources
are sufficient.

58. Bb4xa3 (17)   Rd1-a1 (20)

After 58. ... Rh1 White would defend
himself as in the game, i.e. 59. Nc3
Rxh3 60. gh Rxh5 61. Ne4, or
60. ... Rf3 61. Bc1 Rxf5 62. h6. Finally,
in response to 58. ... h4, White also
has a reliable method for holding the
game balanced, viz. 59. Nc1! (much
worse would be 59. Nc3 Rh1 60. Bd6

Rxh3 61. Ne4 Rf3, because the Knight
obstructs the White King's approach to
the Pawn). 59. ... Rh1 60. Nd3 Rxh3
61. Bd6. For example, 61. ... Rf3
62. Kd4 h3 63. Ke4 Rf1 64. Ke3, or
61. ... Rh1 62. Kd4 h3 63. Nf2.

59. Kc4-b3 (0)   Ra1-h1 (0)
60. g4xh5 (1)   Rh1xh3+ (0)
61. Na2-c3 (0)   Rh3-f3 (0)
62. Ba3-c1! (2)   Rf3xf5 (2)
63. h5-h6 (1)   g7-g6 (9)

63. ... g5, would be no better, since
64. Ne4 Kg6 65. h7 Kxh7 66. Nxf6
Rxf6 67. Rxg5 would force a draw.

64. Nc3-e4 (0)   Rf5-h5 (3)
65. Bc1-b2 (4)

A draw. After 65. ... f5, 66. h7 would
follow. Could Black pose more difficult
problems for his opponent? Of course
he could. But the question of whether
Kasparov could win requires a special
study.

Time: 3.50—3.59.

10 September 1985

GAME THREE

Queen's Gambit Declined

G. Kasparov   A. Karpov

The plot of a chess duel is always
unpredictable. When the Champion and
the Challenger started their new contest
on a high note, it seemed that this would
set the tone for every subsequent game.
But a World Championship match has
a logic of its own. The ultimate result
is so important that a contestant has

to be rational in expending his energy, and his creative spirit must necessarily be curbed by the tasks set by the overall match strategy. Tension cannot be maintained all the time; now and then a player needs some rest.

That is why the third game is markedly different in character from the preceding two. Possibly, the lovers of chess were even disappointed to some extent. Indeed, merely twenty moves were played in the game, and the opponents agreed to draw it in a position where fighting resources were not yet completely exhausted. But it would be unjust to call the game dull or peaceful. The combatants were very inventive in their handling of one of the well-tested lines of the Queen's Gambit. In short, whereas the third game was less dramatic and spectacular than the first two, it was no less instructive.

1. d2-d4 (0)	Ng8-f6 (1)
2. c2-c4 (0)	e7-e6 (0)
3. Ng1-f3 (0)	. . .

The first interesting moment. After his undoubted success in the Nimzo-Indian Defence (game one), Kasparov is the first to vary. Mikhail Botvinnik used to advise keeping to one's opening repertoire until its shortcomings became evident. Nowadays, however, the conduct of a competition is more flexible, and players usually vary their openings in order to find out weak spots in the opponent's preparations.

3. . . .	d7-d5 (1)
4. Nb1-c3 (2)	Bf8-e7 (0)
5. Bc1-g5 (1)	h7-h6 (0)
6. Bg5xf6 (6)	Be7xf6 (0)

Another point of interest. The reader will readily notice that this position has repeatedly occurred in games between Karpov and Kasparov, who have played it as both White and Black. The World Champion willingly adopted this variation with the White pieces in their previous match. The Challenger, who gained rich experience in defending this position as Black, also succeeded in finding some new possibilities for White (e.g., his game against I. Timman in the USSR vs Rest of the World Match, London, 1984).

7. Qd1-b3 (1) . . .

A little surprise in the opening. The approved lines begin with 7. e3, 7. Qd2, or 7. Qc2 (the move previously adopted by Kasparov himself). Although the White Queen's thrust is not an innovation, it has never before played in top chess competitions.

7. . . . c7-c6 (28)

Karpov takes nearly half an hour to decide on this solid move to strengthen Black's position in the centre. But, of course, his long meditation means he is choosing a strategic plan, rather than a single move. It is known that the main idea of Black's counterplay in this variation is associated with undermining the centre with c7-c5, Black even being ready to sacrifice a Pawn in order to activate his pieces, in particular his King's Bishop. A double-edged possibility was at Black's disposal at this moment: 7. . . . c5 8. dxc 0-0, but one has to be in a proper mood to decide on such a continuation. Karpov, for whom White's previous move seemed to be unexpected, decided not to take the risk.

8. e2-e3 (3) . . .

Kasparov is also cautious. A sharp alternative is the plan suggested by E. Kuzminykh: 8. 0-0-0 Nd7 9. e4 dxe 10. Nxe4 0-0 11. g4. The choice depends on many subjective considerations, but it is perhaps now that Kasparov has to some extent given up his opening advantage.

8. . . .	Nb8-d7 (12)
9. Ra1-d1 (3)	0-0 (4)
10. Bf1-d3 (1)	b7-b6 (2)

Strangely enough, this natural move is an innovation. Reference sources give only the manoeuvre 10. ... Qb6, tested in the Hulak—Zvetkovic game (Yugoslavia, 1984) where, after 11. Qc2 dxc 12. Bxc4 c5 13. 0-0 cxd 14. exd, Black ran into difficulties.

11. c4xd5 (4)	. . .

Kasparov decides to take advantage of the temporary weakening of the a8-h1 diagonal to seize the initiative, even at the price of discharging the central tension.
A slower way of consolidating, 11. 0-0 followed by e3-e4, deserves consideration.

11. . . .	c6xd5 (7)
12. e3-e4 (6)	d5xe4 (5)
13. Bd3xe4 (1)	Ra8-b8 (0)
14. 0-0 (5)	. . .
(No. 9)	

Outwardly, Kasparov's operation looks attractive. White's development is superior, and he commands more space. Moreover, White now has at his disposal a new and important motif for activating his forces further—the breakthrough d4-d5. Despite all this, it is very hard for White, as further play will testify,

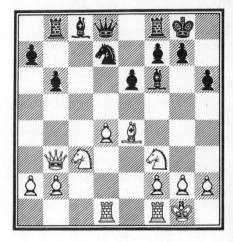

No. 9

to make use of these positive factors, because Black's position is very strong.

14. . . .	b6-b5 (7)

A happy choice of move! On the one hand, Black threatens eventually to drive away the White Knight from its useful position on c3; on the other hand, the Black Queen may now go to b6 or a5, both of which seem attractive. The tempting 14. ... Bb7 would be wrong though, in view of 15. Qa4.

15. Rf1-e1 (12)	. . .

One can hardly object to this manoeuvre, by which White harmoniously completes the mobilisation of his forces. Yet, in retrospect, one gets the impression that the struggle for the initiative in this position requires more specific actions. Since it is evident that White's main trump is the breakthrough d4-d5, which would be disadvantageous now because of Black's retort Nc5, Kasparov should perhaps have played the preliminary

15. Bb1, enhancing the above threat.

   15. . . .   Qd8-b6 (8)

Both 15. . . . Qa5 and 15. . . . b4 are quite playable here, which suggests that Black has completely equalized the game.

   16. Be4-b1 (34) . . .

Very remarkably, White's obvious advantages somehow turn into disadvantages. The secret of it is that, although all White's pieces are optimally placed, White is incapable of launching active operations anywhere, because there are no vulnerable spots in the enemy camp. Paradoxically enough, it is Black whose task is now easier. He has a clear plan to regroup his forces, namely Rf8-d8, Nd7-f8, and Bc8-b7, which would guarantee him good prospects.

  Therefore, after prolonged thought, Kasparov decides to force matters and head for a draw.

   16. . . .   Bc8-b7 (11)

Perhaps 16. . . . Rd8, to counter 17. d5 or 17. Qc2 which the further consolidation of his forces using 17. . . . Nf8, would be still more reliable.

   17. Qd1-c2 (4) g7-g6 (0)
   18. d4-d5 (0)   . . .

At last! The long anticipated breakthrough has finally occurred, but its effectiveness is relatively small, because Black is now ready for it.

   18. . . .   e6xd5 (11)

It's the only way! Karpov avoids a cunning trap. The tempting 18. . . . Bxc3

would be met by the brilliant 19. Rxe6! , shattering the Black King's shelter. Here is an illustrative variation: 19. . . . fxe 20. Qxg6+ Bg7 21. Qh7+ Kf7 22. dxe+ Qxe6 (obviously, after 22. . . . Kxe6 23. Qxg7, White's threats are also irresistible). 23. Rxd7+! Qxd7 24. Ne5+. As it is, the game becomes much simpler.

   19. Nc3xd5 (2) Bb7xd5 (0)
   20. Rd1xd5 (0) Rf8-d8 (3)

No. 10

In spite of several exchanges, the battlefield does not appear to be empty. On the contrary, White's active pieces seem to offer some chance of success. True, the possible sequels—21. Qd2 Nf8 22. Rxd8 Rxd8 23. Qxh6 Bxb2 24. h4, and 21. a3 Nf8 22. Ba2 Rxd5 23. Bxd5—are fairly harmless for Black, but the players' decision to cease the struggle seems somewhat premature. Certainly in view of White's position. Still, as we have already said, the match strategy had a logic of its own.

  Game drawn.
  Time: 1.35-1.40

GAME FOUR

Queen's Gambit Declined

A. Karpov   G. Kasparov

A surprising feature of the dispute between Karpov and Kasparov is their readiness, playing either colour, to defend the same key lines of currently popular openings as if they wanted to compete with each other in the originality and depth of their handling of these lines. It is interesting to note that, in some schemes, the dispute which started in their previous match is renewed. The following game is one example of this.

1. d2-d4 (0)   d7-d5 (2)
2. c2-c4 (2)   e7-e6 (1)
3. Nb1-c3 (3)   Bf8-e7 (3)
4. Ng1-f3 (7)   Ng8-f6 (0)
5. Bc1-g5 (0)   h7-h6 (1)
6. Bg5xf6 (0)   Be7xf6 (0)

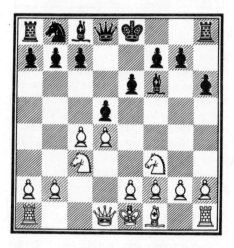

No. 11

A familiar position? This position was more than once seen in their previous games. Karpov had it playing White three times, and Kasparov demonstrated an original method of fighting for the initiative in the preceding game of the present match. But more remarkable is that this dispute has not ended, as we now know, with this (fifth) attempt to settle it. And one can hardly assert that one day it won't be continued...

7. e2-e3 (0)   0-0 (0)
8. Qd1-c2 (1)   Nb8-a6!? (10)

A prepared surprise! Kasparov himself and other leading exponents usually preferred 8. ... c5, to reply to 9. dxc with either 9. ... Nc6 or 9. ... dxc (as, incidentally, was played in the 27th game of their previous match). The idea behind the move in the text is the speediest mobilisation of pieces and the preparation for active operations on the Queen's side.

9. Ra1-d1 (23)   ...

By aiming at the Black d5-Pawn, Karpov strives to impede Black's intended undermining of the White centre Pawns.

9. ...   c7-c5!? (3)

All the same, he does it! To attain his object, Kasparov is ready to sacrifice material.

10. d4xc5 (13)   Qd8-a5 (4)
11. c4xd5 (1)   Na6xc5 (0)
12. Qc2-d2 (4)   ...

Karpov's intuition tells him that it is high time to take preventive measures. Obviously, after 12. dxe Bxe6, White would be in a dangerous situation, as he would be considerably behind in deploying his K-side forces. Accordingly, Karpov first of all relieves the pin on his Knight and consolidates his position in the centre.

12. ...   Rf8-d8 (17)
13. Nf3-d4! ?(3) e6xd5 (8)
14. Bf1-e2 (0)   ...

Having blocked all the roads to his camp (along the diagonals a5-e1 and h8-a1 and the d-file), White is now able to complete the development of his pieces unimpeded.

14. ...   Qa5-b6 (8)

Another possibility would be to simplify the game by 14. ... Ne6 15. Nb3 Bxc3 16. Nxa5 Bxd2+ 17. Rxd2 d4, but Kasparov prefers to retain the tension.

15. 0-0 (0)   Kc5-e4 (1)
16. Qd2-c2 (3)   ...

The Exchange at e4 would, of course, be advantageous to Black.

16. ...   Ne4xc3 (7)
17. Qc2xc3 (0)   Bc8-e6 (2)

The thrust 17. ... Bf5 also looks tempting.

The outcome of the opening should perhaps be equally satisfying for both sides. White has the better pawn configuration and a stable stronghold on d4—just what Karpov likes to have. Black has active pieces—much to Kasparov's liking.

18. Qc3-c2 (15) ...

A subtle manoeuvre. In order to neutralize his opponent's impending initiative, Karpov withdraws his Queen to a safe, yet promising, position.

18. ...   Ra8-c8 (5)
19. Qc2-b1 (0)   Rc8-c7 (13)
20. Rd1-d2 (10) Rd8-c8 (5)

All these moves seem to be quite appropriate. To counterpoise White's pressure along the d-file, Black concentrates his forces on the adjacent open line. However, it is from this moment that, almost imperceptibly, but steadily, the scales begin to tilt in White's favour. Therefore, with hindsight, we may perhaps judge Kasparov's twentieth move as unhappy or, at least, indiscreet. It would be safer to exchange on d4.

21. Nd4xe6! (3) f7xe6 (0)

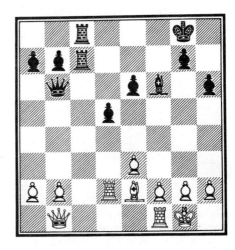

No. 12

The character of the game has radically changed. Both sides having equal forces, there are opposite-colour Bishops on the board. In the endgame, they are the forerunners of peace, whereas in the middlegame, the disturbers of peace. Taking into consideration the weakness of the white squares on Black's K-side and the vulnerable pawn island in the centre, one can already at this stage infer that Karpov's white-bound Bishop is more valuable than his black-bound counterpart. However, this advantage does not seem very considerable, because Kasparov's heavy pieces look more active than Karpov's. Still, as we know, the World Champion finally succeeds in exploiting his advantage. Interestingly, he plays the following seventeen moves solely "on the white keys".

22. Be2-g4 (0)	Rc7-c4 (7)
23. h2-h3 (1)	Qb6-c6 (2)
24. Qb1-d3 (6)	...

The time to invade has not yet come. The thrust 24. Qg6 can be met by 24. ... Qe8.

24. ...	Kg8-h8 (3)

In the opinion of Kasparov, 24. ... a5 would be simpler, and 25. f4 (threatening f4-f5) is not dangerous because of 25. ... Rc5.

25. Rf1-d1 (6)	a7-a5 (4)

As will be seen from the further progress of the game, Black's actions on the Q-side promise him nothing. Therefore it would perhaps be more rational to give up his aggressive plan and begin to simplify the game by 25. ... Rc1. Or he could revert to the simplifying tactics a little later.

26. b2-b3 (2)	...

This displays Karpov's confidence in the impenetrability of White's Q-side.

26. ...	Rc4-c3 (4)
27. Qd3-e2 (1)	Rc8-f8 (2)

And this is a sign of Kasparov's being worried about his position.

28. Bg4-h5! (11)	...

A profound idea. The Bishop is to be transferred to the b1-h7 diagonal, where it will meet no opposition.

28. ...	b7-b5 (8)

Kasparov believes that 28. ... Bd8 was worth considering, and could be followed by 29. Bg6 (29. e4 Bb6) 29. ... Bc7 30. Bd3 Qd6 31. g3 Qe5 32. Qg4 Qf6, and White would not be able to improve his position.

29. Bh5-g6 (0)	Bf6-d8 (2)
30. Bg6-d3 (5)	b5-b4 (0)
31. Qe2-g4 (0)	...

Threatening 32. Qg6. It becomes evident that White firmly holds the initiative.

31. ...	Qc6-e8 (2)
(No. 13)	
32. e3-e4 (5)	...

Taking aim at another target. Now it is Black's centre pawn island that is under fire. The opening-up of the game, though double-edged (the Black pieces also come to life), has been assessed by Karpov very precisely. The alternative would be the more restrained 32. h4.

32. ...	Bd8-g5 (7)
33. Rd2-c2 (1)	...

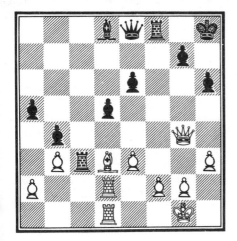

No. 13

Not of course 33. Re2, in view of 33. ... Rf4.

| 33. ... | Rc3xc2 (8) |

In Kasparov's opinion this last move was a serious positional mistake while 33. ... Qc6 34. ed Qxd5, or 33. ... Qc8 34. ed ed 35. Qxc8 Rfxc8 36. Re2 Rc1 37. Rxc1 Rxc1+ 38. Kh2 Rc8 39. Bg6 Bf6 could lead to a passive but stable defence.

| 34. Bd3xc2 (0) | Qe8-c6 (0) |

Kasparov, true to his fighting spirit, looks for any chance of activating his pieces. At the same time, the Black Queen's withdrawal from the King's side (and this is only the beginning of its inroad into White's Q-side) is fraught with grave consequences, as will be seen later. The modest 34. ... Qf7 would undoubtedly be safer.

| 35. Qg4-e2 (3) | Qc6-c5 (2) |
| 36. Rd1-f1 (4) | ... |

The necessary precaution. Black threatened 36. ... Rxf2 37. Qxf2 Be3.

| 36. ... | Qc5-c3 (0) |

In the same over-optimistic spirit. Still it was very hard to foresee that the tempting activation of the Queen would only worsen, rather than improve, Black's standing.

| 37. e4xd5 (2) | e6xd5 (0) |
| 38. Bc2-b1! (0) | ... |

The position has crystallized. Black's temporary initiative has evaporated, whereas White has only just begun to play his trumps. It will be sufficient for him to transfer his Queen to one of the squares on the b1-h7 diagonal, and the Black King becomes an accessible target. Strangely enough, it is very hard to oppose this straightforward plan because, as we have already mentioned, opposite-colour Bishops always favour the attacker in the middlegame.

| 38. ... | Qc3-d2 (5) |
| 39. Qe2-e5 (11) | ... |

There is no point in White's departing from the main line to snatch a Pawn by 39. Qxd2 Bxd2 40. Rd1 Bg5 41. Rxd5 because by playing 41. ... Rd8, Black would force the Exchange of Rooks and the other (neutralizing) property of opposite-colour Bishops would show itself in the ensuing endgame. At the same time 39. Qe6 is worth considering.

| 39. ... | Rf8-d8 (3) |

Kasparov says this was a crucial error; on the other hand, 39. ... Bf6 40. Qf5 Kg8 41. Bd3 Rd8 would have given hope for a stubborn defence.

40. Qe5-f5 (0)	Kh8-g8 (0)

No. 14

Here the game was adjourned and Karpov sealed his move. It is clear that White has the initiative, but the question is whether his initiative is enough to win the game. The adjournment session has shown that it is and that Black's defensive resources are far smaller than one would suppose.

41. Qf5-e6+ (6)	Kg8-h8 (0)
42. Qe6-g6 (0)	Kh8-g8 (0)
43. Qg6-e6+ (0)	Kg8-h8 (0)
44. Bb1-f5! (0)	...

A very strong move. Karpov creates the additional threat of 45. Re1, which could not be played at once because of 44. ... Rf8.

44. ...	Qd2-c3 (0)

Hurrying to the defence of his King, but there is no time...

45. Qe6-g6 (0)	Kh8-g8 (0)
46. Bf5-e6+ (3)	Kg8-h8 (0)
47. Be6-f5 (0)	Kh8-g8 (0)
48. g2-g3 (6)	...

The way Karpov plays this ending is very instructive. Taking advantage of the fact that his opponent has no counterplay, the World Champion steadily improves the position of his pieces, making no haste to force matters. White's immediate plan is to place his King on g2, and then transfer his Rook from f1 via d1 and d3 to e3 or f3.

48. ...	Kg8-f8 (4)
49. Kg1-g2 (5)	Qc3-f6 (10)

Perhaps 49. ... Be7 would be more stubborn, to meet 50. Rd1 by 50. ... Rd6. Although this would not change the general assessment.

50. Qg6-h7 (2)	Qf6-f7 (0)

Otherwise, White would simply respond with 51. f4, winning a piece.

51. h3-h4 (1)	Bg5-d2 (1)

There is nothing to be done about it, Black has to withdraw yet another piece, leaving his King almost without protection. In the event of 51. ... Be7, White could immediately decide the game by playing 52. Re1, threatening either 53. Be6 or 53. Bg6.

52. Rf1-d1 (0)	Bd2-c3 (0)
53. Rd1-d3 (10)	...

White's plan is fulfilled. Once the long-range artillery has come into action, his attack becomes irresistible.

53. ...	Rd8-d6 (13)

Kasparov should perhaps have attempted to drive the White Queen away from its active position by playing 53. ... Qg8 54. Qg6 Qf7. Now the game is ended by force.

54. Rd3-f3! (1)	...

A study-like finesse. On the other hand, White would gain nothing by 54. Re3, in view of 54. ... g5, and Black would luckily escape.

54. ...	Kf8-e7 (7)

The Black King has to leave his refuge. It turns out that Black's attempts to stop up the f-file by 54. ... Rf6, or 54. ... Bf6, would fail against the decisive 55. Re3, because in the former case the defence 55. ... g5 is insufficient in view of 56. Qh8+ (the Bishop's action being blocked), while in the latter case 55. ... g5 would be followed by 56. Qxh6+ (the Rook's action being blocked).

55. Qh7-h8! (21)	...

Again the best move. Should White succumb to the temptation of a direct attack upon the Black King by 55. Re3+ Kd8 56. Qh8+ Kc7 57. Qc8+, he would merely risk letting it escape to a relatively safe refuge. As it is, the decisive 56. Re3+ is threatened.

55. ...	d5-d4 (12)

To 55. ... Be5, Karpov would reply with 56. Bh3, and if 56. ... Rf6, then 57. Re3! Rxf2+ 58. Kg1.

56. Qh8-c8 (3)	Rd6-f6 (6)

57. Qc8-c5+ (17)	Ke7-e8 (5)
58. Rf3-f4 (4)	Qf1-b7+ (1)
59. Rf4-e4+ (1)	Ke8-f7 (2)

Black's ingenious 59. ... Re6! ? (intending to answer 60. Bxe6? with 60. ... Qxe4+) would be refuted by the equally ingenious 60. Qc4! Rxe4 61. Qg8+ Ke7 62. Qxg7+, followed by 63. Qxb7.

60. Qc5-c4+ (8)	Kf7-f8 (0)
61. Bf5-h7! (4)	...

Oh, these white squares!

61. ...	Rf6-f7 (2)
62. Qc4-e6 (1)	Qb7-d7 (1)
63. Qe6-e5! (1)	

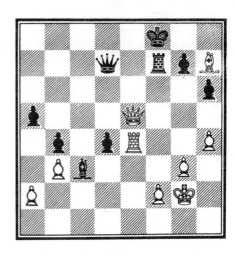

No. 15

Black resigns. His defensive resources are exhausted. After 63. ... Re7, White would decide the issue by 64. Qf4+ Rf7 65. Qb8+, while 63. ... Qd8 would be answered by 64. Qc5+ Re7 65. Rf4+ Ke8 66. Qc6+ Qd7 67. Bg6+, and 63. ... Qe7 by 64. Qb8+.

An impressive achievement on Karpov's part! This game has been called a "white-key symphony".

Time: 4.00-3.37.

14 September 1985

GAME FIVE

Ruy López

G. Kasparov   A. Karpov

Everyone was interested in the strategy Kasparov would follow now that the score was even. Would he take the line of minimun risk and quiet play, lying in wait for his chance, or would he attempt to take immediate revenge for his loss of the previous game?

Much to the delight of all who love chess, the latter happened. Kasparov revealed his aggressive intentions, opening the game with his King's Pawn. Karpov accepted the challenge.

1. e2-e4 (1)	e7-e5 (0)
2. Ng1-f3 (0)	Nb8-c6 (1)
3. Bf1-b5 (0)	. . .

This time the Ruy López, the opening which occurred in the forty-fourth and forty-sixth games of their previous contest. In those games Karpov succeeded (both times as Black) in keeping the balance. Yet he did it only after a hard and complicated struggle, during which White had a lasting initiative.

3. . . .	a7-a6 (0)
4. Bb5-a4 (0)	Ng8-f6 (0)
5. 0-0 (1)	Bf8-e7 (0)
6. Rf1-e1 (0)	b7-b5 (0)
7. Ba4-b3 (0)	d7-d6 (2)

8. c2-c3 (0)	0-0 (0)
9. h2-h3 (0)	Bc8-b7 (5)
10. d2-d4 (0)	Rf8-e8 (0)

This build-up, proposed by Karpov's second Zaitsev, has recently become very popular in tournament chess.

11. Nb1-d2 (1)	Be7-f8 (8)
12. a2-a4 (4)	Qd8-d7 (7)
13. a4xb5 (16)	a6xb5 (0)
14. Ra1xa8 (1)	Bb7xa8 (0)
15. d4-d5 (1)	

All these moves were played in the forty-sixth game of the previous match and continued 15. ... Nd8 16. Nf1 h6 (the threat was 17. Bg5) 17. N3h2 Nb7 18. Bc2 Nc5 19. b4 Na6 20. Ng4, with a clear advantage for White.

15. . . .	Nc6-a5! (5)

This move, gaining tempo, looks more logical than 15. ... Nd8, as in the game cited above.

16. Bb3-a2 (4)	c7-c6 (3)
17. b2-b4 (0)	Na5-b7 (0)

The line 17. ... Nc4 18. Nxc4 bxc 19. Bg5! (19. Bxc4 cxd 20. Bxd5 Nxd5 21. exd Qb5; if 20. exd, then 20. ... Qb7 or 20. ... Rc8) would lead to complications advantageous to White: for example, 19. ... cxd 20. Bxf6 dxe 21. Nxe5 Qa7 22. Bxc4 dxe 23. Bd8! .

The position that has arisen after Black's seventeenth move Nb7 deserved detailed examination. (**No. 16**)

The first impression is that White commands more space, while Black's pieces, especially the Bishop on a8 and the Knight on b7, are placed very passively. That White has a positional advantage

56

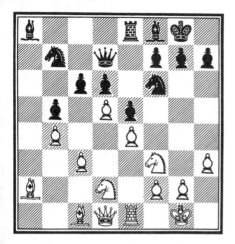

No. 16

seems to be beyond doubt. However, all is not so simple as one would think. As Nimzowitsch pointed out, a cramped position is sometimes like a compressed spring which may expand suddenly. Therefore, we should first of all establish whether White can keep his centre set-up, and especially the Pawn on d5, intact. Obviously, it is this Pawn that plays the key part, blocking the diagonal for the Black Bishop on a8 and controlling the squares c6 and e6, thereby restricting the mobility of the Black Knight on b7.

Let us attempt to hold the Pawn on d5 by the method employed by Kasparov in the game already cited above: 18. Nf1 cxd 19. exd h6 20. N3h2 Nd8 21. Ng4 Nh7 and, because of the threat of f7-f5, Black fights on for the d5-square.

In the present game, Kasparov carries out a different plan, bringing his c-Pawn into action, which looks a rather good idea.

18. c3-c4 (2)	Re8-c8 (20)
19. d5xc6?! (12)	. . .

But this move raises serious objections. It seems to us that White's task consists in keeping Black's position cramped. Kasparov is evidently of the opinion that, when the game is opened up, his pieces, which have already taken aim at Black's K-side, will be more active than Black's. Maya Chiburdanidze's recommendation of 19. Qe2, to maintain the central tension, appears more logical.

19. . . .	Qd7xc6 (0)
20. c4-c5 (0)	. . .

White's idea reveals itself: after 20. . . . dxc there would follow 21. Bxf7+. However, the f7-square can easily be defended; moreover, the Black Knight may now be conveniently placed on e6.

20. . . .	Nb7-d8 (16)
21. Bc1-b2 (4)	. . .

No. 17

At first sight the White Bishops look menacing, but Black's King's side is reliably protected, while the Black pieces have now come into play. Therefore Karpov dares further complications, rightly judging that White's resources are insufficient for a serious attack.

21. ...   d6xc5! (17)
22. b4xc5 (0)   ...

After 22. Nxe5 Qa6 23. Qa1 c4 24. Bc3 Qa3 25. Re3, Black can play 25. ... Bxb4 26. Nexc4 bxc 27. Bxf6 c3! , with a good game.

An alternative is 22. Bxe5 Nd7 23. Bb2 c4 24. Bc3, but this would mean shifting to another track.

22. ...   Qc6xc5 (0)
23. Bb2xe5 (3)   ...

After 23. Nxe5, 23. ... Qc2 would be unpleasant.

23. ...   Nf6-d7 (3)
24. Be5-b2 (15) Qc5-b4! (1)

This is stronger than 24. ... Qc2 25. Qa1 Qa4 26. Nd4 Nc5 27. Re3, with a sharp game. After the move in the text, the initiative is completely Black's.

No. 18

25. Nd2-b3?(30) ...

Kasparov thought about this move for half an hour, but failed to find a way out. His was a difficult choice. After 25. Qa1, there could follow 25. ... Nc5, while 25. Qb1 could be met by 25. ... Ne6. His position was perhaps defensible, but now it is critical.

25. ...   Nd7-c5 (7)
26. Bb2-a1 (10) ...

White gives up a Pawn in the hope that open lines will allow him a chance for active play with his pieces. What else could he do? After 26. Nxc5; the variation 26. ... Qxb2 27. Re2 Qa3 28. Nd3 Bxe4 29. Bxf7+ Nxf7 30. Rxe4 b4 is unpleasant for him.

26. ...   Ba8xe4 (10)
27. Nf3-d4 (12) ...

After 27. Ng5, there could have followed the spectacular 27. ... Bc2! 28. Qxc2 Qxe1+ 29. Kh2 Bd6+ 30. g3 Ne4! , winning (suggested by Yuri Kotkov).

27. ...   Nd8-b7 (4)
28. Qd1-e2 (11) Nb7-d6 (4)
29. Nb3xc5 (1)   Qb4xc5 (2)

White has no compensation for the lost Pawn. Black's task now is to simplify. Being pressed for time, Karpov strives to play solidly and securely to adjourn the game.

30. Qe2-g4 (3)   Rc8-e8 (1)
31. Re1-d1 (2)   Be4-g6 (2)
32. Qg4-f4 (2)   Qc5-b4! (7)
33. Qf4-c1 (1)   Bg6-e4 (11)
34. Rd1-e1 (1)   Qb4-a5 (3)
35. Ba2-b3 (1)   Qa5-a8 (0)

36. Qc1-b2 (2)	b5-b4 (3)
37. Re1-e3 (4)	Be4-g6 (2)
38. Re1xe8 (1)	Qa8xe8 (0)
39. Qb2-c1 (0)	Nd6-e4 (2)
40. Bb3-d5 (1)	Ne4-c5 (1)
41. Nd4-b3 (2)	

Here the game was adjourned. Karpov sealed his move 41. ... Nc5-d3 (7). Black's extra passed Pawn should ensure him a win.

Kasparov resigns without resumption. Time: 2.28-2.33.

GAME SIX

Queen's Gambit Declined

| | |
| A. Karpov | G. Kasparov |

The first five games of the present match gave chess fans much excitement. Having won the first game, the Challenger took the lead. He also nearly succeeded in winning the second game, which was drawn. And then the World Champion turned the tables by scoring full points in the fourth and fifth games.

It is about such a situation that Kasparov wrote in his book *Ordeal by Time*: "Changing my game under enemy fire could be disastrous. Therefore, it was first of all necessary to gain time, that is to hold out against my rival's onslaught in the next few games." This was Kasparov's motto in the sixth game.

This game was played after a free day and the first time-out taken by the Challenger.

1. d2-d4 (1)	d7-d5 (1)
2. c2-c4 (0)	e7-e6 (0)
3. Nb1-c3 (2)	Bf8-e7 (1)
4. Ng1-f3 (1)	Ng8-f6 (0)
5. Bc1-g5 (0)	h7-h6 (0)
6. Bg5xf6 (0)	Be7xf6 (0)
7. e2-e3 (0)	0-0 (0)
8. Qd1-d2 (0)	...

In the fourth game of the present match, Karpov played 8. Qc2, but gained no advantage. Therefore, the World Champion adopts the move in the text, which, with a different order of moves, he employed in the previous match.

| 8. ... | d5xc4 (8) |

Kasparov rejects 8. ... Nc6, although in the 19th game of the previous match he managed after 9. Rc1 a6 10. Be2 dxc 11. Bxc4 e5 12. d5 Ne7, to keep the game balanced. Perhaps his belief that Karpov will surprise him in the opening is not groundless.

9. Bf1xc4 (2)	Nb8-d7 (0)
10. 0-0 (5)	c7-c5 (2)
11. Rf1-d1 (0)	c5xd4 (4)

White is better developed, and commands more space. Therefore, Black should play very purposefully in order not to get into trouble. His main problem is to bring his Queen's Bishop into play.

12. Nf3xd4 (0)	Nd7-b6 (5)
13. Bc4-e2! (0)	...
(No. 19)	

In the Belyavsky-Portisch game (Tilburg, 1984), White placed his Bishop on b3, where it remained passive. Karpov plays more precisely: he transfers his Bishop to f3, whence it will be able to attack the Black Pawn on b7.

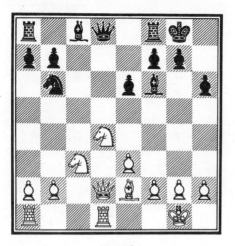

No. 19

13. . . .	Bc8-d7 (6)
14. Be2-f3 (5)	Ra8-b8 (4)
15. Nc3-e4 (12)	. . .

White launches active operations. Now 16. Qa5 threatens; therefore Kasparov decides to discharge the position.

15. . . .	Bf6xd4 (7)
16. Qd2xd4 (0)	Bd7-a4! (7)

Worse is 16. . . . Bc6 17. Qc5, and if 17. . . . Bd5 then 18. Nc3, while after 17. . . . Qc7, 18. Nd6 would be strong.

17. Qd4xd8 (7)	Rf8xd8 (1)
18. Rd1xd8+ (0)	Rb8xd8 (0)
19. Ne4-c5 (0)	. . .

By playing very consistently White has attained his object—the Black Pawn on b7 must fall. However, by way of compensation, Black can activate his Rook.

19. . . .	Rd8-d2 (2)
20. b2-b3 (5)	. . .

This move seems very natural: White relieves his Pawn with a gain of tempo. However, the immediate 20. b4 deserves serious consideration. For instance, 20. . . . Bc6 21. Nxb7 Bxf3 22. gxf and if 22. . . . Rb2 23. a3 Nc4, then 24. Nc5 g5 25. Rd1 Nxa3 26. Rd8+ Kg7 27. Rd7; having given the Pawn back, White has much activated his pieces. If, however, Black were to respond with 22. . . . Nd7, then White would gain tempo, as compared with the actual game, and may possibly have a winning chance in sharp variations arising from the pawn advance on the Q-side.

20. . . .	Ba4-c6 (0)
21. Bc5xb7 (0)	Bc6xf3 (0)
22. g2xf3 (0)	Nb6-d7! (3)

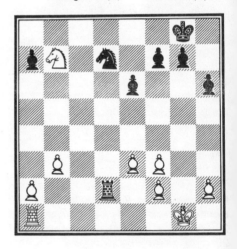

No. 20

That White's K-side is weakened provides an important motif for Black's counterplay. Therefore, the Black Knight heads for e5 to attack White's Pawn on f3, simultaneously preventing the White Knight from occupying, for the moment, the c5-square.

23. Kg1-g2 (25)   g7-g5 (3)

In this way, Black improves his King's position and prepares, at the same time, a threat to the White King.

24. b3-b4 (11)   Nd7-b6 (17)

Another possibility is 24. ... Ne5 25. Nc5 (threatening 25. ... Nd3) Nc4 26. Kg3 Na3! , and it would be very hard for White to make headway. Kasparov prefers a more dynamic plan, threatening to fork the White Pawns on b4 and e3 with his Knight: 25. ... Nd5.

25. Kg2-f1 (7)   ...

Neither 25. Kg3 Nd5 26. b5 h5, with the unpleasant threat of 27. ... h4+, nor 25. b5 Nc4! (25. ... Nd5 26. Kg1) 26. Kg3 (or g1) Na3, can be attractive for White. Nor can he throw caution to the winds by playing 25. a4 Nd5 26. b5 Nxe3+ 27. Kg1 Nc2 28. Ra2 Rd1+ 29. Kg2 Ne1+ 30. Kf1 Nxf3+ 31. Ke2 Rd7, because it is Black who has an extra Pawn now.

25. ...   Nb6-d7 (1)

The Knight again heads for the unprotected Pawn on f3. Here, too, the reckless line 26. a4 Ne5 27. b5 Nxf3 28. a5 Nxh2+ 29. Kg1 (if 29. Kg2, then 29. ... Ng4 30. b6 axb 31. a6 Nxe3+ 32. Kg3 Nd5 33. a7 Nc7 34. Rc1 Ra2) 29. ... Nf3+ 30. Kg2 Ne5 31. b6 axb 32. a6 Nc6 33. a7 Nxa7 34. Rxa7 Rd7 35. Ra8+ Kg7 36. Rb8 would lead White nowhere: Black does not risk a loss in this position (no better is 33. Rb1, to which Black can reply with 33. ... Na7 34. Rxb6 Rd7). The line 26. Na5 Ne5 27. b5 Nd3 28. Nc6 Rxf2+ 29. Kg1

Rb2 30. Nxa7 Ne5 is risky for White, who should now think of a draw.

26. Kf1-g2 (21)   Nd7-b6 (1)
27. Kg2-f1 (14)   Nb6-d7 (0)

After 28. Kg2 Nb6, the position will have been repeated three times, hence the game was drawn. Any attempt by White to play for a win would be fraught with danger.

Time: 2.23-1.12.

21 September 1985

GAME SEVEN

Nimzo-Indian Defence

G. Kasparov   A. Karpov

This encounter proceeds rather unconventionally. The events in it are highly intriguing, and the fierce, relentless battle lasts to the end. Perhaps the most distinguishing feature of this game is the unpredictability of the contestants' decisions. Indeed, even the highly authoritative council of Grandmasters, which was lively discussing the twists and turns of the duel in the press room, often failed to guess which move would be played.

Having already played over fifty games against each other, Karpov and Kasparov now know each other so well that when deciding on a plan or even a single move, they sometimes seem to be guided by circumstances and considerations unknown to anybody else, and their judgement seems to be based on psychological factors rather than objective, pure chess criteria.

It is from this point of view that we

shall attempt to answer the questions posed by this intricate game.

1. d2-d4 (1)	Ng8-f6 (4)
2. c2-c4 (0)	e7-e6 (0)
3. Nb1-c3 (0)	Bf8-b4 (0)

Again the Nimzo-Indian Defence.

4. Ng1-f3 (1)	0-0 (5)

This natural developing move should not have arrested our attention—the more so that it does not yet determine the future structure. But when commenting on a game between two top chess players, a game whose development may be affected even by seemingly negligible nuances in the opening moves, we should dwell on this 4. . . . 0-0. Strangely enough, it is this "natural developing move" that is the origin of Black's further troubles.

In the Nimzo-Indian Defence, when success largely depends on the flexibility of a player's strategical plans and delicate manoeuvring in the opening phase, an early castling, which precedes the establishment of a pawn configuration, generally reduces very substantially Black's opportunities, especially if the White Queen's Bishop may go to g5.

5. Bc1-g5 (2)	. . .

Of course! The pin of the Knight is very unpleasant for Black here.

5. . . .	d7-d6 (2)

The attempt to seize the initiative, at the price of weakening the castled position of the Black King by 5. . . . h6 6. Bh4 g5 7. Bg3 Ne4, is risky. After 8. Qc2 f5 9. e3 b6 10. h4 g4 11. Ne5

Nxg3 12. fxg Qf6 13. 0-0-0, Black has serious problems (Gulko-Rashkovsky, 44th USSR Championship, 1976).

In the event of 5. . . . c5 6. e3 Qa5 7. Bxf6! ? Bxc3+ 8. bxc Qxc3+ 9. Nd2 gxf 10. Rc1 Qa5 11. Qg4+ Kh8 12. Qh4, as was played in the Taimanov-Esteves game (Leningrad, 1973), the defects of Black's K-side pawn configuration give him a great deal of trouble.

Karpov chooses the most restrained plan to strengthen his position in the centre.

6. e2-e3 (9)	Nb8-d7 (2)
7. Qd1-c2 (18)	b7-b6 (1)

This method of development, whose object is to set up control over the white centre squares, is characteristic of many lines in the Nimzo-Indian Defence. However, in this position, where Black has already castled Kingside and his Knight can be unpinned only at the cost of considerable positional concessions, the fianchettoing of the Queen's Bishop is no longer attractive. Moreover, the White King may castle long, which will facilitate White's active operations on the King's side.

Black should perhaps have preferred 7. . . . e5 (or 7. . . . h6 8. Bh4 e5). For instance, in the Larsen-Matanovic game (Monte Carlo, 1967), after 8. Be2 Re8 9. 0-0 Bxc3 10. bxc, Black's position, though somewhat passive, is quite solid.

8. Bf1-d3 (2)	Bb4xc3+ (4)
9. b2xc3 (5)	. . .

Needless to say, in the event of 9. Qxc3 Bb7, Black's task would be much simpler.

9. . . .	h7-h6 (20)

Probably, it is on this move that Karpov makes the brave decision to start counterplaying on the King-side, although this plan is doubtless risky.

The alternative is the less drastic 9. ... Qe8 10. e4 e5, but here Black would have to defend himself in an unpromising position arising after 11. 0-0 Bb7 12. Rae1.

10. Bg5-h4 (0)	Bc8-b7 (3)
11. Nf3-d2! (3)	...

The challenge to a relentless duel. Taking advantage of the possibility of Queen-side castling, Kasparov is preparing for an action against the Black King, without stopping at a pawn sacrifice.

No. 21

11. ...	g7-g5!? (26)

Tit for tat! Needless to say, to accept the sacrifice would be dangerous, because after 11. ... Bxg2 12. Rg1 Bb7 13. 0-0-0, White would have at his disposal the open g-file, a powerful

pawn centre, and actively placed pieces. Still, the plan of counterplay adopted by the World Champion does require strong nerves although, of course, there is nothing else for it. In the event of 11. ... e5 12. 0-0 Qe7 13. Bf5!?, Black can hardly be envied.

12. Bh4-g3 (0)	Nf6-h5 (0)
13. Qc2-d1?! (22)	...

How bizarre a Grandmaster's thoughts can be! The natural continuation 13. f3 Nxg3 (otherwise, White simply plays 14. Bf2 and 15. 0-0-0) 14. hxg Kg7 15. g4, followed by the Knight's transfer via f1 to g3, Q-side castling and doubling the Rooks on the h-file, could obviously lead to a tempting position in which White would have the initiative.

The more resolute 13. f4! ?, immediately taking aim at the adversary's K-side, is also attractive. At any rate, both these plans seem logical, whereas Kasparov's idea is admittedly difficult to comprehend. Clearly, in the event of Black's exchanging on g3, the White Queen will be quickly transferred to the h-file. But Black can play differently.

13. ...	Nh5-g7 (2)

Karpov did not take much time to play this move, by which he wishes to stress that Kasparov's 13. Qd1 has only slowed down the pace of White's initiative, because now White will have to lose tempo to be able to castle (without which he has nothing to count on), while Black may use this time to consolidate.

14. h2-h4 (3)	f7-f5! ? (3)
15. h4xg5 (0)	h6xg5 (0)
16. f2-f3 (1)	Qd8-e7 (8)

As a result, Black has almost succeeded in blocking all roads to his King. Indeed, he has nearly completed the mobilisation of his forces, which are now placed rather well. Still, it's a long way to the haven of rest.

17. Qd1-b3! ? (3) . . .

Kasparov looks for a chance to sharpen the game. In comparison with 17. Qe2, his last move is at least more intricate. Threatening either to double the Rooks on the h-file after castling to the Q-side, or to open up the game with c4-c5, the Challenger poses an uneasy dilemma for the World Champion: which of these threats should be averted with greater priority?

17. . . .   Kg8-f7 (5)

Karpov strives to neutralise the action of White's heavy pieces but, as further play will reveal, his decision is somewhat debatable.

It would very likely be more appropriate to resort to the blockading method, characteristic of the Nimzo-Indian Defence, and continue 17. . . . c5. Then, after 18. 0-0-0 Nf6, Black's position would be quite stable.

18. 0-0-0 (8)   . . .

Kasparov is in no hurry to carry out the intended breakthrough. He seems to be sure that his opponent will not interfere with his intentions. It would, of course, be more consistent to play 18. c5! dxc 19. Nc4 without delay.

18. . . .   Rf8-h8 (1)

Karpov, on the other hand, consistently

executes his plan. But, perhaps, it is not too late to respond with 18. . . . c5.

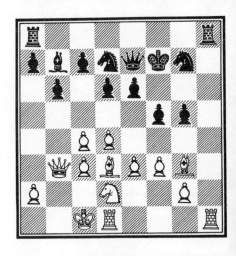

No. 22

19. c4-c5! (2)   . . .

The beginning of the hand-to-hand fight. The game is opened up and, through gaping breaches, White pieces are moving fast to attack the Black King. With such a turn of events, pawns are no longer counted.

19. . . .	d6xc5 (5)
20. Nd2-c4 (3)	c5xd4 (13)
21. c3xd4 (2)	f5-f4 (19)

One of the many riddles of this game. Although the threats of 22. Ne5+ and 22. e4 are unpleasant for Black, he is not in so bad a way as to take extreme measures. For instance, the attempt at counterplay by 21. . . . Rxh1 22. Rxh1 Bd5 23. e4 Bxc4 24. Bxc4 b5! ? 25. Bxb5 Rb8 is worth considering. Black could also play 21. . . . Bd5 at once. But this is just the case when the choice of move is dictated by psychological factors rather than objective considerations.

22. Bg3-f2 (10) ...

One more puzzle! Why not 22. exf? To 22. ... Bd5, White could reply with 23. Qc2, while after 22. ... Nh5, there would be the attractive possibility of a direct attack, viz., 23. Rxh5! Rxh5 24. f5 Bd5 25. Qc2. It is indeed surprising that Kasparov, who is always ready to sacrifice anything for an attack, should suddenly turn so stingy and not give away his Rook for the Black Knight.

Despite this, the move actually played still leaves the initiative with White.

22. ... Ng7-h5 (3)

Needless to say, after 22. ... fxe there would have followed 23. Nxe3 with many threats.

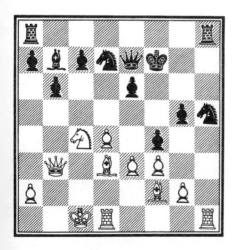

No. 23

23. Bd3-c2? (22)

This time, White's move is not a puzzle, but rather is a misconception. After the natural 23. e4, with an additional threat of 24. d5, White could retain a dangerous initiative which would be hard for Black to oppose. At the same time, the dreams of an attack along the b1-h7 diagonal, possibly evoked by Kasparov's reminiscences of the hardships he had borne in the fourth game, never come true.

23. ... f4xe3 (8)
24. Bf2xe3 (2) ...

After 24. Nxe3, White would have to reckon with 24. ... Nf4.

24. ... Bb7-d5 (1)

Having consolidated his position in the centre, Black may feel confident of his future. Thus Karpov has managed to turn the tables.

25. Qb3-d3 (2)   Ra8-g8 (1)

White's threats have been parried, while Black's extra Pawn has remained.

26. Nc4-e5+ (10) ...

26. g4 promises nothing. After 26. ... Nf4 27. Bxf4 gxf 28. Rxh8 (or 28. Rh7+ Rxh7 29. Qxh7+ Kf8 30. Qh6+ Ke8) 28. ... Rxh8 29. Qg6+ Kf8, the Pawn on f3 would merely be an additional source of worry to White.

26. ... Nd7xe5 (7)
27. d4xe5 (0)   Nh5-f4? (2)

The time has come for the last riddle. It

can readily be explained, though, by Karpov's being under severe time pressure and by his mental fatigue. Evidently, by playing 27. ... c6 (Rotmir Kholmov recommends 27. ... c5!?, with the idea of 28. ... c4, which is also good) Black could have ensured a safe refuge for his King, whereupon his material advantage could be followed up.

28. Be3xf4 (7)	g5xf4 (0)
29. Rh1xh8 (0)	Rg8xh8 (0)
30. Qd3-g6+ (0)	Kf7-f8 (0)

No. 24

31. Rd1xd5! (0)

This spectacular blow saves the day. One can readily see that after 31. ... exd 32. Qf5+ White has perpetual check. Game drawn, after an exceptionally hard-fought struggle.

Time: 2.18-2.28.

GAME EIGHT

Queen's Gambit Declined

A. Karpov   G. Kasparov

A World Championship match is not only a battle for the highest chess title, but also a creative polemic over the various aspects of the strategy, tactics and theory of this ancient game. The contest between Karpov and Kasparov is characterised, as we have already noted above, by the contestants' readiness to play the crucial lines of popular openings with the pieces of either colour. In the present game, they resume the theoretical dispute over the Tartakower-Makagonov-Bondarevski Variation of the Queen's Gambit which was started in their previous match.

1. d2-d4 (2)	d7-d5 (0)
2. c2-c4 (0)	e7-e6 (0)
3. Nb1-c3 (0)	Bf8-e7 (1)
4. Ng1-f3 (12)	Ng8-f6 (0)
5. Bc1-g5 (11)	h7-h6 (2)
6. Bg5-h4 (0)	...

Having tested his opponent's views of the Petrosyan Variation (6. Bxf6), Karpov decides to change the battle-ground and to start a discussion of another popular line in the Queen's Gambit.

6. ...	0-0 (0)
7. e2-e3 (1)	b7-b6 (1)
8. Bf1-e2 (6)	Bc8-b7 (2)
9. Bh4xf6 (0)	...

"Where is the logic?" the reader may ask, "White shies away from the Exchange on one move, only to exchange two moves later with a loss of tempo! " The substantiation of White's ninth move is that Black has revealed his idea—to undermine the centre with c7-c5. The Exchange at f6, followed by b2-b4 is intended to obstruct this plan.

9. . . .	Be7xf6 (0)
10. c4xd5 (0)	e6xd5 (0)
11. b2-b4 (1)	c7-c5 (3)

In spite of all obstacles, Black strikes at the centre. Yet, this leads to the appearance of an isolated Pawn on d5.

12. b4xc5 (0)	b6xc5 (0)
13. Ra1-b1 (1)	. . .

In this way White gains important tempo.

13. . . .	Bb7-c6 (2)
14. 0-0 (0)	Nb8-d7 (0)
15. Be2-b5 (0)	. . .

This move is also impressive: the Pawn on d5 is further weakened.

15. . . .	Qd8-c7 (0)

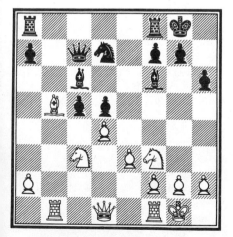

No. 25

This is the critical position, whose assessment determines the fate of the whole variation. This position was repeatedly seen in the previous match. In the twelfth game, White continued 16. Qd2; in the 38th, 39th, and 42nd—16. Qc2. All these games ended in draws.

16. Qd1-d3 (13)	. . .

At last a novelty? Alas, no. This move was played in the Dydyshko-Vladimirov game at the eighth USSR Spartakiad in 1983.

16. . . .	Rf8-d8 (7)
17. Rf1-d1 (16)	. . .

It is only now that Karpov varies from the game cited above, which continued 17. Qf5?! cd 18. ed g6 19. Qh3 Bxb5 20. Nxb5 Qf4, with a good game for Black.

17. . . .	Ra8-b8 (17)

To relieve the pressure in the centre by 17. ... c4 would be a mistake. After 18. Qf5 Nb6 19. Ne5, White's initiative would be built up unhampered.

18. Bb5xc6 (9)	Qc7xc6 (15)
19. Rb1xb8 (6)	. . .

This looks quite logical: White starts exchanging pieces, further emphasising the weakness of the d5-Pawn. However, before proceeding with active operations he should perhaps have interposed 19. h3.

19. . . .	Rd8xb8 (3)
20. d4xc5 (0)	Bf6xc3 (0)
21. Qd3xc3 (0)	Qc6xc5 (0)
22. Qc3xc5 (6)	Nd7xc5 (0)
23. h2-h3 (0)	. . .

No. 26

Up to now the d5-Pawn has been immune, but now White threatens to capture it. After 23. ... Rd8 24. Nd4, Black's play would be confined to a passive defence. Kasparov prefers to sacrifice the Pawn in order to gain counterplay.

23. ...	Nc5-e4! ? (23)
24. Rd1xd5 (2)	Rb8-b1+ (2)
25. Kg1-h2 (0)	Ne4xf2 (5)

The attempt to protect the seventh rank by 25. ... Rb7 would hardly be successful, because after 26. Rd4! Nxf2 27. Kg1 Rb2 28. a4 Black would be faced with the very difficult problem of freeing his Knight from the enemy camp without suffering an appreciable loss.

After the move in the text, the balance just restored is again disturbed.

26. Rd5-d8+ (2)	Kg8-h7 (0)
27. Rd8-d7 (0)	a7-a5 (5)
28. Rd7xf7 (0)	Rb1-b2 (2)
29. a2-a4 (7)	Nf2-d1 (4)
30. Rf7-e7 (0)	...

Some commentators recommended 30. e4 here as a move posing more difficult problems for Black; for example, 30. ... Ne3 31. Kg3 Rxg2+ 32. Kf4, and all White's pieces are excellently placed. However, instead of 31. ... Rxg2+, Black has at his disposal the stronger 31. ... Rb4! 32. e5 Rxa4 and, having restored the material balance, Black has nothing to fear. Of course, White should not play 33. e6 Re4 34. e7 Rxe7, but the line 32. Kf4 Nxg2+ 33. Ke5 Ne3 is hardly better, as only Black has the chance of winning from this position.

30. ...	Rb2-b4 (6)
31. Nf3-d4 (11)	Nd1xe3 (2)

These simplifications lead by force to a drawable Rook and Pawn ending, which can be lost only by those who are unfamiliar with the principles of its conduct.

32. Nd4-c6 (1)	Rb4-c4 (0)
33. Re7xe3 (0)	Rc4xc6 (0)
34. Re3-e5 (0)	Rc6-c3 (0)

Needless to say 34. ... Ra6 is also playable, but since, after 35. h4 Kg6 36. g4 Kf6 37. Rf5+ Ke6 38. h5, the Pawn will have to be returned anyway, it is better to do so at once. And perhaps 34. ... g5 35. Rxa5 Rc4 36. Kg3 Rf4 would be only a little more precise.

35. Re5xa5 (0)	Rc3-a3 (0)
36. h3-h4 (1)	Kh7-g6 (12)
37. g2-g4 (12)	...

The continuation 37. h5+ Kf6 38. g3 would also promise very little: while the White King would be making his way to the a-Pawn, Black would have time to create counter-chances on the other wing.

68

37. . . .	Kg6-f6 (12)
38. Ra5-f5+ (7)	Kf6-e6 (0)
39. Rf5-f4 (0)	. . .

To 39. a5, Black would respond with 39. . . . Ra4 40. Kg3 Ra3+ 41. Kf2 Ra4, and the White King may not leave the g4-Pawn.

39. . . .	g7-g5 (4)
40. h4xg5 (0)	h6xg5 (0)
41. Rf4-b4 (0)	Ke6-e5! (38)

No. 27

Kasparov seals the strongest move, immediately forcing matters. After 41. . . . Kd6, Black would still have to display his endgame technique. Karpov probably wants to see how his opponent will defend his position.

42. Kh2-g2 (1)	Ra3-a2+ (1)
43. Kg2-f3 (1)	Ra2-a3+ (0)
44. Kf3-e2 (0)	Ra3-g3! (0)
45. Ke2-d2 (0)	Rg3-g2+ (1)

Now the Rook starts checking from the other side, which drives the White King back.

46. Kd2-e3 (6)	Rg2-g3+ (0)
47. Ke3-e2 (0)	Rg3-a3 (1)
48. Ke2-d2 (3)	Ra3-g3 (0)
49. Rb4-c4 (0)	Ke5-d5 (0)

Game drawn.
Time: 2.16-2.57.

26 and 27 September 1985

GAME NINE

Ruy López

G. Kasparov   A. Karpov

In his book *Inexhaustible Chess* Anatoly Karpov wrote: "The Ruy López is characterised by unusually profound conceptions, delicate and intricate manoeuvres, frequent shifts of fighting from one flank to the other, etc.

"In order to win with the White pieces, a player must be able to build up his advantage patiently, to stifle Black's counterplay gradually, and to display virtuosity in attack. On the other hand, Black, if he wishes to win, should also demonstrate a number of sporting qualities, such as defensive skill, the ability to defend himself patiently and laboriously, and the art of counter-attacking at the right moment."

The World Champion's apt and pithy characteristic of the Ruy López can well be applied to the ninth game, which may be divided into two distinctly different phases. First, both players manoeuvred for a long time in their own camps, White threatening to start active play now on the K-side, now on the Q-side, Black taking preventive measures, always ready to repulse White's attack.

Just before the control, when the spectators began to think that it would never come to a hand-to-hand fight, Kasparov opened up the position in the centre and on the Q-side, whereupon the game became extremely sharp. The game was adjourned, and the adjourned position was differently assessed by the experts, some favouring White, some Black. The finale turned out exceptionally beautiful; having sacrificed one by one three Pawns, White won a piece, but Black's defence rose to the occasion, and the result was a drawn game.

1. e2-e4 (0)	e7-e5 (0)
2. Ng1-f3 (0)	Nb8-c6 (0)
3. Bf1-b5 (0)	a7-a6 (0)
4. Bb5-a4 (0)	Ng8-f6 (0)
5. 0-0 (0)	Bf8-e7 (1)
6. Rf1-e1 (0)	b7-b5 (0)
7. Ba4-b3 (0)	d7-d6 (4)
8. c2-c3 (0)	0-0 (0)
9. h2-h3 (0)	...

The above order of moves is the result of many decades of searching. After 9. d4 Bg4, Black has, in our opinion, more chances for counterplay.

9. ...	Bc8-b7 (2)
10. d2-d4 (0)	Rf8-e8 (0)

This is the most popular line nowadays. However, Black's possibilities are far from being exhausted by this one move: 10. ... Qd7, 10. ... Na5, 10. ... exd, and 10. ... h6 are also playable.

11. Nb1-d2 (0)	Be7-f8 (2)
12. a2-a4 (0)	h7-h6 (2)

Karpov rejects 12. ... Qd7, which he employed in the fifth game. Although he won that game, the World Champion undoubtedly expects that Kasparov will have prepared something new in reply. Therefore Black shifts to another system, invented by the Hungarian Master Breyer and re-introduced into modern tournament play by Furman and Borisenko.

13. Bb3-c2 (0)	Nc6-b8 (0)

This transfer of the Black Knight from c6 to d7 was Breyer's invention. Nowadays, chess theorists are looking for the possibility of Black's active play in the sharp variation 13. ... exd 14. cxd Nb4 15. Bb1 c5.

14. Bc2-d3 (3)	c7-c6 (1)
15. Nd2-f1 (12)	...

White adheres to the standard plan in such positions: the White Knight heads for g3. After 15. b4 Nbd7 16. Nb3 the Knight can be placed on a5, although it is yet to be demonstrated that its position there would be advantageous.

15. ...	Nb8-d7 (4)
16. Nf1-g3 (0)	Qd8-c7 (10)

After 16. ... g6 17. h4 Bg7 18. h5, the game would immediately become sharp.

Karpov chooses a more elastic continuation, concealing, for the time being, his intentions. **(No. 28)**

The time has come to sum up. The opening has led to a position in which White commands more space and may start an offensive on either wing, while Black has a solid, almost impenetrable, but rather passive set-up.

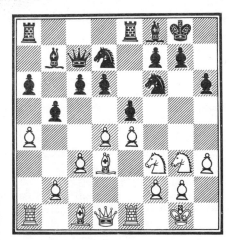

No. 28

17. Bc1-d2 (8)   g7-g6 (20)
18. Qd1-c1 (11)   Kg8-h7 (5)
19. b2-b3 (20)   . . .

19. h4 looks tempting here; for example, 19. ... Bg7 20. h5. If, however, Black starts active operations in the centre by 19. ... c5, then 20. axb c4 21. b6! (after 21. bxa cxd 22. axb Rxa1 23. Qxa1 Qxb7, Black has good play on the white squares for the lost Pawn) 21. ... Nxb6 22. Bc2 leads to a promising position for White. However, after long meditation, Kasparov hesitates to push his King's Rook's Pawn, having apparently come to the conclusion that the time is not yet ripe for an offensive. The move in the actual game, incidentally, parries the threat of c6-c5.

19. ...   Bf8-g7 (2)
20. Qc1-c2 (7)   . . .

White is getting ready for Black's possible breakthrough d6-d5, as a result of which Black's Queen and Bishop tandem could come into play quite forcibly.

20. ...   Nd7-f8 (20)

Karpov, in his turn, is not in a hurry to start counterplaying. He wishes first to improve the position of his pieces.

21. Bd2-e3 (23)   Nf8-e6 (3)
22. Ra1-d1 (6)   Ra8-c8 (9)
23. Bd3-f1 (4)   Bg7-f8 (8)

Twenty-three moves have already been played, yet not a single piece has been exchanged.

24. Rd1-d2 (5)   Qc7-b8 (2)
25. Qc2-b1 (5)   . . .

White also withdraws his Queen from the c-file, for fear of complications associated with c6-c5.

25. ...   Bb7-a8 (1)

Again Black threatens his opponent with the breakthrough c6-c5 and again White averts the threat.

26. b3-b4 (5)   Ba8-b7 (4)
27. a4xb5 (5)   a6xb5 (4)

Worse would be 27. ... cxb 28. d5 Nf4 29. Rc1, followed by c3-c4.

28. Re1-d1 (2)   Qb8-c7 (3)

The plan of White's active play depends on whether he would be able to carry out the breakthrough c3-c4. It is around this advance that further play is developing.

29. Rd1-c1 (8)   Bf8-g7 (11)
30. Rc1-d1 (4)   . . .

Here the intended 30. c4 seems playable, but Kasparov postpones it till a later time.

| 30. . . . | Rc8-d8 (3) |
| 31. d4xe5 (5) | d6xe5 (0) |

The game will now be opened up, although this results in the Rooks being exchanged.

32. Rd2xd8 (0)	Re8xd8 (2)
33. Rd1xd8 (0)	Ne6xd8 (0)
34. c3-c4 (1)	. . .

At last White has made up his mind to advance the c-Pawn.

34. . . .	b5xc4 (2)
35. Bf1xc4 (0)	Nf6-e8 (3)
36. Qb1-a2 (5)	. . .

In our opinion, 36. h4 would be more dangerous for Black.

| 36. . . . | Ne8-d6 (1) |
| 37. Bc4-b3 (0) | Nd6-b5 (1) |

Karpov strives to counterplay. After the more cautious 37. . . . Bc8, there could follow 38. Qa5.

| 38. h3-h4 (0) | . . . |

White starts playing actively on the K-side too. Now Black should respond vigorously, because the threat of h4-h5 is unpleasant for him.

38. . . .	Nb5-d4 (9)
39. Be3xd4 (2)	e5xd4 (0)
40. h4-h5 (0)	Qc7-e7 (5)

Black's pieces are also coming to life: apart from the h4 square, they take aim at the White Pawn on b4. The control moves having been played, one would expect the game to be adjourned: but the opponents decide to play on, their

following moves leading to a much more complicated situation.

| 41. Qa2-d2 (11) | c6-c5 (1) |

Black's Bishop, which has so far lain in ambush, has finally come into play.

| 42. Qd2-c2!?(1) | . . . |

No. 29

In this sharp situation the game is adjourned, and the World Champion seals his 42nd move.

| 42. . . . | c5xb4(3) |
| 43. h5xg6+ (0) | . . . |

Here 43. Qc4 gxh 44. Nxd4 h4 45. Ndf5 Qg5, leading to unclear complications, also comes into consideration, but after the adjournment analysis Kasparov comes up with a neater, though far from obvious, plan of attack.

| 43. . . . | f7xg6 (2) |
| 44. Qc2-c4 (0) | h6-h5 (0) |

It would seem that, having thus defended himself from the mating threats, Black should now seize the initiative, but...

45. e4-e5! (0)   Bb7xf3 (32)

The variation 45. ... h4 46. Nh5! looks dangerous; for instance, 46. ... gxh 47. Qg8+ Kh6 48. Bc2, leading to an inevitable mate; or 46. ... Bxf3 47. Qg8+ Kh6 48. Nxg7 Qxg7 49. Qxd8, giving material advantage.

46. g2xf3 (1)   Bg7xe5 (0)
47. f3-f4! (0)   Be5xf4! (8)

Upon the retreat of the Bishop, 48. f5, to open up the Black King's position, would be very strong. Therefore, Karpov's decision to give up a piece, thus reconciling himself to a draw, seems quite reasonable.

48. Qc4-g8+ (1)   Kh7-h6 (0)
49 Bb3-c2 (0)   Qe7-g7! (3)

49. ... Qf6 would lose, because of 50. Ne4.

50. Qg8xd8 (0)   Bf4xg3 (0)
51. f2xg3 (0)   Qg7-e5 (0)
52. Qd8-f8+ (0)   Kh6-g5 (0)
53. Kg1-g2 (2)

Here the game was drawn, in view of 53. ... Qe2+ 54. Kh3 Qg4+ (not, of course, 54. ... Qxc2?? 55. Qf4 mate!) 55. Kg2 Qe2+.

Time: 2.38-3.13.

28 September 1985

GAME TEN

Sicilian Defence

A. Karpov   G. Kasparov

From now on games in the match will have two-digit numbers. And this is not just a statistical detail. The number of games in the match being limited, the contestants have crossed the line beyond which the importance of each following game steadily increases. Hence the players' fighting mood and uncompromising attitude towards the present game, which has already been indicated by their choice of opening.

1. e2-e4 (1)	c7-c5 (1)
2. Ng1-f3 (0)	d7-d6 (0)
3. d2-d4 (0)	c5xd4 (0)
4. Nf3xd4 (0)	Ng8-f6 (1)
5. Nb1-c3 (0)	a7-a6 (0)
6. Bf1-e2 (0)	e7-e6 (1)
7. 0-0 (0)	Bf8-e7 (0)
8. f2-f4 (1)	0-0 (0)
9. Kg1-h1 (0)	Qd8-c7 (1)
10. a2-a4 (1)	Nb8-c6 (1)
11. Bc1-e3 (1)	Rf8-e8 (0)

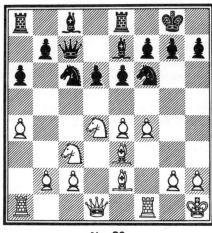

No. 30

This position, arising from one of the crucial lines in the currently popular Scheveningen Variation, has become the subject of heated debates in the match. Its spirit is dear to both the Champion and the Challenger. For Karpov it offers the opportunity to seize the intiative, based on White's greater command of space and the harmonious placement of his pieces. For Kasparov it is attractive because of the potential for active counterplay inherent in its structure.

The contestants have already played two very interesting games with this line—the forty-fifth game in their previous match and the second game in the present match. However, the arguments in favour of their conceptions seem far from being exhausted. Therefore, a new trial of strength begins.

12. Be3-g1 (4)   . . .

This elastic manoeuvre is probably the reason for Karpov's returning to this variation. Previously, he preferred the academic plan of strengthening his position in the centre by 12. Bf3.

12. . . .   Ra8-b8 (14)

Kasparov's patent. He consistently plays this move, allowing the possibility of counterplay with b7-b5. Other possibilities are 12. ... e5 13. Nxc6 (or 13. Nf3 exf) 13. ... Qxc6 14. Qd3 exf 15. Rxf4 Be6 (Arnasson-Iljic, Bor, 1984), and 12. ... Bd7 13. Nb3 Nb4 14. a5 Bc6 (Karpov-Quinteros, Hanover, 1983).

13. Qd1-d2 (10)   . . .

A player's choice of means to mobilise his forces is, of course, a matter of taste. Still, after the withdrawal of the White Bishop from e3, it seems that the third rank could be used to transfer the Queen to the K-side via d1-d3-g3. Such was, by the way, Keres' handling of similar positions. There is, though, a more recent example, the Kudrin-Arnasson game (Bor, 1984), which continued 13. Qd3 Nxd4 14. Bxd4 e5 15. Ba7 Ra8 16. Be3 exf 17. Bxf4 Be6 18. Rad1 Red8 19. Qg3, with better chances for White.

Karpov's original handling of this position is also not without venom.

13. . . .   e6-e5 (22)

Nowadays, this double-edged, undermining advance in the centre is considered to be according to plan and a must. The only question to be settled is whether Black should preliminarily exchange the Knights on d4.

It is probably over this problem that Kasparov pondered. In similar situations, he tends to exchange the Knights at once. But he might not like the variation 13. ... Nxd4 14. Bxd4 e5 15. Ba7 Ra8 16. Bg1 exf 17. Qxf4, when White's pieces would become quite active, and the White Queen could easily be transferred to the K-side. Still, with hindsight, we can state that it is this way of proceeding that Kasparov should have preferred.

14. Nd4-b3 !? (5)   . . .

Here 14. Nf5 (or 14. fxe Nxe5! 15. Nf5), to take possession of the white squares, seems tempting. However, in the given case, when the Bishop at g1 cannot be quickly brought into play on the K-side, the above straightforward idea does not promise White very much. The more so that, after the natural retreat of the Black Bishop to f8, White would be burdened with cares about his pawn on e4.

The move Karpov plays is obviously more elastic, because the tension is now maintained and White may start operations in any part of the board at will.

14. . . .   Nc6-a5 (5)
15. Nb3xa5 (23) Qc7xa5 (0)
16. Bg1-a7 (0)   . . .

16. b4, by the way, is unplayable. After 16. ... Qxb4 17. Rab1 Nxe4 18. Rxb4

Nxd2 19. Rd1 d5!, White would be incapable of trapping the strayed Knight.

16. ...   Rb8-a8 (0)
17. Ba7-e3 (0)   ...

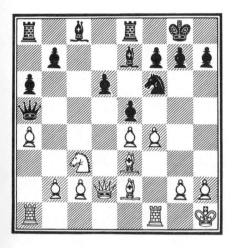

No. 31

One may recall that a similar position was reached in a previous game between Karpov and Kasparov. Indeed, with the White Bishop on f3 and the Black Queen on c7, we would have a position from the 45th game of the previous match. This seemingly negligible difference, however, affects the assessment of the position. Strange as it may seem, the difference turns out to be quite advantageous to White. Indeed, the f-file is now unobstructed, the two White Bishops keep Black's Q-side under heavy fire, while the Black Queen's position on a5, where it can be attacked, is unstable. After prolonged thought Kasparov takes an unexpected decision.

17. ...   Qa5-b4?! (26)

The experts were immediately sceptical about this manoeuvre because, of course, its drawbacks are easier to see than its advantages. Quite probably, Kasparov himself did not consider it to be a perfect solution. But it is Hobson's choice.

Consider other possibilities. Most commentators suggest 17. ... exf, to meet 18. Bxf4 by 18. ... Be6, and Black would be all right, because after 19. Bxd6 he has at his disposal the counterblow 19. ... Nxe4. However, the capture with the Rook—18. Rxf4!—is much stronger, because after 18. ... Be6 (what else?) White can respond with 19. b4! Qc7 (not 19. ... Qxb4? 20. e5) 20. Nd5 Bxd5 21. exd, with a clear positional advantage.

Kholmov recommends the waiting 17. ... Rb8. In one of the variations he gives, viz. 18. b4 Qc7 (the line 18. ... Qxb4? 19. Rab1 Qa5 20. Bb6 Nxe4 21. Nxe4 Qxd2 22. Nxd2 exf is obviously disadvantageous to Black) 19. a5 Be6 20. Bb6 Qc6, Black stands rather well. But his other variation—18. b4 Qc7 19. Nd5! Nxd5 20. exd exf 21. Bxf4 b5—is far less convincing. If, for example, instead of 21. Bxf4, White continues 21. Ba7 Ra8 22. Bd4 Bg5 23. Bd3 it immediately becomes clear that Black's extra Pawn is not much consolation for the complete passivity of his pieces. In any case, Kasparov could hardly have liked such a dismal prospect.

Therefore, one should not criticise Black's last move too severely: its object is to sow the wind, even at the risk of reaping a hurricane. When deciding on this move, psychological considerations seemed to be not the least important. Indeed, the unfathomable complications now begin to require that the players should re-adjust themselves to the new situation; this will perhaps be hard for both, and will to some extent equalise their chances.

18. Qd2-d3!(9) ...

The best answer. After 18. Bd3, there could follow an interesting exchange of tactical blows, as suggested by Kholmov: 18. ... Be6 19. a5 Rac8 20. Rfb1 exf 21. Bb6 Bd7 22. Ra3 Rxc3! 23. Rxc3 Bc6, which testifies to Black's considerable potential for counterplay.

18. ... Bc8-e6 (7)

Black must go on with his plan. To gain counterplay, he should release the tension in the centre. After 18. ... Bd7, as was recommended by some commentators, 19. Ra3 would only gain in strength, because, in the event of 19. ... b5, White would have an additional resource: 20. Rb3 Qa5 21. fxe dxe 22. Rxf6! Bxf6 23. Qxd7.

19. f4-f5 (4)   Be6-d7 (7)
20. Ra1-a3!(2) ...

Both consistent and strong. The threat of 21. Rb3 Qa5 22. Bb6 looks rather unpleasant for Black.

20. ...   Qb4-a5 (6)

20. ... d5 would be unconvincing, if only because of 21. exd e4 22. Qd1 Qa5 23. Rb3 Bb4 24. Na2!? Bd6 25. Rxb7 Qxa4 26. Nc3 Qa5 27. Bd4.

21. Ra3-b3 (2) b7-b5!? (6)

Kasparov did not, of course, take a risk simply in order to switch now to the unpromising defence by 21. ... Qc7. For good or ill, he must sacrifice a Pawn!

22. a4xb5 (2)   a6xb5 (1)
23. Nc3xb5 (2) ...

The positional way 23. Nd5 Nxd5 24. Qxd5 would also suffice, but why shouldn't he capture the Pawn?

23. ...   Bd7-c6 (2)

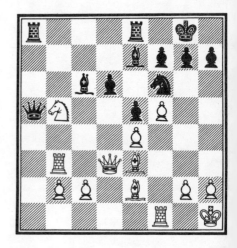

No. 32

The time has come to give tentative estimates of the results of Kasparov's dangerously defiant sally. For the sacrificed Pawn he has succeeded in obtaining more space for his men, pressure on White's centre Pawn, and some prospects of a future attack along the files "a" and "b"—in short, Black has now as good compensation as he enjoys in the Volga Gambit. Still, White's position looks strong enough to withstand Black's onslaught. And then White's extra Pawn may tell. However, it's a thorny path to attain one's object.

24. Be2-f3 (23) ...

Strangely enough, it is this fairly natural move that eventually deprives White of the fruit of his previous work. True, it was hardly possible, at the board, to take into account all the consequences of the impending tactical storm, but subsequent analysis has revealed that 24. Nc3 would be a stronger continuation. After 24. . . . Rab8, there could follow 25. Rxb8 Rxb8 26. Bc1!? (Kholmov's recommendation; in the event of 26. b3 Qa8 27. Bf3 Rb4 28. Bg5 Rd4 29. Qe3 h6 30. Bxf6 Bxf6, Black's task would be simpler) 26. . . . Qa8 27. Bf3 Rb4 28. Re1 Rd4 29. Qe2. Although there would still be a long, long way to go, White would have successfully fulfilled his first defensive task.

| 24. . . . | Ra8-b8!? (10) |
| 25. c2-c4 (6) | . . . |

Only in this way can White hope to retain his material advantage. In the event of 25. Nxd6 Rxb3 26. cxb Rd8 27. Nc4 Rxd3 28. Nxa5 Bxe4, or 25. Nc3 Rxb3 26. cxb Rb8, White's extra Pawn would be of no value to him.

| 25. . . . | Qa5-a8! (2) |

The most important step in Black's plan of counterplay. It is surprising that the Black Queen, which is now in the forking zone of the White Knight, turns out to be immune.

| 26. Be3-g5 (20) | . . . |

The Pawn has to be given up and, with it, any hope of success. Still, neither 26. Nc7 Rxb3 27. Qxb3 Rb8 28. Qc3 Qb7 29. Nd5 Bxd5 30. cxd Qxb2, nor 26. Ra3 Bxe4, would be promising for White.

| 26. . . . | Bc6xe4 (6) |

| 27. Bf3xe4 (3) | Nf6xe4 (1) |
| 28. Bg5xe7 (4) | . . . |

And here 28. Nc7 would be still worse because of 28. . . . Nf2+! 29. Rxf2 Rxb3.

| 28. . . . | Re8xe7 (0) |
| 29. Rb3-a3 (0) | . . . |

Had Karpov wished to sharpen the situation, he could have played 29. f6! ?. But it seems that he has had enough tension in this game.

| 29. . . . | Qa8-c6 (1) |
| 30. b2-b4 (2) | . . . |

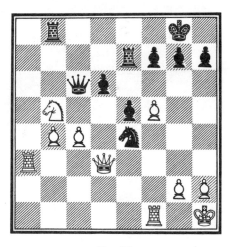

No. 33

The smoke of the tactical battle has cleared, and it is now evident that the game should end in a draw. However, the reader is to witness one more exciting moment.

| 30. . . . | h7-h5 (11) |

Why not 30. . . . h6, which would be more reliable? After all, the Black King needs, so to speak, just a ventilation pane, and not a window flung wide open. Fortunately, this difference does not affect the ultimate result, but the solid 30. ... h6 would mean Karpov remaining on the alert for a while. As it is, the game is quickly drawn—perhaps to the satisfaction of both players.

31.	Nb5-a7! ?(5)	Re7xa7! ?(0)
32.	Ra3xa7 (0)	Rb8xb4 (1)
33.	Qd3-f3 (3)	...

With the Black Pawn at h6, White would not have this counterblow at his disposal. Still, in that case, Karpov would doubtless prevent the Exchange sacrifice.

33.	...	Rb4xc4 (0)	
34.	Qf3xh5 (2)	Ne4-f2+!	(0)
35.	Kh1-g1 (0)	Nf2-h3+!	(0)
36.	Kg1-h1 (0)	...	

The Black Knight is immune both at f2 (because of a back-row mate) and at h3 (because of the check on the diagonal).

36.	...	Nh3-f2+ (0)
37.	Kh1-g1 (0)	

Game drawn. One of the most complicated and interesting games in this match. Time: 2.15-2.06.

1 October 1985

GAME ELEVEN

Nimzo-Indian Defence

G. Kasparov   A. Karpov

In 1927, during the World Championship match between Capablanca and Alekhine,

Grandmaster Rudolf Spielmann published his sensational article "The Riddle of the World Title Battle". Lamenting the errors committed by Capablanca in that match, Spielmann wrote: "I must admit that I am incapable of giving any reasonable explanation for them. But if anything at all may shed light on this strange phenomenon, it is the fact that in all the previous World Title matches one may observe blunders very similar to those committed by Capablanca...

"Chess players who were the greatest masters of their time, who reached the highest peaks of skill and who, when playing in tournaments, gave evergreen, brilliant paragons of their creativeness, committed—as soon as it came to a World Championship match—blunders of the worst kind! Maybe it was the immensity of the stake that disturbed their balance? Or maybe it was the enormous strain caused by the struggle with the strongest rival of all that exhausted their strength and overtaxed their nerves? Maybe, maybe... But one would look in vain for a really satisfactory solution to this riddle...

"In truth, World Championship matches are under a curse."

Since these lines were written, nearly 60 years have elapsed, 18 World Championship matches have been played and in almost each of them blunders were made which put commentators in a spot.

The outcome of the eleventh game of the present match was also decided by an obvious blunder made by Karpov but, unlike Spielmann, we shall not "plead a curse", but instead attempt to give a rational explanation of what happened.

1.	d2-d4 (3)	Ng8-f6 (0)
2.	c2-c4 (0)	e7-e6 (0)

3. Nb1-c3 (0)   Bf8-b4 (2)
4. Ng1-f3 (1)   0-0 (4)

Karpov persistently adheres to the line chosen in the seventh game, although his last move was criticised by some commentators.

5. Bc1-g5 (0)   c7-c5 (2)

And here Karpov varies. In the seventh game, there followed 5. ... d6 6. e3 Nbd7, with the better game for White.

6. e2-e3 (1)   c5xd4 (2)

As a result of this rather peculiar handling of the opening, the players might expect to find themselves in unexplored territory but, alas, there is nothing new under the sun. And soon the game transfers to a well-known position arising from the Queen's Gambit.

7. e3xd4 (2)   h7-h6 (3)
8. Bg5-h4 (1)   d7-d5 (3)
9. Ra1-c1 (24)   d5xc4 (12)

In this way Black obtains a position characteristic of the Queen's Gambit Accepted, but with a loss of tempo.

10. Bf1xc4 (0)   Nb8-c6 (0)
11. 0-0 (2)   Bb4-e7 (0)

White threatens 12. d5; therefore, the Bishop's retreat is practically forced.

12. Rf1-e1 (7)   ...
(No. 34)

Interestingly, a similar position occurred in the ninth game of the 1981 Merano Match, but there the White Rook was still at f1. In that game, Karpov played

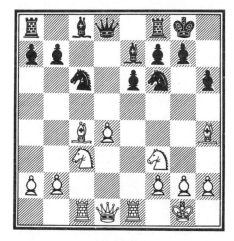

No. 34

his Knight to h5 and, having exchanged the black-squared Bishops, had a good game. In the diagrammed position however, after 12. ... Nh5 there can follow 13. Bxe7 Nxe7 14. Ne5 Nf6 15. Re3, and the transfer of the White Rook to the K-side in conjunction with White's lead in development may give him a dangerous attack.

12. ...   b7-b6 (18)
13. a2-a3 (24)   ...

The 24 minutes which Kasparov took over this move did not help him make up his mind to play 13. d5, although it would seem that White could thus develop a strong initiative. The following variations will illustrate the dangers Black might then encounter:
    1) 13. ... exd 14. Nxd5 Nxd5 15. Bxd5 Bxh4 16. Bxc6 Rb8 17. Qa4 Bf6 18. Qxa7, and White is a Pawn ahead;
    2) 13. ... Nxd5 14. Bxd5 exd 15. Nd4! (15. Qxd5 Qxd5! 16. Nxd5 Bxh4 17. Nxh4 Nd4, and 18. ... Ne6,

or 17. Rxc6 Bd8 18. Ne7+ Bxe7 19. Rxe7 Be6 20. a3 Rfe8 would only lead to simplifications) 15. ... Bxh4 16. Nxc6 Bxf2+ 17. Kxf2 Qf6+ 18. Kg1 Qxc6 19. Nxd5 Qb7 (19. ... Qd7 20. Rxc8!) 20. Re7, winning the Exchange.

Why does Kasparov not play 13. d5? An analysis reveals that in the latter variation, instead of 16. ... Bxf2+, Black can play the stronger 16. ... Qd6! 17. Nxd5 Kh8, and White's initiative would hardly give him much, because Black's position shows no weaknesses.

13. ...	Bc8-b7 (1)
14. Bh4-g3 (0)	...

After 14. Ba2, there may follow 14. ... Nd5 15. Bg3 Nxc3 16. Rxc3 Bf6, with complete equality; accordingly, Kasparov at once withdraws his black-squared Bishop to avoid exchanging it.

14. ...	Ra8-c8 (20)

It seems that this natural move only adds to Black's problems. By playing 14. ... Bd6 15. Ne5 (15. Bh4 Be7 leads to repetition) 15. ... Bxe5 16. dxe Qxd1 17. Rcxd1 Nh5 18. Rd7 Rab8, Black could succeed in equalising the game.

15. Bc4-a2 (2)	Be7-d6 ! ? (25)

After 16. Qd3 and 17. Bb1, White could create rather dangerous threats to the Black King along the b1-h7 diagonal. Offering to exchange the Bishops, Karpov, therefore tries to facilitate his defensive task. White seems to have the retort 16. Bh4, and to meet 16. ... Be7 he could play 17. Qd3 Re8 18. Bb1, with the threat of 19. Rxe6.

However, in reply to 16. Bh4 Karpov could strike an ingenious counterblow requiring precise calculation: 16. ... g5! 17. Bg3 (the sacrifice 17. Nxg5 hxg 18. Bxg5 is refuted by 18. ... Nxd4) 17. ... Bxg3 18. hxg g4 19. Ne5 Qxd4! 20. Nxc6 Qxd1 21. Ne7+ Kg7 22. Rcxd1 Rce8, and the White Knight would be trapped.

Of course, White could attempt to refute the above variation by 20. Nxf7! ?, but the ensuing complications are practically incalculable. Therefore, having thought about his next move for 23 minutes, Kasparov decides to change the character of the game drastically.

No. 35

16. d4-d5! ?(23)	Nf6xd5 (2)
17. Nc3xd5 (1)	Bd6xg3 (0)
18. h2xg3 (3)	e6xd5 (0)
19. Ba2xd5 (0)	Qd8-f6 (10)

After this natural move, Karpov seems to be able to breathe freely. Indeed, the tension has been released and Black apparently has to play just one or two careful moves in order to equalize the game completely. One cannot exclude the possibility, however, that 19. ... Qd7, preventing the White Queen from going to a4, would be a more straightforward method of simplifying the game further.

> 20. Qd1-a4 (10) Rf8-d8 (3)
> 21. Rc1-d1 (18) Rd8-d7 (12)

By playing 21. ... Qxb2 22. Bxc6 Rxd1 23. Bxb7! , Black could only lose material, but the move in the text does not look a happy idea either. Here 21. ... Rd6 would be safer; for instance, 22. Bxc6 Bxc6 23. Rxd6 Qxd6 24. Qxa7 Bxf3 25. gxf Qd2, and it would be dangerous for White to continue 26. Re7 Qxb2 27. Rxf7, because of 27. ... Rc1+ 28. Kg2 Rc2, and the f2-square cannot be defended.

> 22. Qa4-g4 (7)   ...

No. 36

Because of Black's inaccuracy of the previous move, his position is again under a threatening cloud, and he ought to defend himself with the utmost care and precision. Thus, after 22. ... Rdc7 23. b4, White would have the advantage. But it seems to us that by playing 22. ... Re7, Karpov would have sufficient chances to maintain the equilibrium. For example, 23. Bxc6 Rxe1+ 24. Rxe1 Qxc6 25. Re7 Rc7, or 23. Rxe7 Qxe7 24. Bxc6 Rxc6 25. Rd7 Rc1+ 26. Kh2 Bxf3 27. gxf Qe6 (or 27. ... Qg5), and Black cannot lose.

Yet, having successfully overcome his difficulties in the opening, Karpov has evidently lost his concentration, for an instant he forgets his usual caution and, almost without thinking, replies:

> 22. ...   Rc8-d8?? (0)

There follows a fairly simple combination.

> 23. Qg4xd7 (1)   Rd8xd7 (0)
> 24. Re1-e8+ (0) Kg8-h7 (0)
> 25. Bd5-e4+ (0)

Black resigns. After 25. ... g6 26. Rxd7, he loses a piece.
> Time: 2.09-2.03

3 October 1985

GAME TWELVE

Sicilian Defence

> A. Karpov   G. Kasparov

This game is of a very special importance. It may outwardly appear to be the least interesting of the games played so far in the match. Indeed, it lasted for less than two hours, merely 18 moves were played, and it was drawn in a simple position. Yet, the game is adorned by the most interesting innovation of the match, which appears to have overthrown one of the most solid set-ups White can build in the Sicilian Defence.

1. e2-e4 (0)	c7-c5 (2)
2. Ng1-f3 (0)	e7-e6 (0)
3. d2-d4 (0)	c5xd4 (0)
4. Nf3xd4 (0)	Nb8-c6 (1)
5. Nd4-b5 (2)	. . .

Karpov's favourite plan, against which many players, including Kasparov himself, have had to defend.

5. . . .	d7-d6 (0)
6. c2-c4 (1)	Ng8-f6 (0)
7. Nb1-c3 (0)	a7-a6 (0)
8. Nb5-a3 (0)	. . .

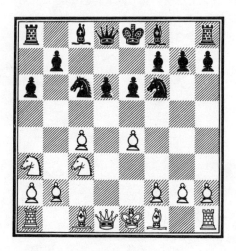

No. 37

The diagrammed position can be encountered in every monograph on the Sicilian Defence. Without fear of exaggeration, one can state that in recent years this position has occurred in at least a thousand games. It has been played, too, at all levels: by World Champions and Grandmasters, by professionals and amateurs. It has been extensively analysed by numerous analysts. Both theory and practice would seem to establish, exactly and irrefutably, two important facts about this position. First, White's pawn outposts at e4 and c4 will for a long time be preventing any diversions associated with the undermining b7-b5 or d6-d5, thus guaranteeing White an enduring positional advantage. Second, in spite of the solidity of his set-up, Black is doomed to a laborious defence, when for a long time he will be able to move his pieces only in the three back rows, hoping to carry out one of the standard undermining manoeuvres that would free his game only after a long preparation.

In the diagrammed position, the following moves used to be played automatically: 8. ... Be7 9. Be2 0-0 10. 0-0, and then either 10. ... b6 (as, by the way, Kasparov himself played in the third game of the previous match), or 10. ... Bd7 in the spirit of restrained manoeuvring.

Suddenly, like a bolt from the blue, there followed:

$$8. . . . \qquad d6\text{-}d5!!(1)$$

Two exclamation marks for the unexpectedness of his preparation and the boldness of his fantasy! Kasparov attempts to cut the Gordian knot at its stoutest spot. When the move was actually posted on the demonstration board, all the experts experienced something like shock. That a Pawn was sacrificed was obvious to everyone. But what for?!

9. e4xd5 (13)	e6xd5 (0)
10. c4xd5 (2)	Nc6-b4 (1)

11. Bf1-c4 (10)   Bc8-g4 (2)

Only now has Kasparov's idea begun go be revealed, though far from completely. Black's pieces now have freedom of movement and can be rapidly advanced to the front lines. But is Black's dawning initiative worth a Pawn? The question is especially pertinent because White is not behind in development.

We can only state that, after the most obvious 12. f3 and 12. Qa4+, Black would evidently hold the initiative. However, at this stage, without close analysis, it is very hard to make the final assessment of Kasparov's whole conception.

Karpov seems to have come to the same conclusion. After long meditation he decides against entering into a dispute over an unfamiliar subject. Having been surprised, the World Champion takes the correct, practical decision—he postpones the debate until better days and discharges the situation by exchanges.

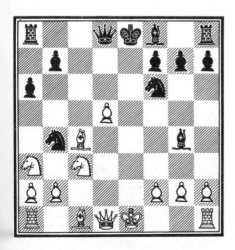

No. 38

12. Bc4-e2 (8)   . . .

Now the game should end quickly.

12. . . .   Bg4xe2 (0)
13. Qd1xe2+ (4) Qd8-e7 (0)
14. Bc1-e3 (18)   Nb4xd5 (1)
15. Na3-c2 (5)   . . .

It would be safer for White to play 15. Nxd5 Nxd5 16. Nc2, because now Black could, rather advantageously, complicate matters to a certain extent by 15. ... Nxc3 16. bxc g6 17. 0-0 Bg7. Yet the game ends without new conflict.

15. . . .   Nd5xe3 (9)
16. Nc2xe3 (0)   Qe7-e6 (0)
17. 0-0 (7)   Bf8-c5 (1)
18. Rf1-e1 (4)   0-0 (3)

Game drawn.

Journalists have called Kasparov's eighth move "the novelty of the year". Its mystery, however, will remain hidden for the time being.

Time: 1.28-0.21.

8 October 1985

GAME THIRTEEN

Nimzo-Indian Defence

G. Kasparov   A. Karpov

This encounter was awaited with especial interest because, firstly, it marked the beginning of the second, and decisive, half of the contest, and secondly because it was preceded by Karpov's time-out. In the four-day pause before the game, the contenders had time enough to rest well and to prepare properly for the games to follow. Chess fans could justifiably expect that the thirteenth game would be both interesting and hard-fought. Their expectations were not disappointed.

1. d2-d4 (1)   Ng8-f6 (0)
2. c2-c4 (0)   e7-e6 (0)
3. Nb1-c3 (0)   Bf8-b4 (0)

In spite of all the difficulties he had to overcome in the previous games thus opened, Karpov firmly adheres to the line which he probably mapped out during his preparation for the match.

4. Ng1-f3 (0)   c7-c5 (1)

K-side castling, as in games 7 and 11, does not seem to satisfy Karpov any longer, because of White's unpleasant retort 5. Bg5.

5. g2-g3 (0)   . . .

As in the first game, Kasparov resorts to the Romanishin system, one of the currently most popular lines in the Nimzo-Indian Defence. The fianchettoing of the King's Bishop, successfully adopted by Alekhine has recently attracted theoreticians by its originality and dynamism. In this system, White opposes Nimzowitsch's idea of exerting pressure on the central squares d5 and e4 by employing the Catalan motif, i.e. by putting pressure on the centre along the h1-a8 diagonal. Although the negative side of such a set-up—the weakening of White's pawn configuration on the Queen's side—is clear, Romanishin's system has many adherents.

5. . . .   Nb8-c6 (0)

The bitter experience gained from the first game has evidently been sufficient for

Karpov to lose his confidence in the unloading variation 5. . . . Ne4 6. Qd3 Qa5. Also, the move in the text has been less investigated.

6. Bf1-g2 (0)   Nf6-e4 (2)

The Knight goes to e4 after all. His incursion, which is very much consistent with Black's whole concept, is intended to emphasise the vulnerability of White's pawn structure and to mount the tension in the spirit of the system being played.

In the event of 6. . . . cxd 7. Nxd4, there could arise, though via a different sequel of moves, a position typical of the English Opening. Such transformations, by the way, are peculiar to many modern openings.

7. Bc1-d2 (1)   . . .

Here is one more motif, this time the "Queen's Indian". The purpose of this move is to mobilise White's forces as speedily as possible, while retaining the Pawn centre. In the Gulko-Balashov game (51st USSR Championship Semifinal, 1983), there followed 7. Qd3 cxd (7. . . . Qa5 is also worth considering) 8. Nxd4 Nxc3 9. bxc Ne5 10. Qc2 Be7 11. Qb3 0-0 12. Bf4, with some pressure.

7. . . .   Bb4xc3 (7)

After 7. . . . Nxd2 8. Qxd2, Black gives up his trumps in the centre, although he gains the Bishop pair instead. In the Farago-Suba game (Baile-Erculane, 1982), the continuation was 8. . . . cxd 9. Nxd4 0-0 10. 0-0 a6 11. Nc2 Be7 12. Rfd1 Qc7 13. Rac1, with White having the initiative.

8. b2xc3 (1)	0-0 (2)
9. 0-0 (0)	f7-f5 (6)

Black should hardly have hastened to play this drastic move. The elastic 9. . . . d6, successfully tested in the Sharif-Byrne game (22nd Olympic Team Tournament, Haifa, 1976) looks more reliable. The above-mentioned game continued 10. Qc2 (10. Be3 seems stronger) 10. . . . Nxd2 11. Qxd2 Qe7 12. Qe3 Bd7!, with a good game for Black. Also interesting is 9. . . . Na5 (see game 17).

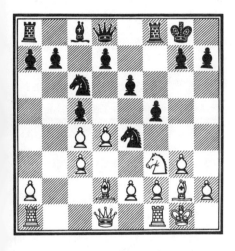

No. 39

10. Bd2-e3! (34) . . .

An unexpected and ingenious move, which emphasises that Black's set-up also has defects, e.g. the weakness of the black squares and the backwardness of his Q-side development.

White offers a Pawn in order to retain his black-squared Bishop. This strategic device—sacrificing a Pawn for the initiative is the leitmotif of Kasparov's play in most games of the present match.

10. . . . Ne4xc3 (47)

After his lengthy deliberation, Karpov accepts the sacrifice and thus commits himself to defend a rather difficult position. But this is his best practical chance, because he should now be able to use his material advantage as a defensive trump. Had the Champion played passively, e.g. 10. . . . d6, or 10. . . . b6, White could have developed his initiative unhindered by 11. Qd3, followed by 12. Nd2.

11. Qd1-d3 (18) c5xd4 (3)

In the event of 11. . . . Ne4 12. dxc Qe7 (or 12. . . . Qa5 13. Nd2 Nxc5 14. Qd6) 13. Nd2 Nxc5 14. Qa3, White would be able to exert considerable pressure as a result of having sacrificed the Pawn.

12. Nf3xd4 (2) Nc3-e4 (1)

It is on this reciprocal sacrifice that Karpov bases his plans. Indeed, after 13. Bxe4 fxe 14. Qxe4 d5, Black would at last succeed in deploying his forces. However, White may take his time over restoring material equality. His motto is the initiative!

13. c4-c5 (13) . . .

It would be unfair to criticise Kasparov's vigorous move, which aims at cramping Black's position, the more so because it probably evokes pleasant reminiscences of the first game. On the other hand, Black will now have a target for his counterplay, which he would have lacked should White have increased his pressure with 13. Rfd1!?. Still, in assessing similar positions, general considerations prevail, and the choice of a move is a matter of player's intuition and style.

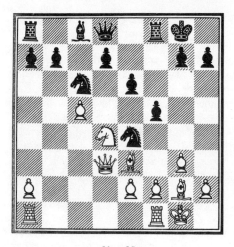

No. 40

13. . . .   Nc6xd4 (29)

Again an important decision. Having played 13. c5, Kasparov offers his opponent a wide, though far from easy, choice of defensive plans. While 13. . . . Nxc5?? should be rejected at once, because of 14. Nxc6, there are at least four plausible replies at Black's disposal: 13. . . . Nb4, 13. . . . d5, 13. . . . b6, and 13. . . . Nxd4. Probably Karpov discarded 13. . . . Nb4, in view of 14. Qc4 Nd5 15. Nxf5! Nxe3 16. fxe d5 (16. . . . Nd2 17. Qd4; 16. . . . Rxf5 17. Bxe4) 17. cxd Nxd6 18. Nxd6 Qxd6 19. Rxf8 Qxf8 20. Rd1. Equally unattractive is 13. . . . d5, because of 14. cxd Qxd6 15. Nxc6 Qxc6 16. Rfc1. However, the other two continuations would be roughly equivalent and satisfactory from Black's point of view, and Karpov has decided on the Exchange of the Knights, because this line seems clearer. Possibly the immediate 13. . . . b6 would be more appropriate, because after 14. Nxc6 dxc 15. Bxe4 (or 15. Qxd8 Rxd8 16. cxb axb 17. Bxb6 Rd2) 15. . . . fxe 16. Qxe4 there

would follow 16. . . . Qd5!?, and by returning material Black could simplify the game.

14. Be3xd4 (4)   . . .

After 14. Qxd4, the standard 14. . . . b6 would only gain in strength, because after 15. Bxe4 Black could interpose with 15. . . . bxc.

14. . . .   b7-b6 (7)

Black does not seem to have anything else. In the event of 14. . . . d5 15. cxd Qxd6, White has the dangerous reply 16. Qe3! b6 17. Rfd1.

15. Bg2xe4 (5)   f5xe4 (0)
16. Qd3xe4 (0)   Bc8-a6 (0)

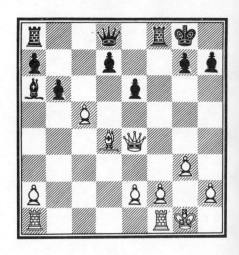

No. 41

The tension has diminished, and it seems that, owing to the opposite-colour Bishops, the game has become drawish.

Yet, all is not so simple. As is known, in the presence of heavy pieces, these

Bishops differ not only in colour but also in strength, their value increasing in proportion to the active possibilities open to their armies. Evidently, it is White who has the initiative now and his centralised Bishop looks far more dangerous than its Black counterpart.

By continuing 17. Rfc1! ?, White could at this juncture pose rather difficult problems for his opponent to solve. For example, after 17. ... bxc he can play 18. Rxc5! ?, threatening 19. Rh5; or 17. ... Rc8 18. cxb Rxc1 (18. ... axb 19. Rxc8 Bxc8 20. Rb1) 19. Rxc1 axb 20. Qe3 b5 21. Qe5! Rf7 22. Qd6; or 17. ... b5 18. c6! ? and, in the event of 17. ... Bb5, 18. Qe3. However, having played strongly in the preceding phase of the game, Kasparov now seems to lose the thread of his initiative, and the game in unexpectedly and rapidly drawn.

> 17. c5xb6?! (2)   a7xb6 (0)
> 18. Qe4-e5?! (18) ...

Even at this moment 18. a4! ? would still give better prospects for White. At any rate, Black would probably have to give up his b-Pawn (18. ... b5?, for instance, would be bad, because of 19. axb Bxb5 20. Rxa8 Qxa8 21. Qe5). As it is, White's advantage disappears into thin air.

> 18. ...   Qd8-f6 (7)
> 19. Qe5-e3 (2)   ...

After 19. Qd6, 19. ... e5! ? would suffice.

> 19. ...   Qf6-h6! (1)

Kasparov seems to have underestimated the strength of this manoeuvre. The rest of the moves are simple.

> 20. Qe3xh6 (0)   g7xh6 (0)
> 21. Rf1-e1 (1)   Ba6-c4 (2)
> 22. a2-a3 (1)   b5-b5 (1)
> 23. Ra1-d1 (2)   Rf8-f5 (3)

Not, of course, 23. ... Rxa3? because of 24. Bc5.

> 24. Bd4-b2 (6)   Rf5-d5 (1)

Kasparov offers a draw, which is accepted.
  Time: 2.00-2.03.

10 October 1985

GAME FOURTEEN

Sicilian Defence

A. Karpov   G. Kasparov

In this game, Karpov adopts a new and rather unusual move in a well-known theoretical position. While the plusses and minuses of the move were the subject of a lively discussion in the press room, your commentators could not help recalling a similar dispute in the chess media, which took place half a century ago during the World Championship match between Alekhine and Euwe. In the seventh game of that match, after 1. e4 e6 2. d4 d5 3. Nc3 Bb4 4. Nge2 dxe 5. a3 Be7 6. Nxe4 Nc6, Alekhine unexpectedly played 7. g4.

This move, to which, for example, Romanovsky attached two exclamation marks and two question marks, caused a real storm in the chess world. It was condemned by almost all commentators. "Underestimating his opponent! " exclaimed some. "Violating the Steinitzian positional principles,"—declared others. Within a period of a year the *Shakhmaty v SSSR* magazine published this game three times—with notes by Botvinnik, Levenfish and, finally, by Alekhine himself. He wrote: "In my opinion, the move has been too severely criticised in the press. After the opponent's correct reply, White would still be able to reach a complicated position with chances for both sides, and it is far from certain that he will get an inferior game."

It seems to us that, apart from chess reasons proper, the choice of that move had been dictated by clearly psychological considerations. For a theoretician, such as Max Euwe was at that time, the necessity of playing in an unknown, irrational position was both unexpected and highly undesirable. After 7. ... b6 8. Bg2 Bb7 9. c3 Nf6 10. Neg3 0-0 11. g5 Nxe4 12. Nxe4 Kh8 13. Qh5 Qe8 14. Nf6! , the game entered into the combinational groove so desired by Alekhine and ended in his convincing victory.

In spite of all the criticism, Alekhine's pioneering ideas always attracted the attention of the chess world. In 1939, Panov employed such a "bayonet" move in the Scheveningen Variation, and the idea was immediately taken up by Paul Keres, who developed, on its basis, a system subsequently called the Keres Attack, which is now considered a most formidable weapon for White.

Nowadays, when chess has become much more dynamic and very concrete, a choice of move—even if superficially it may appear to be the most "anti-positional" continuation—is primarily motivated by its expediency and by the advantages it may offer. And the only question is whether these advantages are sufficient to counterbalance its obvious positional shortcomings.

1. e2-e4 (1)	c7-c5 (1)
2. Ng1-f3 (0)	e7-e6 (1)
3. d2-d4 (0)	c5xd4 (0)
4. Nf3xd4 (0)	Nb8-c6 (0)
5. Nb1-c3 (2)	d7-d6 (1)

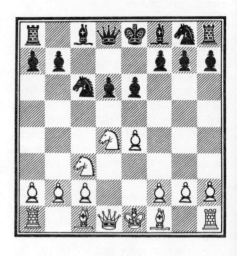

No. 42

The order of moves chosen by Kasparov, who delays the deployment of his King's Knight to f6, signifies his intention to avoid the Keres Attack, which would be possible with the conventional sequel: 1. e4 c5 2. Nf3 e6 3. d4 cxd 4. Nxd4 Nf6 5. Nc3 d6 6. g4! ? The purpose of the latter move is to drive back the Black Knight and to seize more space on the K-side. Experience has shown that Black's defensive task is far from simple.

The Keres Attack has long been Karpov's favourite line. Although in the first game of the previous match Kasparov (as Black) succeeded in solving his opening problems in this variation, he did not risk adopting it a second time.

6. g2-g4! ?(1)   . . .

"Nobody has ever played this move in such a position," was the experts' consensus. The first reaction of those in the press room was distinctly negative: the advanced Pawn may not only become a target for Black's pieces, but is also responsible for a complex of weak squares around it. And what about the plusses? They are the same as those White has in the Keres Attack: the threat of g4-g5, and the associated spatial advantage, though the g-Pawn will now be advanced without a gain of tempo. Still, has nobody ever played g2-g4 in this position previously? Your commentators decided to rummage reference books for an answer. In the very recent monograph *Sicilian Defence. Scheveningen Variation* by Kasparov and Nikitin (Moscow, Fizkultura i Sport Publishers, 1984), we came across the relatively unknown game between Zaitsev and Vogt (1980), which opened as follows: 1. e4 c5 2. Nf3 e6 3. d4 cxd 4. Nxd4 d6 5. Nc3 Be7 6. g4! (the mark put by the authors of the monograph!) 6. ... a6 7. Be3 b5 8. Bg2 (Kasparov and Nikitin are of the opinion that 8. Rg1 Bb7 9. a3 is more precise because to 9. ... h5, White may respond with 10. g5) 8. ... Bb7 9. 0-0 h5 10. gxh Nd7 11. a3 Qc7 12. f4 Ngf6 13. Qe2 Rxh5 14. f5! e5! 15. Ne6 fxe 16. fxe Qc4! 17. exd Kd7. Game drawn.

One can see that such ideas are in the air and, of course, Zaitsev is Karpov's second and coach.

It took Kasparov nearly an hour to play the following three moves—the psychological effect of the innovation is evident.

6. ...   h7-h6 (21)

Kasparov regards g4-g5 as a threat and,

first of all, prevents this advance. Indeed, after 6. ... Nge7, there would follow 7. g5, further cramping Black's position.

7. h2-h4(4)   ...

Karpov is consistent. Otherwise, he would have to reckon with the positional threat of g7-g5.

7. ...   a7-a6 (14)

The immediate attack on the h4-Pawn would give Black nothing. To 7. ... Be7, White would reply 8. Be3, and it would be dangerous for Black to capture the h-Pawn because of 9. Nxc6 bxc 10. Rxh4! Qxh4 11. Qxd6 Bd7 12. g5! , with a strong attack. Also good is 9. Rxh4! Qxh4 10. Ndb5 Qd8 11. Nxd6+ Kf8 12. Bc5 Nge7 13. Qf3 Ne5 14. Qg3, with mounting pressure.

8. Bf1-g2 (29)   Bf8-e7 (22)
9. Bc1-e3 (9)   ...

The h4-Pawn is *en prise*, but to capture it at this moment would be no less dangerous, because of the same Exchange sacrifice: 10. Nxc6 bxc 11. Rxh4! Qxh4 12. Qxd6 Bd7 13. g5!

9. ...   Nc6xd4 (2)
10. Qd1xd4 (2)   e6-e5 (0)
11. Qd4-d1 (9)   ...

The line 11. Qc4 Bxg4 12. Nd5 Rc8 13. Qb4 would lead to great complications, but it is hardly promising for White in view of 13. ... Nf6 14. Qxb7 Nxd5. For example, 15. exd Rxc2 16. Qxa6 Re2+ ! 17. Kf1 Rxb2, etc.

11. ...   Bc8-e6 (5)

But here Black must not capture the h-Pawn because of 12. Nd5, with the terrible threat of 13. Bb6 and 14. Nc7. In the event of 11. ... Nf6, 12. Bf3 would be good for White, threatening g4-g5.

12.	Nc3-d5 (4)	Ra8-c8 (1)	
13.	c2-c3 (9)	. . .	

As a result of the opening, there has arisen a complicated position with roughly even chances.

13.	. . .	Ng8-f6 (8)
14.	Nd5xe7 (8)	Qd8xe7 (10)

Would 14. ... Kxe7 not be better for Black? Analysis reveals that, after 15. g5 Ng4 16. Bd2 hxg 17. hxg Rxh1+ 18. Bxh1 Qb6, Black could seize the initiative; for instance: 19. Qe2 Rh8 20. Bf3 Rh2! The correct move is 15. Bf3, taking time over the advance g4-g5. In that case, 15. ... d5 would be premature, because of 16. exd Bxd5 17. g5! It seems that after 15. Bf3 Black's best answer is 15. ... Nd7, with a complicated game and chances for both sides.

15.	g4-g5 (7)	. . .

White immediately avails himself of the opportunity to play this move. But 15. Bf3 would perhaps be more elastic.

15.	. . .	h6xg5 (3)
16.	h4xg5 (0)	. . .

After 16. Bxg5 Qc7 17. Bxf6 gxf, Black's chances are as good as White's.

16.	. . .	Rh8xh1+ (0)
17.	Bg2xh1 (0)	Nf6-g4! ? (3)

This thrust had to be well calculated,

because the Knight could easily get into trouble on this square.

18.	Be3-d2 (0)	Qe7-f8! (0)

That is the point! By this peculiar manoeuvre the Black Queen seizes possession of the h-file, from which it will be able to give support to the Knight.

19.	Qd1-f3 (13)	Qf8-h8 (3)
20.	Bh1-g2 (4)	. . .

The line 20. b3 Qh4 21. Ke2 d5! would lead to variations similar to those in the actual game.

20.	. . .	Qh8-h4 (4)
21.	b2-b3 (3)	. . .

No.43

White prepares a refuge for his King on e2, which will also allow him to threaten moving the Rook to h1. But Black has his trumps too.

21.	. . .	d6-d5! (12)
22.	Qf3-g3 (0)	. . .

Not, of course, 22. exd Bxd5 23. Qxd5 Qxf2+ 24. Kd1 Rd8!, as White would be forced to part with his Queen. After the text move, the tension, which was about to soar up, is again released and the game heads for an even end game, not devoid, however, of nuances. Indeed, the Black Knight is stuck at g4, and, moreover, White has a Bishop pair.

22.	...	Qh4xg3	(0)
23.	f2xg3 (0)	Rc8-d8	(0)

23. ... d4 could hardly promise more than the move played, in view of 24. Rc1.

24.	Ke1-e2 (2)	Ke8-e7	(2)
25.	Bd2-c1 (6)	...	

White's last attempt to gain the advantage.

25.	...	d5-d4	(10)
26.	Bc1-a3+ (7)	Ke7-e8	(4)
27.	c3xd4 (3)	e5xd4	(0)
28.	Ra1-h1 (0)	Ng4-e5	(2)

At last the Knight is free.

29.	Rh1-h8+ (2)	Ke8-d7	(1)
30.	Rh8xd8+ (0)	Kd7xd8	(0)
31.	Ba3-b2 (2)	Be6-g4+	(0)

If 31. ... Nc6, then 32. e5!, and the White Bishops would begin to come to life.

32.	Ke2-d2 (0)	Ne5-f3+	(2)

Game drawn. After 33. Bxf3 Bxf3 34. Kd3, White would win a Pawn, but in the ensuing end game with opposite-colour Bishops it would be worthless to him.

Time: 2.07-2.12

12 October 1985

GAME FIFTEEN

Petroff Defence

G. Kasparov   A. Karpov

As regards its creative value, of course, the fifteenth game cannot be compared with the many spectacular, hard-fought games played in the match. Whereas relentless battles were fought throughout all the phases of those games, here the real fight was in fact already over in the opening. The sharp, conflicting situation that developed in the very beginning of the game resulted in a rapid extermination of both players' fighting units, a release of tension, and complete equality. Although merely twenty-two moves were played, the game lasted for over three hours and brought much excitement to both the spectators and the players themselves.

1.	e2-e4 (1)	e7-e5	(1)
2.	Ng1-f3 (0)	Ng8-f6	(0)

Again and again we are witnessing attempts to surprise the opponent in an opening. For the first time in this match Karpov adopts the Petroff Defence, although it has long been in his repertoire.

One may recall that the last game of their previous match also opened with the Petroff, and Kasparov (as White) gained the opening advantage. It is also widely known that Karpov does not belong to those chess players who can readily abandon their opinions after a failure. There could, therefore, be no doubt whatever that, in his preparations for the present match, Karpov would make every effort to "mend" his old weapon. The experts were rather surprised by the fact that the World Champion had not adopted the Petroff Defence earlier in this match.

3. Nf3xe5 (0) d7-d6 (0)

Theorists of the distant past were distrustful of the move 2. ... Nf6, considering the sole variation to be 3. Nxe5 Nxe4 4. Qe2 Qe7 5. Qxe4 d6 6. d4 with an advantage for White, until the first Russian chess Master, Petroff, demonstrated that interposing 3. ... d6 would happily solve all Black's opening problems. Thanks to Petroff and Jaenisch's thorough analyses, the defence with the move 2. ... Nf6 is often called the Russian Defence.

4. Ne5-f3 (0) Nf6xe4 (0)
5. d2-d4 (0) . . .

A disadvantage of the Petroff Defence is that, after 5. Qe2, Black is forced to reply with 5. ... Qe7 and, after 6. d3, to withdraw his Knight, which usually results in exchanging the Queens, leading to positions where, with accurate play, White has no difficulty in maintaining the balance. In other words, if White merely aims at a draw, Black should better avoid playing this defence, provided his aim is different from White's. If, however, White is in an aggressive mood, then the Petroff Defence may offer him rich possibilities to fight for a win. In that case, though, Black would be able to reciprocate. Incidentally, the move 5. d4 was both widely employed and extensively analysed at the end of the past century, and it was re-introduced into modern tournament practice by Bobby Fischer in the sixties.

5. ... d6-d5 (2)
6. Bf1-d3 (0) Nb8-c6 (2)

Here Black frequently plays 6. ... Be7 and only then moves his Queen's Knight to c6. It is of interest to note that Bilguer's famous *Handbook* (edited by E. Shallop) gives an exclamation mark to the move 6. ... Nc6 and mentions that the defensive line 6. ... Nc6 and 7. ... Be7 was suggested by Jaenisch. As an illustration, the *Handbook* gives: 6. ... Nc6 7. 0-0 Be7 8. c4 Bg4 9. Nc3 Nxc3 10. bxc 0-0 with level chances.

7. 0-0 (0) . . .

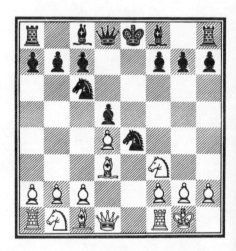

No. 44

7. ... Bc8-g4 (4)

Opening theory recommends 7. ... Be7 here, transferring to a more usual line. However, Karpov's ambitious move is not a novelty. In the *Handbook* of 1922, edited by Schlechter, one can find the continuation (with transposition): 8. Re1 f5 9. c4! Bd6 10. cxd Bxf3 11.

Qxf3 Nxd4 12. Qe3 Qf6 13. Bxe4 fxe
14. Qxe4+ Kf7 15. Bg5! Qxg5 16. Qxd4
with a clear advantage for White (Ca-
pablanca-Marshall, New York, 1909).
Instead of the bad move 8. ... f5, the
Handbook recommends 8. ... Be7!
giving the illustrative variation 9. Bxe4
dxe 10. Rxe4 Bxf3! 11. Qxf3 Nxd4
12. Qd3 Ne6, with an even game.

8. c2-c4 (0)	Ne4-f6 (1)
9. Nb1-c3 (46)	...

Notice how long Kasparov ponders over
the position before he decides on this
move. Indeed, having saved tempo by
refraining from playing Be7, Black
seriously threatens to capture White's
d4-Pawn. Kasparov therefore decides to
give it up for the sake of a rapid development of his pieces. Curiously enough,
after 9. Re1+ Be7, there might have
arisen (with transposition) a set-up
from the 28th game of the previous
match, which continued: 10. cxd Bxf3
11. Qxd3 Qxd5 12. Qh3 Nxd4 13.
Nc3 Qd7, and was soon drawn. Here 9.
Be3, aimed at strengthening the support
of the d-Pawn, also comes into consideration. Now complications begin.

9. ...	Bg4xf3 (2)
10. Qd1xf3 (0)	Nc6xd4 (0)
11. Rf1-e1+ (15)	...

It would also be interesting to attempt
the withdrawal of the Queen to d1 at
once.

11. ...	Bf8-e7 (0)
12. Qf3-d1 (0)	Nd4-e6 (4)

The Black Knight is thus masking the
e-file. After 12. ... Nc6, 13. Bg5 looks
strong.

13. c4xd5 (5)	Nf6xd5 (0)
14. Bd3-b5+ (0)	c7-c6 (0)
15. Nc3xd5 (0)	...

By so playing, White renders Black's
extra Pawn on the Q-side quite worthless, because now two White pawns
will be able to hold three Black.

15. ...	c6xb5 (0)
16. Qd1-b3 (13)	...

Complications, requiring very close analysis for their assessment, could result
from 16. Bf4; this move prevents Black
from castling because of 17. Nxe7+
Qxe7 18. Bd6, winning the Exchange.
In this case it would be dangerous for
Black to play 16. ... Nxf4, in view of
17. Rxe7+ Kf8 18. Re5 Qd6 19. Qd4.
But after 16. ... Bd6 17. Bxd6 Qxd6
18. Nf6+ Ke7 19. Nd5+, Black would
also be in difficulties.
But Black does have a defence against
16. Bf4, viz. 16. ... Rc8. For example,
17. Qb3 0-0 18. Rad1 Bc5 19. Nc7 Qf6 20.
Nxe6 fxe 21. Rxe6? Qxf4, and the White
Rook has no satisfactory retreat, because
22. Rxf6 can be met by 22. ... Qc4!
Still, after the best continuation 17. Be5!
(suggested by M. Yudovich), White could
maintain strong pressure.

16. ...	0-0 (11)

Not wishing to tempt providence, Karpov voluntarily gives up his extra Pawn
in order to complete the development
of his pieces.

17. Nd5xe7+ (3)	Qd8xe7 (0)
18. Qb3xb5 (0)	a7-a6 (7)
19. Qb5-b3 (3)	Rf8-d8 (6)
20. Bc1-e3 (1)	Ra8-c8 (7)
21. Ra1-c1 (0)	...

Rooks are supposed to occupy open files, but this betokens exchanges.

21. . . .   h7-h6 (14)
22. h2-h3 (18)   Ne6-d4 (16)

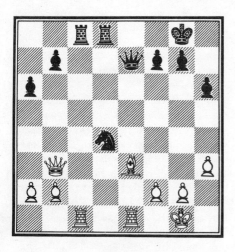

No. 45

Game drawn. After 23. Bxd4, Black first plays 23. . . . Rxc1 24. Rxc1 and then 24. . . . Rxd4, with complete equality.

Time: 1.47-1.17.

15 October 1985

GAME SIXTEEN

Sicilian Defence

A. Karpov   G. Kasparov

Like adepts in all other spheres of creative work, chess players have their hours of triumph sometimes. At such moments, they experience an uncommon feeling of elevation, when their thought throbs with wonderful strength, their fantasy soars on mighty wings, and their decisions are taken, as it were, by intuition. Happy is he who has experienced these moments.

The 15th of October, 1985, is certain to be remembered by Kasparov. That night he defeated Karpov in one of the most impressive games he ever played.

But let us begin with the sixteenth game prehistory. The reader may remember that in the twelfth game Kasparov virtually overwhelmed both his opponent and the experts by coming up with a novelty that called in question whether one of White's standard set-ups against the Sicilian Defence was really advantageous. True, there was no fighting in that game. Having been surprised by the innovation, Karpov showed both prudence and wisdom by refusing to enter into a dispute over an unfamiliar subject without due preparation, and the game was quickly drawn.

The crucial test of the innovation introduced by Kasparov was postponed. But the intriguing question, whether the dispute would take place at all, remained open. And would Karpov, after close analysis, succeed in finding defects in Kasparov's ingenious concept? Would Kasparov himself want to repeat the experiment? Indeed, some inventions are short-lived and intended to surprise the opponent but once.

The fourteenth game, also opening with the Sicilian Defence, did not help to clear the situation, because Karpov chose another variation and, in his turn, made an attempt to surprise his opponent by a new and bold idea.

However, the first opening moves played in the sixteenth game immediately put those present on their guard. Indeed, after the introductory moves...

1. e2-e4 (1)	c7-c5 (0)
2. Ng1-f3 (0)	e7-e6 (1)
3. d2-d4 (0)	c5xd4 (0)
4. Nf3xd4 (0)	Nb8-c6 (0)

... which have of late become conventional in their encounters, Karpov plays...

5. Nd4-b5 (1)   . . .

as in the twelfth game. Now it is Kasparov's turn to reveal his intentions. The moves flashed by ...

5. . . .	d7-d6 (0)
6. c2-c4 (0)	Ng8-f6 (0)
7. Nb1-c3 (1)	a7-a6 (0)
8. Nb5-a3 (0)	. . .

and, without hesitation, Kasparov replies...

8. . . .	d6-d5! (1)
9. c4xd5 (1)	e6xd5 (0)
10. e4xd5 (0)	Nc6-b4 (1)

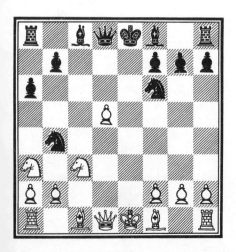

No. 46

The implication of these moves is that Karpov has come to the conclusion that Kasparov's concept is not faultless and should be put to the test, whereas Kasparov is quite sure that his innovation is viable.

11. Bf1-e2 (0)   . . .

Played instantaneously. Karpov evidently relies on a rapid deployment of his forces. Indeed, after 11. ... Nbxd5 12. 0-0 Be7 (12. ... Nxc3 13. Qxd8+ Kxd8 14. bxc is obviously risky for Black, and 12. ... Bxa3 is also bad for him, because of 13. Qa4+) 13. Nxd5 Nxd5 14. Qa4+ Bd7 15. Qb3, White would seize the initiative.

It will be recalled that the stem-game here continued 11. Bc4 Bg4 12. Be2 (the continuations 12. f3 Bf5, and 12. Qd4 b5 13. Bb3 Bc5!?, are yet to be analysed) 12. ... Bxe2 13. Qxe2+ Qe7 14. Be3 Nbxd5, and the tension was completely released.

11. . . .   Bf8-c5!? (0)

Surprise for surprise! Kasparov rates the initiative above a Pawn, and his strategy is that of a gambit. Will the whole variation some day be called Kasparov's Gambit?

12. 0-0 (6)	0-0 (1)
13. Be2-f3 (16)	. . .

At first sight the move seems logical. The Pawn on d5 is now reliably protected and, as soon as White's Q-side pieces (and, first of all, his "strayed" Knight on a3) are brought into play, White's position will be excellent. However, the further development of the game shows that White's task is very difficult to fulfil.

Since, without committing any obvious mistake, Karpov soon runs into difficulties, one cannot help concluding that his whole plan has miscarried, and it is just this tempting manoeuvre of the White King's Bishop that is the root of the problem.

At this moment Karpov should perhaps have abandoned his ambitious plans, in order to attempt to neutralise his opponent's budding initiative. To this end, he could play either 13. Nc2 or 13. Nc4, either of which would lead to a roughly level game. But has Karpov taken up the gauntlet just to bring an olive branch in it?

13. ...   Bc8-f5 (1)

In this way Kasparov discloses two main defects in White's set-up, namely the strayed passive Knight on a3, and the weakness of the d3-square. These factors should prove decisive in further play.

14. Bc1-g5 (2)   ...

The a3-Knight cannot now be brought into play, because after 14. Nc4, the manoeuvre 14. ... Nc2 15. Rb1 Nd4 is very unpleasant for White. Nc4. If Qxd5, N(e)-d2. If Nxd5, (17)Nxc5 Bxb1 (18)Qxd4etc.

14. ...   Rf8-e8 (16) is not bad

Black's motto is the speediest mobilisation of his forces. But the move in the game also carries a threat—to meet 15. Nc4 by 15. ... Bd3 16. Be2 Rxe2 17. Nxe2 Bxc4.

15. Qd1-d2 (10) b7-b5 (11)

The trap shuts and the hapless Knight will remain inactive till the end of the battle.

16. Ra1-d1 (14) ...

Since White's position immediately becomes very difficult, the opinion has been expressed that it is the Rook's move that causes this deterioration. But in fact 16. Qf4, suggested by some commentators, would not have relieved White either, because of 16. ... Bg6 17. Bxf6 (otherwise Black would have played 17. ... Nd3) 17. ... Qxf6! 18. Qxf6 gxf and, in spite of the simplifications, the threat of 19. ... Nd3 would be as strong as ever. It seems that White's strategic error was made at an earlier point in the game.

16. ...   Nb4-d3 (5)
17. Na3-b1 (8)   ...

Having travelled all over the board via the intricate route g1-f3-d4-b5-a3, the Knight has returned to the square originally occupied by its colleague. Yet, what else is there to do? Black threatens 18. ... b4 and, to 17. Be2?, he could reply with 17. ... Nxf2. Kasparov thinks that 17. d6 should have been played here.

17. ...   h7-h6!? (4)
18. Bg5-h4 (6)   ...

Here 18. Be3 is unplayable, if only because of 18. ... Bxe3 19. fxe Qb6.

18. ...   b5-b4 (4)
19. Nc3-a4 (11) ...

In the event of 19. Ne2, the variation 19. ... g5!? 20. Bxg5 Nxf2!? is unpleasant for White.

19. ...   Bc5-d6!? (5)

This move is more dynamic than 19. ...

96

Ba7. The threat of 20. ... Bf4 enables Black to gain time for building up his initiative.

20. Bh4-g3 (7) Ra8-c8 (26)

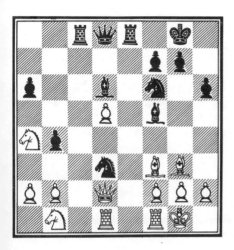

No. 47

A glance is enough to see that White has got the worst of it as a result of the opening. His extra Pawn is of no significance, whereas his pieces are very poorly placed. Indeed, what can one say if the White Queen, both Rooks, and both Knights have not a single square accessible to them? Still, Karpov does not lose heart.

21. b2-b3 (5) ...

White's task is to rid himself, whatever the price, of the Black Knight on d3, by which he is bound hand and foot. White can play neither 21. Be2, because of 21. ... Ne4 22. Qxd3 Nxg3, nor 21. Bxd6 Qxd6 22. Be2, because of 22. ... Nf4 (also playable is 22. ... Nxb2) 23. Bf3 Ne4 24. Bxe4 (or 24. Qd4 Ng5)

24. ... Bxe4. Karpov intends withdrawing his Knight to b2.

21. ... g7-g5! (14)

When such a move is played on the board, it seems obvious. It is actually much more difficult to find than a forced sacrificial combination. Its purpose is to prevent at any cost the intended regrouping of the White pieces. Now 22. Nb2 would be decisively met by 22. ... Nxb2 23. Qxb2 g4! 24. Be2 Rc2. Moreover, in some variations it would be important for the outpost on f4 to be secured for the Black Knight.

22. Bg3xd6 (17) ...

Karpov should perhaps have somewhat enlivened the game by playing 22. h4, the more so that he would not have to fear 22. ... g4 in view of the simple 23. Be2, and if 23. ... Ne4 then 24. Qxh6. Yet even this would not significantly improve the situation for him. By continuing 22. ... Nf4! and, in the event of 23. Rc1 (23. Bxf4 Bxf4 24. Qxb4 fails to 24. ... Bd6, followed by 25. ... g4), 23. ... Ne4!?, Black maintains a formidable initiative.

22. ... Qd8xd6 (1)
23. g2-g3 (0) ...

Here 23. Nb2 is again bad, because of 23. ... Nxb2 24. Qxb2 g4; and after 23. Be2, the continuation 23. ... Nf4 24. Bc4 Ng4 25. g3 Rxc4! 26. bxc Re2 27. Qd4 Be4 would decide the issue.

23. ... Nf6-d7! (11)

Again a very strong manoeuvre. Its main purpose—to relieve its colleague on d3, should it be exchanged by 24. Nb2—is quite obvious. But there is a second motive, more profound and better hidden, which will become evident a little later.

24. Bf3-g2 (4) ...

All the same, White should have played 24. Nb2. Of course, after 24. ... N7e5 25. Bg2 Qb6!? 26. Nxd3 Nxd3, he would as before have the worst of it, but at least the number of his opponent's fighting units would decrease.

24. ... Qd6-f6! (5)

That is the point! The Knight on a4 has no retreat. Tarrasch once remarked that a Knight on the edge of the board is always ineffectively posted. What would his comment be in the case of two such idle Knights?

25. a2-a3 (4) a6-a5 (1)
26. a3xb4 (0) a5xb4 (0)
27. Qd2-a2 (1) ...

The White pieces have no scope at all. How can White free himself?

27. ... Bf5-g6!? (4)

There is no hurry. 27. ... Nf4 here, in order to counter 28. Nb2 with 28. ... Rc2, looks tempting. But the simple 28. Qb2 would have rendered this idea worthless.

28. d5-d6 (12) ...

White is running out of moves. Thus, 28. Bh3 is unplayable, because of the spectacular 28. ... N7e5, and 29. Bxc8 is met by 29. ... Nf3+ 30. Kh1

Be4, with a crushing attack. For instance, 31. Qe2 Qg6! 32. Qe3 (32. Rxd3 Nd4+) 32. ... Qh5, or 31. Bh3 Nd2+ 32. f3 (32. Bg2 Bxg2+ 33. Kxg2 Qf3+ 34. Kg1 Nxf1 35. Rxf1 Ne1!) 32. ... Bxf3+ 33. Bg2 Bxg2+ 34. Kxg2 Re2+, or 31. Bg4 h5! 32. Bxh5 Qh6! 33. g4 Qd6. The move 28. Nd2 fails to 28. ... Re2.

28. ... g5-g4! (11)

Not, of course, 28. ... Qxd6, since after 29. Nd2 Re2 30. Nc4! White would at last be able to breathe freely. With the move in the game, Black further tightens the ring.

29. Qa2-d2 (8) Kg8-g7 (3)
30. f2-f3 (3) ...

The situation has become intolerable for White, and Karpov decides to bring it to a crisis, for as Schiller said: "Better an end with horror than a horror without end."

30. ... Qf6xd6 (1)
31. f3xg4 (2) Qd6-d4+ (2)
32. Kg1-h1 (0) Nd7-f6! (5)

No. 48

Black's attack is irresistible. White cannot satisfactorily defend himself against the threats of 33. ... Nxg4 and 33. ... Ne4. A spectacular finale follows.

33. Rf1-f4 (6)	Nf6-e4 (3)
34. Qd2xd3 (2)	Ne4-f2+ (0)
35. Rf4xf2 (1)	...

Or 35. Kg1 Nh3++ 36. Kh1 Qxd3 37. Rxd3 Nxf4.

35. ...	Bg6xd3	(0)
36. Rf2-d2 (0)	Qd4-e3!	(2)

Another winning line is 36. ... Re3 37. Nb2 Rc3 38. Nxc3 bxc 39. Rxd3 Rxd3 40. Nxd3 c2.

37. Rd2xd3 (0)	Rc8-c1!	(1)
38. Na4-b2 (0)	Qe3-f2!	(0)
39. Nb1-d2 (0)	...	

Too late. . .

39. ...	Rc1xd1+ (0)
40. Nb2xd1 (0)	Re8-e1+ (0)

White resigns.
Time: 2.29-2.20.

17 October 1985

GAME SEVENTEEN

Nimzo-Indian Defence

G. Kasparov	A. Karpov

Almost all World Championship matches have significantly contributed to the theory of openings, thereby making some particular opening the fashion. This has happened not only because world's strongest chess players have, as a rule, kept up with the latest theoretical developments and, sometimes, have even been ahead of them, blazing the trail. The other reason is that the specific nature of the struggle in the match compels the contestants to deepen, rather than broaden, their opening repertoires, greatly elaborating a few systems to be used for both White and Black.

In the present match, the Nimzo-Indian Defence has become Karpov's main defensive weapon against White's 1. d4. In contrast to their previous match, Kasparov now invariably allows this defence by playing his Queen's Knight to c3 on the third move. In the seventeenth game this opening occurs for the fifth time. Both the Champion and the Challenger firmly uphold their opinions in this theoretical dispute, and their adherence to principle cannot be but admired.

1. d2-d4 (2)	Ng8-f6 (0)
2. c2-c4 (0)	e7-e6 (0)
3. Nb1-c3 (0)	Bf8-b4 (1)
4. Ng1-f3 (0)	...

In reply to Black's 3. ... Bb4, Kasparov has always moved his King's Knight to f3, keeping in reserve the possibility of developing his Queen's Bishop to g5 should Black now castle short.

4. ...	c7-c5 (5)
5. g2-g3 (0)	Nb8-c6 (0)
6. Bf1-g2 (0)	Nf6-e4 (0)
7. Bc1-d2 (0)	...

Kasparov's patent, which he first tested in the 13th game. Previously, White here played 7. Qd3.

7. . . .	Bb4xc3 (7)
8. b2xc3 (0)	0-0 (1)
9. 0-0 (0)	. . .

No. 49

This position has already been the subject of a dispute between the contestants. In the 13th game, Karpov continued 9. . . . f5, which was condemned by most commentators as weakening the dark squares. By responding with the unexpected 10. Be3!? Kasparov sacrificed a Pawn and seized the initiative.

9. . . .	Nc6-a5! (6)

This attack against White's weak Q-side Pawns looks quite logical, the more so that it will be difficult for White to protect his c4-Pawn. Thus, after 10. Qa4, there would follow 10. . . . d6, threatening 11. . . . Bd7, while 10. Qc2 would be met by 10. . . . Nd6. However, Kasparov does not even try to defend this Pawn.

10. d4xc5 (43)	. . .

The viability of the variation initiated by 9. . . . Na5 depends on the assessment of White's 10. Bf4. Let us consider the possible continuations.

Black should not capture on c3, because of 11. Qc2, capturing the Black Knight. The move 10. . . . b6 fails to 11. Ng5. After 10. . . . Nxc4, there may follow the unpleasant 11. dxc, threatening 12. Qd4, while 10. . . . g5 11. Qd3 f5 12. Be3 would only weaken Black's position.

Yet it seems that Black does have a possibility of advantageously complicating the game by the interesting 10. . . . d5, to meet 11. cxd by 11. . . . Nxc3!? (but not 11. . . . exd, in view of 12. dxc). Maybe this is the reason for Kasparov's rejecting 10. Bf4.

10. . . .	Qd8-c7 (6)

Not, of course, 10. . . . Nxc4 or 10. . . . Nxc5, because of 11. Bf4. Now one gets the impression that White's Pawns should fall one by one. But what will be his compensation?

11. Nf3-d4 (37)	. . .

Another possibility would be 11. Be3 Nxc4 12. Bd4. Of course, after 12. . . . Nxc5 13. Bxg7! Kxg7 14. Qd4+ f6 15. Qxc4, White's prospects would be better. The line 12. . . . f6 13. Qd3 d5 14. cxd Ned6 15. Nd2 Nxd2 16. Qxd2 Rd8 (worse is 16. . . . e5 17. Bd5+ Kh8 18. Be3) is, however, rather unclear.

11. . . .	Ne4xd2 (2)
12. Qd1xd2 (0)	Na5xc4 (0)
13. Qd2-g5! (0)	. . .

White has a temporary lead in development which compensates him for the weakness of his Q-side Pawn configuration and even for the possible loss of a Pawn. However, White should now play vigorously and purposefully. His last move's aim is to weaken Black's K-side.

13. ...   f7-f6 (11)
14. Qg5-f4 (4)   Nc4-e5 (4)

Karpov chooses the most reliable method of defence. After 14. ... Qxc5 15. Nb3 Qb5, there would have arisen a problematic position in which Black's extra Pawn would perhaps have been counterbalanced by White's initiative. The game might have continued 16. Rfd1 d5 17. e4.

Similar situations have quite often been observed in the match.

15. Nd4-b3 (4)   Ra8-b8 (5)

By this manoeuvre, followed by 16. ... b6 and 17. ... Bb7, Black completely equalizes the game.

16. Qf4-d4 (6)   b7-b6 (2)

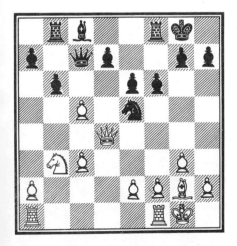

No. 50

17. f2-f4 (1)   Ne5-f7 (1)

By adhering to the same solid line of play, Black deliberately avoids the exchange of tactical blows 17. ... bxc 18. Qxc5 Qxc5 19. Nxc5 Rb5! which would immediately have led to simplifications.

18. Rf1-d1 (2)   Rf8-d8 (3)
19. c3-c4 (5)   Bc8-b7 (10)
20. Bg2xb7 (1)   Rb8xb7 (4)
21. c5xb6 (0)   Rb7xb6 (6)

A more complicated game would have resulted from 21. ... axb 22. c5 b5.

22. c4-c5 (2)   Rb6-c6 (4)
23. Ra1-c1 (4)   d7-d5 (14)
24. c5xd6 (2)   ...

White also has to simplify.

24. ...   Rd8xd6 (1)
25. Qd4-e3 (1)   Rd6xd1+ (7)
26. Rc1xd1 (1)   g7-g6 (1)
27. Rd1-c1 (3)   ...

Here 27. Nd4 Qb6 28. Kf2 Rd6 would be risky for White.

27. ...   Rc6xc1+ (11)
28. Qe3xc1 (2)   Qc7-b6+ (2)
29. Qc1-c5 (1)

Game drawn.
Time: 2.01-1.57.

GAME EIGHTEEN

Sicilian Defence

A. Karpov   G. Kasparov

The eighteenth game was postponed by the Challenger, his decision to take a time-out proving rather unexpected and, for this reason, attracting attention.

Indeed, experience has shown that such radical steps are usually taken only in critical situations inevitably arising in every World Title match. At the same time, everything seemed to indicate that Kasparov's star was in the ascendant. However, the present, exceedingly tense, contest has a logic all its own. It is perhaps the favourable situation in the match that might, paradoxically, account for Kasparov's apparently strange decision. Having brought about a dramatic reversal to take the lead in the middle phase of the match, the Challenger very likely thought it necessary to have a sober and objective look at the state of affairs, giving himself the opportunity to cool down, to rest on the eve of the match's decisive phase, and to make his plans for the concluding battles.

Undoubtedly, Karpov also welcomed this chance to rest and think over his problems. In short, in the eighteenth game both the Champion and the Challenger had to bring forward their fresh programmes and arguments. It fell to this game to set the tone for the contestants' mood and fighting spirit at the finish of the match.

1. e2-e4 (0)	c7-c5 (1)
2. Ng1-f3 (0)	d7-d6 (0)

A curious moment. In spite of his success in the preceding three Sicilian games when he continued 2. ... e6, Kasparov now adopts the standard line of the Scheveningen Variation.

3. d2-d4 (0)	c5xd4 (0)
4. Nf3xd4 (0)	Ng8-f6 (1)
5. Nb1-c3 (0)	a7-a6 (0)
6. Bf1-e2 (0)	a7-e6 (0)
7. 0-0 (0)	Bf8-e7 (0)
8. f2-f4 (4)	0-0 (0)
9. Kg1-h1 (1)	Qd8-c7 (0)
10. a2-a4 (0)	Nb8-c6 (0)
11. Bc1-e3 (0)	Rf8-e8 (0)

These moves are played, as it were, in the same breath. The resulting position has come to be a peculiar "launching pad" in games between these contestants. It has been repeatedly tested both in their previous match and in the present. For the reader's reference, it will be recalled that in the fifth game of the previous match Karpov here chose 12. Re1, and the tenth game of the present match— 12. Bg1; in all the remaining games, as here he continued 12. Bf3. This opening scheme is currently one of the most popular in master play.

12. Be2-f3 (3)	Ra8-b8 (2)
13. Qd1-d2 (4)	Bc8-d7 (5)

The immediate discharge of tension in the centre, by 13. ... Nxd4 14. Bxd4 e5 15. Ba7 Ra8 16. Be3 Bd7 17. a5 Rac8, was tested in the forty-fifth game of the previous match, but after that game Kasparov began deploying his Queen's Bishop as an initial step.

No. 51

14. Nd4-b3 (7)   . . .

The beginning of a theoretical dispute. In the second game of this match, Karpov continued 14. Qf2 which led, after 14. ... Nxd4 15. Bxd4 e5 16. Be3, to the release of the central tension. It seems that such a release is favourable to Black rather than to White.

This time Karpov avoids simplifying the game, and the character of the struggle changes significantly. White commands more space and, therefore, has the greater freedom of movement. His task is to prepare for active operations in the centre and on the K-side, whereas Black's objective is to organise counterplay on the Q-side, combining it with preventive measures in the centre. A very large number of games have already followed this strategic scheme, but the richness of its content and the sharpness of the ensuing conflict continue to win round new adherents. It will be instructive, therefore, to trace the world's strongest chess players disclosing the deeply hidden possibilities open to both sides in this position.

14. ...   b7-b6 (20)

A typical device. Black should first of all prevent the binding a4-a5. Also, he intends to start counterplaying with Nc6-a5.

15. Be3-f2!? (1)   . . .

An important step in White's plan is his consistent preparation for the advance e4-e5. To this end, White has to transfer his Bishop to g3 and free the e-file for his Rook. And at g3, incidentally, the White Bishop will be able to control the h2-b8 diagonal, which may prove useful in future tactical skirmishes.

15. ...   Bd7-c8!? (10)

At first sight this move seems illogical: why has Black withdrawn the already developed Bishop? This regrouping, however, is not only necessary but also rather typical of such positions. Black is getting ready for White's intended breakthrough in the centre and, with this in mind, he vacates the d7-square for his Knight, while his Bishop will be transferred to the long diagonal.

16. Bf2-g3 (21)   Nf6-d7 (11)
17. Ra1-e1 (46)   Bc8-b7 (22)

The manoeuvre 17. ... Na5 also comes into consideration, but Kasparov is primarily concerned with his opponent's main positional threat.

18. e4-e5!? (3)   . . .

Karpov willingly gives up a Pawn in order to open up the centre.

No. 52

The critical moment. The opponents have already used all their arguments for and against this breakthrough. What will be the outcome of the confrontation?

18. ...   Rb8-d8! (4)

The best move, and possibly the only one, by which Black completes the consolidation of his forces just before the inevitably opening up of the game. It would now be imprudent for Black to play 18. ... dxe 19. fxe Ncxe5 20. Bxb7 Rxb7, whereupon White would have the pleasant choice between the immediate restoration of the material balance by 21. Qe2 and the mounting of the pressure by 21. Nd4. Needless to say, Black's 18. ... d5 would only have facilitated White's flank operations, such as f4-f5. But now the d-file will become an important trump in Black's counterplay.

19. Qd2-f2 (8)   ...

White would have gained nothing by 19. exd Bxd6 20. Ne4, in view of 20. ... Nc5.

19. ...   Re8-f8 (1)

The last in a series of preventive manoeuvres, after which Black may regard his position as quite safe. All roads to the Black King are securely blocked, and the long-awaited moment when Black may start active operations in the centre and on the Q-side is about to come.

20. Bf3-e4 (6)   ...

One of White's last attacking resources. After 20. Ne4, White would have had to reckon with the loss of the e5-Pawn.

20. ...   d6xe5 (14)
21. f4xe5 (0)   Nd7-c5 (1)

For the first time in this game Black has moved a piece beyond his three back rows, but this event is magnificently staged. Black's forces have become active and it is White's turn to be on the alert in order not to yield the initiative.

22. Nb3xc5 (5) b6xc5!? (5)

Kasparov again demonstrates that he has excellently grasped the situation. What could be more natural and tempting than to recapture at c5 with the Bishop, thus gaining valuable time? But it is just then that the withdrawal of the Bishop from the K-side could have negative consequences and, after 23. Qf3 (in the event of 23. Qf4, Black could sacrifice a Pawn by 23. ... f5!? 24. exf Qxf4 25. Rxf4 Rxf6 26. Rxf6 gxf 27. Bxc6 Bxc6, gaining counterplay sufficient for equality) 23. ... Nd4 24. Qh5, fresh possibilities would suddenly be open to White. After the move in the game, however, Black will have an important trump for his counterplay in the centre.

104

23. Bg3-f4!? (3) ...

A useful manoeuvre.

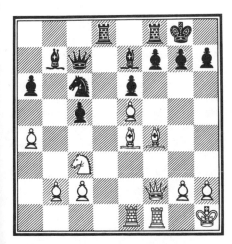

No. 53

Here Kasparov was suddenly lost in thought. With time pressure just round the corner, the dissipation of twenty minutes could hardly be explained, because Black's 23. ... Nd4 is a must. But it turned out that the Challenger was not thinking about this move, but about the World Champion's offer of a draw. Neither the sporting nor the pure chess considerations could justify refusal. Indeed, in the final position, both sides had their trumps and their problems. But the most important thing was that, in the closing stages of the match, the situation dictated that the players should above all be cool and cautious. Kasparov therefore accepted the World Champion's offer.
Game drawn.
Time: 1.52-1.56.

24 October 1985

GAME NINETEEN

Nimzo-Indian Defence

G. Kasparov   A. Karpov

One cannot help being impressed by Kasparov's truly encyclopaedic knowledge of openings. But even more striking is his incessant research in this field, his desire to be at least one step ahead of "official" theory.

It is for this reason perhaps that in the last games of the match Karpov attempted to go off the beaten track, to adopt lines which are seldom played, so as to be able to start the fighting in the opening phase, and to forestall his opponent in the posing of problems.

This tendency is especially pronounced in the present game, but where it leads to is another question.

1. d2-d4 (1)	Ng8-f6 (0)
2. c2-c4 (0)	e7-e6 (0)
3. Nb1-c3 (0)	Bf8-b4 (2)
4. Ng1-f3 (0)	...

The Nimzo-Indian Defence has thus appeared for the sixth time in this match, the Challenger invariably answering with his King's Knight's move.

4. ...   Nf6-e4 (3)

A rare line, to which handbooks of openings have paid little attention. Nevertheless, this continuation has been played in top-level chess, viz., in the 19th game of the World Championship return match between Euwe and Alekhine in 1937, which continued: 5. Qc2 d5 6. e3 c5 7. Bd3, and Black had to withdraw his Knight to f6, thereby admitting the failure of his plan.

This is probably why the handbooks of openings published in the forties attach an interrogation mark to 4. ... Ne4. However, Konstantinopolski, in the *Shakhmaty v SSSR* magazine No. 6, 1938, and Botvinnik, in his book on the return match, published in the following year, refrain from so severe a verdict for the Knight's move, rightly believing that it is only Black's next move, 5. ... d5, that deserves criticism.

"Black should have played 5. ... f5, "points out Konstantinopolski, "and, in the event of 6. e3, 6. ... b6 7. Bd3 Bb7 8. 0-0 Bxc3 9. bxc 0-0, with a solid position."

"The move 5. ... f5, followed, should the opportunity arise, by the fianchettoing of the Black Queen's Bishop, would of course be in the spirit of this defence," agrees Botvinnik.

Curiously enough, the variation with 4. ... Ne4 occurred even before that game between Euwe and Alekhine, namely, in the Balogh-Keres postal game played in 1936-37. Their game went as follows: 5. Qc2 f5 6. g3 b6 7. Bg2 Bb7 8. Nd2! (this forces the Exchange of the white-squared Bishops, because 8. ... d5 would be disadvantageous to Black) 8. ... Bxc3 9. bxc Nd6 10. Bxb7 Nxb7 11. e4 0-0 12. 0-0 Nc6 13. Ba3 Ne7 14. Rae1 c5 15. f4. Although White commands more space, Black's position is also quite strong.

So now, nearly 50 years after those games, the move 4. ... Ne4 is again put to the test at the top level.

| 5. Qd1-c2 (5) | f7-f5 (0) |
| 6. g2-g3 (11) | . . . |

Kasparov sticks to his guns by persistent-ly employing this plan, with the development of his King's Bishop to g2. After 6. e3 b6 the game would transpose to well-known lines.

| 6. . . . | Nb8-c6 (11) |

In the seventeenth game of the match, the manoeuvre Nb8-c6-a5 gave Black a satisfactory game. Accordingly, Karpov attempts to carry out the same plan of attacking White's c4-Pawn. There is, however, a significant difference between the two games: in the 17th game Black's Pawn was already at c5, whereas here the White c-Pawn is not blockaded and can be advanced.

7. Bf1-g2 (10)	0-0 (18)
8. 0-0 (5)	Bb4xc3 (0)
9. b2xc3 (0)	Nc6-a5 (0)
10. c4-c5	. . .

No. 54

Karpov thinks for a long time before deciding on his next move. Indeed, the diagrammed position is crucial for his plan of development. Black's main problem is to make his Queen's Bishop useful.

The reply 10. ... b6 suggests itself at this juncture, although it looks rather risky and requires the ensuing variations to be calculated far ahead. For example, 11. Ng5 Nxg5 12. Bxg5 Qxg5 13. Bxa8 is not dangerous for Black, who can reply with 13. ... c6, and the White Bishop would be unlikely to extricate itself from the enemy camp. In the event of 11. Nd2, Black would answer with 11. ... Nxd2 12. Bxd2 Bb7 13. c4 Bxg2 14. Kxg2 Nc6 15. d5 Ne7, with a satisfactory game.

It seems to us that if Karpov were to play 10. ... b6, then his unconventional opening strategy might be justified. But he chooses another continuation, and runs into difficulties which eventually prove insurmountable.

10. ...	d7-d6 (21)
11. c3-c4! (22)	...

This ingenious rejoinder reveals the main defects of Black's set-up, namely the absence of his black-squared Bishop and the unsteady position of his Knight on a5.

What ought Black to do now? White threatens, first of all, to play 12. Nd2; and it would be very dangerous for Black to accept the sacrifice, because 11. ... dxc 12. dxc Nxc5 is met by 13. Ba3.

11. ...	b7-b6 (13)
12. Bc1-d2!? (19)	...

It is very possible that Karpov has underestimated the strength of this move.

12. ...	Ne4xd2 (17)
13. Nf3xd2 (3)	d6-d5?! (0)

This indicates that Black's life is far from comfortable. He is now doomed to defend himself in a very difficult, unpromising situation. Another possibility, 13. ... Bb7 14. Bxb7 Nxb7 15. c6 Na5 16. d5 Qe7 17. Qd3, would also be disadvantageous to Black, whose Knight would be out of play. Still, in this variation, Karpov would have had more chance of gaining counterplay than after the move in the actual game.

14. c4xd5 (5)	e6xd5 (0)
15. e2-e3 (5)	...

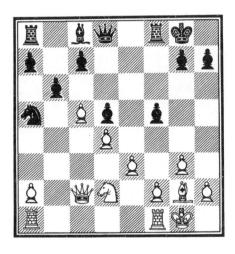

No. 55

The outcome of the opening can be briefly summarised as follows: White has a clear positional advantage; his Bishop is far more active than its Black counterpart, while his Knight will be able to occupy the vital e5-square, which is Black's main weakness.

Black's chief trouble is that there is no counterplay in sight for him, and it is quite unclear how he might oppose White's clear-cut strategy.

15. ...   Bc8-e6 (5)

Neither 15. ... Ba6 16. Rfc1 Nc4, in view of 17. Bf1, nor 15. ... b5, because of 16. Qc3 Nc4 17. a4, could improve the situation for Black.

16. Qc2-c3 (3)   ...

The necessary preventive measure, by which Kasparov wards off the threat of 16. ... b5.

16. ...   Rf8-f7 (7)
17. Rf1-c1 (2)   Ra8-b8 (5)
18. Ra1-b1 (3)   Rf7-e7 (6)
19. a2-a4 (4)   ...

White carefully prevents any possible counterplay on the Q-side with c7-c6 and b6-b5.

19. ...   Be6-f7 (2)
20. Bg2-f1 (5)   ...

Taking advantage of Black's lack of active possibilities, Kasparov is consistently improving the position of his pieces before he launches active operations on the Q-side.

20. ...   h7-h6 (5)
21. Bf1-d3 (4)   Qd8-d7 (4)
22. Qc3-c2 (6)   ...

Kasparov does not want to be enticed away by tactical complications associated with 22. Qa3, but adheres to his course of gradually mounting the pressure on Black's position.

22. ...   Bf7-e6 (0)
23. Bd3-b5 (2)   Qd7-d8 (2)

After 23. ... c6, Black would only be

burdened with additional cares about his b6-Pawn.

24. Rc1-d1 (2)   g7-g5 (6)

Seeing that Kasparov is not in a hurry, Karpov decides to start playing actively on the K-side but, in so doing, he only creates new weaknesses in his own position. Although the game will now be sharper, such a course of action seems to play into White's hands.

25. Nd2-f3 (4)   Re7-g7 (0)

Black cannot bring his Knight into play, because 25. ... Nc4 would be followed by 26. Bxc4 dxc 27. d5.

26. Nf3-e5 (1)   f5-f4 (2)
27. Bb5-f1! (3)   ...

White immediately transfers the Bishop to the defence of his King.

27. ...   Qd8-f6 (1)
28. Bf1-g2 (0)   Rb8-d8 (5)
29. e3-e4! (2)   ...

No. 56

As a result of Black's desperate attempts to start complications on the K-side, White has succeeded in opening up the centre, thereby making the defects of Black's position still more obvious. Black now has weaknesses on both wings and his Knight is as idle as ever.

29. ...	d5xe4 (1)
30. Bg2xe4 (0)	Rg7-e7 (0)
31. Qc2-c3 (2)	Be6-d5 (8)

Exchanges usually facilitate the defender's task in such positions. On the other hand, Black's Bishop plays an important role by covering the approach to Black's camp. Still, the Exchange of Bishops should not be censured, as Black's position can hardly be defended either way.

32. Rd1-e1 (2)	Kg8-g7 (0)
33. Ne5-g4! (2)	...

White starts preparing for the decisive attack. First, he takes possession of the open file.

33. ...	Qf6-f7 (1)
34. Be4xd5 (1)	Rd8xd5 (1)
35. Re1xe7 (1)	Qf7xe7 (0)
36. Rb1-e1 (0)	Qe7-d8 (0)
37. Ng4-e5 (1)	...

Black's position is hopeless, because his King has been denuded of his Pawn cover. White threatens 38. gxf, opening up files on the K-side, and also 38. Qc2 Qf6 39. cxb. Black defends himself against the first threat.

37. ...	Qd8-f6 (1)
38. c5xb6 (0)	Qf6xb6 (0)

Black is forced to recapture with his Queen, because 38. ... cxb would

be followed by 39. Qc7+ Kg8 40. Nd7 Qf7 41. Nf6+!.

39. g3xf4 (1)	Rd5xd4 (0)

This oversight changes nothing. After 39. ... gxf, 40. Kh1 (threatening 41. Rg1+) would be decisive.

40. Ne5-f3(0)	Na5-b3 (1)
41. Re1-b1 (1)	Qb6-f6 (1)
42. Qc3xc7+ (2)	

No. 57

Here the game is adjourned, and Kasparov plays his last move on the board, instead of sealing it. Now Black will inevitably lose much material.

Karpov therefore resigns without resumption.

Time: 2. 32-2.29.

GAME TWENTY

Queen's Gambit Declined

A. Karpov   G. Kasparov

The twentieth game has a special implication. One could not help noticing that in their previous match Kasparov was inferior to Karpov in the end game. In particular, he lost a couple of endings which could have been saved with better play.

This is therefore one possible reason why Karpov, having failed to gain anything tangible out of the middle phase of this twentieth game, decides to put his opponent's endgame technique to the test.

The game drags on, but this time Kasparov is up to the task.

1. d2-d4 (0)	d7-d5 (2)
2. c2-c4 (0)	e7-e6 (0)
3. Nb1-c3 (0)	Bf8-e7 (1)
4. c4xd5 (0)	e6xd5 (0)
5. Bc1-f4 (0)	Ng8-f6 (2)

A significant moment. Kasparov eschews the standard and popular 5. ... c6. After 6. e3 Bf5 7. g4, a number of promising ways of developing White's initiative have recently been found in this system.

6. Qd1-c2 (10)   . . .

White thus prevents the Black Bishop from going to f5, and also seems to threaten to attack the Pawn on c7.

6. . . .	0-0 (17)
7. e2-e3 (5)	. . .

It turns out that 7. Nb5 is not a threat after all. Indeed, this thrust would be met by 7. ... Bb4+ 8. Kd1 Nc6, and Black would have an excellent game for the lost Pawn.

7. . . .   c7-c5! (3)

This move is typical of Kasparov. He is not afraid that he may be left with an isolated Pawn, relying on his skill in piece play. Moreover, in the case under consideration, White has somewhat slowed down his development (6. Qc2), which will allow Black to free himself with the breakthrough d5-d4.

8. d4xc5 (8)	Be7xc5 (5)
9. Ng1-f3 (7)	Nb8-c6 (1)
10. Bf1-e2 (8)	d5-d4!? (3)
11. e3xd4 (5)	. . .

By Q-side castling White could win a Pawn, but this risky undertaking would give Black a strong initiative. For example, 11. 0-0-0 Qa5 12. exd Bb4, with great complications. And should White play 11. Rd1, Black could simply answer with 11. ... Qb6.

11. . . .	Nc6xd4 (6)
12. Nf3xd4 (0)	Qd8xd4 (0)
13. Bf4-g3 (0)	. . .
(No. 58)	

At first sight all Black's difficulties have already been overcome. But this is not quite so. The exposed position of the Black Queen requires Kasparov remaining on the alert. White threatens 14. Rd1 Qb4 15. a3.

13. . . .   Bc8-e6 (34)

It seems that Black could also have

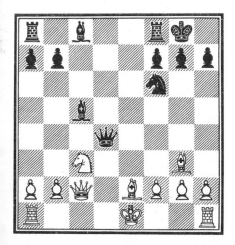

No. 58

replied with 13. ... Bb4 14. 0-0 (or
14. Rd1 Qe4!) 14. ... Bxc3, but then
he would have had to solve the problem
of developing his Queen's Bishop, while
White would also have had the Bishop
pair.

Kasparov prefers the more natural
continuation in the text.

14. 0-0 (4) ...

To 14. Rad1 Qb4 15. a3, Black could
reply with 15. ... Qb3.

14. ... Ra8-c8 (4)
15. Be2-f3 (9) b7-b6 (1)

Another possibility would be 15. ...
Qb4 16. a3 Qb6 17. Na4 Qb5, but Kasparov seems to be unwilling, on principle,
to part with his Bishop pair!

16. Rf1-e1 (14) Qd4-b4 (10)
17. Bg3-e5 (28) Bc5-d4 (0)

Here 17. ... Nd7 is interesting: after
18. Re4?!, Black is not at all forced to

sacrifice his Queen by 18. ... Qa5 19.
Ra4 Nxe5 20. Rxa5 Nxf3+ 21. gxf,
because after 18. ... Bf5! it is White
who is in difficulties.

18. a2-a3 (2) Qb4-c5 (1)
19. Be5xd4 (1) Qc5xd4 (1)
20. Ra1-d1 (0) Qd4-c5 (4)

But 20. ... Qf4, keeping the a4-square
under control, would be more precise.

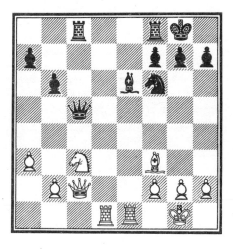

No. 59

21. Qc2-a4 (9) a7-a5(2)

Interesting complications could result
from 21. ... Qc7 22. Nb5 Bd7! 23.
Nxc7 Bxa4, but Kasparov radically solves
the problem of defending his a-Pawn
by advancing it.

22. Qa4-d4 (1) ...

White's plan has become quite clear.
He intends to exchange the Queens,
seize possession of the d-file, and make
an attempt to attack the somewhat

111

weak Black Pawn on b6. All these factors should contribute to his initiative.

22. ...	Qc5xd4 (3)
23. Rd1xd4 (0)	Rf8-d8 (1)
24. Re1-d1 (0)	Rd8xd4 (0)
25. Rd1xd4 (0)	Kg8-f8 (1)
26. Kg1-f1 (0)	...

As is prescribed for the end game, the opponents bring their Kings into play. White would have gained nothing by 26. Rd6 Nd7 27. Bc6, because of 27. ... Ke7 28. Bxd7 Kxd6 29. Bxc8 Bxc8, and Black would then have the advantage.

26. ...	Kf8-e7 (3)
27. Kf1-e2 (0)	Be6-b3 (10)

In this way, Black not only defends himself from the threat of Na4, but also sets up control over the c2-square, where his Rook will be able to penetrate if the White Knight is withdrawn from c3.

28. Ke2-e3 (3)	Rc8-c5 (5)
29. Ke3-d2 (8)	h7-h6 (2)

Here 29. ... Rf5, followed by g5 with an attempt at counterplay on the K-side, deserves consideration, but for the time being Kasparov keeps to his waiting tactics, mainly wishing to find out his opponent's intentions.

30. Bf3-e2 (7)	Nf6-e8 (11)
31. Be2-f3 (5)	Ne8-f6 (1)

The central squares d5 and e4 must be controlled.

32. Rd4-d3 (4)	Rc5-e5 (5)
33. h2-h3 (1)	Re5-c5 (1)
34. Rd3-d4 (0)	Rc5-c8 (1)

35. Bf3-e2 (1)	Rc8-c5 (0)
36. Be2-d3 (1)	h6-h5 (1)
37. g2-g3 (2)	g7-g6 (1)

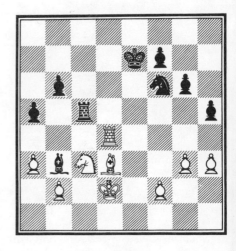

No. 60

Black, without any special need, places his Pawns on squares of the same colour as those controlled by his Bishop, which, in an ending with minor pieces, may give some advantage to White. Accordingly, just before the adjournment, Karpov decides to exchange the Rooks.

38. Nc3-e2 (2)	Nf6-d7 (1)
39. Rd4-e4+ (3)	Rc5-e5 (1)
40. Ne2-d4 (0)	Bb3-d5 (0)
41. Re4-e2 (1)	Re5xe2+ (6)

This move, which could be sealed by Black, Kasparov plays on the board.

42. Bd3xe2 (0)	Nd7-c5 (1)
43. Nd4-b5 (2)	Nc5-e4+ (10)
44. Kd2-e3 (1)	Ne4-d6 (0)
45. Ke3-d4 (4)	Bd5-c6 (3)
46. Nb5xd6 (5)	...

Thus a Bishop ending has arisen. White could not prevent his Knight from being exchanged, as 46. Nc3 would be followed by 46. ... h4 47. gxh Nf5+, 48. Ke5 f6+, with complete equality.

46. ...	Ke7xd6 (1)
47. Be2-c4 (1)	Bc6-e8 (0)
48. h3-h4 (0)	f7-f6 (0)

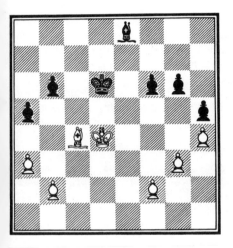

No. 61

Black has a weak Pawn on g6 (and, potentially, also on h5) which he has to protect with his Bishop, thus restricting its scope. However, in such an ending, a single weakness is not yet decisive. In order to win, White should create a position of *zugzwang* and this object may be attained if Black has a second weakness or if the White King is able to penetrate into the enemy camp. For the time being, however, none of these factors exists and Karpov, therefore, decides to manoeuvre his Bishop back and forth to find out whether his opponent has grasped all the nuances of the situation.

49. Bc4-g8 (28)	Kd6-c6 (3)

That the position is still dangerous to Black may be illustrated by the following variation: 49. ... Bd7 50. Bf7' Bf5 51. f3 Ke7 52. Bd5 Kd6 53. Be4, and Black has many problems in the Pawn ending; or 51. ... Bc2 52. g4 Ke7 53. Bd5 Bd1 54. Be4 f5 (54. ... Kf7 55. gxh gxh 56. Kd5) 55. gxf gxf 56. Bxf5 Bxf3 57. Ke5, and Black's position has deteriorated.

50. Bg8-a2 (1)	Kc6-d6 (1)
51. Ba2-d5 (0)	Kd6-e7 (0)
52. Bd5-g8 (4)	Ke7-d6 (1)
53. Bg8-b3 (0)	Kd6-e7 (1)

Possibly the only move. In the event of 53. ... Kc6? 54. Ba4+ b5 55. Bc2, Black would have a second weakness, his b5 Pawn.

54. Bb3-d1 (1)	Ke7-d6 (1)
55. Bd1-e2 (3)	Be8-d7 (7)
56. Be2-d3 (1)	Bd7-e8 (0)
57. Bd3-c4 (0)	Kd6-e7 (1)
58. Bc4-e2 (0)	...

58. Kd5 would be followed by 58. ... Bf7+, and the King would have to retreat.

58. ...	Ke7-d6 (1)
59. g3-g4 (0)	...

At last White has started to advance on the K-side.

59. ...	h5xg4 (2)
60. Be2xg4 (0)	Be8-f7 (30)

Kasparov avoids falling into a well-hidden trap. The tempting 60. ... g5 would be met by 61. h5 f5 62. h6 Bg6 63. Bh5 Bh7 64. Kc4 Kc6 65. Be8+ Kd6 66. Kb5 Kc7 67. Ka6, and Black's position would have become critical.

61. f2-f4 (4)   f6-f5 (7)

This is forced, because White threatens 62. f5!, setting up a distant passed Pawn.

62. Bg4-d1 (1)   Bf7-d5 (0)
63. Bd1-a4 (0)   Bd5-f3 (1)

After 63. ... Bf7 64. Bb5, Black would be in *zugzwang*.

64. Ba4-b3 (2)   Bf3-e2 (4)
65. Bb3-f7 (5)   Be2-h5 (0)
66. Kd4-c4 (0)   Bh5-e2+ (2)
67. Kc4-c3 (0)   Be2-h5 (1)
68. b2-b4 (0)   Kd6-e7 (3)

Black refuses to capture at b4, because after 69. Kxb4 Kc7 70. Kc4! Kd6 71. Kb5 Kc7 72. Ka6, the White King would penetrate into his camp.

69. Bf7-c4 (3)   Ke7-d6 (1)
70. b4xa5 (0)   b6xa5 (0)

No. 62

Black should be extremely cautious, as his Pawn on a5 is now exposed.

71. Kc3-d4 (1)   Bh5-f3 (1)
72. Bc4-f1 (4)   Bf3-d5 (3)
73. Bf1-e2 (0)   Bd5-b7 (1)
74. Be2-d1 (5)   Bb7-d5 (4)
75. Kd4-e3 (9)   ...

White intends to prevent the Black Bishop from getting to the d1-h5 diagonal, while attempting to place his Bishop on f7 or e8 but, as a result, Black manages to improve his King's position.

75. ...   Kd6-c5 (2)
76. Bd1-a4 (0)   Bd5-f7 (0)
77. Ba4-d7 (4)   ...

It would seem that after 77. Kd3 Bc4+ 78. Kd2 Bf7 79. Kc3!, White could at last succeed in putting Black in *zugzwang*. However, Black would then be able to counterattack with 78. ... Kd4! 79. Be8 Ke4 80. Bxg6 Kxf4 81. h5 Kg5, and he would not in the least risk losing the game.

77. ...   Kc5-c4 (10)
78. a3-a4 (0)   ...

A last chance. White intends to swap his a4-Pawn for Black's Pawn on g6.

78. ...   Kc4-c5 (1)

The variation 78. ... Kb4 79. Kd4 Bb3 80. Be8 Bxa4 81. Bxg6 would result in complications clearly advantageous to White. For example, 81. ... Bc2 82. Be8 a4 83. Bxa4 Bxa4 84. h5 Be8 85. h6 Bg6 86. Ke5 Kc5 87. Kf6, winning.

79. Bd7-b5 (1)   Kc5-d5 (8)
80. Ke3-d3 (0)   Kd5-c5 (0)

114

81. Kd3-c3 (1)	Kc5-d6 (1)
82. Kc3-d4 (0)	...

By making every effort White has finally succeeded in driving his opponent's Bishop away from the f7-square, but this only leads to a forced draw.

82. ...	Bf7-b3 (0)
83. Bb5-e8 (1)	Kd6-e7 (3)
84. Be8xg6 (2)	Bb3xa4 (0)
85. Bg6xf5 (0)	Ke7-f6 (2)

No. 63

Game drawn. Black would be able to draw the game even without his Pawn on a4, because it would be sufficient for him to give up his Bishop for the White f-Pawn.

Time: 4.05-4.28.

31 October and 1 November 1985

GAME TWENTY-ONE

Queen's Gambit Declined

G. Kasparov   A. Karpov

This game is characterised by sophisticated manoeuvring, with White having the initiative and exerting positional pressure almost to the end. The players seem to have decided to compete with each other in taking original and paradoxical decisions. The White King, for instance, remains uncastled throughout the game, while Black castles only on move eighteen. When the Queens are exchanged, there arises a complex end game, in which Karpov has to demonstrate all his resourcefulness in order to prevent White's initiative from becoming decisive.

The adjourned position is evaluated by all experts as difficult for Black, because of White's dangerous threat of a Pawn breakthrough in the centre. However, Karpov succeeds in obtaining counterplay on the Q-side, and the position becomes quite sharp. Kasparov, who is leading in the match by two points, seems unwilling to take chances and is satisfied with a draw.

1. d2-d4 (0)	d7-d5 (0)

Karpov rejects 1. ... Nf6, and with good reason! We may recall that in his six games with the Nimzo-Indian Defence he has scored only one and a half points.

2. c2-c4 (1)	e7-e6 (0)
3. Nb1-c3 (2)	Bf8-e7 (0)

Now Kasparov begins to think, and one can readily guess that he is choosing between the variations with 4. Nf3, repeatedly played in both the matches, and the Exchange at d5, whose main line leads to a more vigorous struggle.

4. c4xd5 (20) e6xd5 (0)
5. Bc1-f4 (0) c7-c6 (3)
6. e2-e3 (1) Bc8-f5 (3)

This defence was considered entirely satisfactory for Black until Botvinnik employed, against Petrosyan in the World Championship match (Moscow, 1963), the sharp move 7. g4, whose purpose is to take advantage of the exposed position of the Black Bishop and seize more space on the K-side. Since then the variation has been much analysed and played, White having the last word.

7. g2-g4 (0) Bf5-e6 (0)
8. h2-h4 (1) ...

Botvinnik played 8. h3 against Petrosyan, and in a later game against Spassky (Leiden, 1970) he resolutely pushed his Pawn to h4, thus inviting Black to capture it. This idea has found many adherents, among whom, as the reader can see, is Kasparov himself.

8. ... Nb8-d7 (11)

Why not 8. ... Bxh4? The answer to this question was furnished by the Vaiser-Diaz game (Havana, 1985) in which, after 9. Qb3 g5 10. Bh2! Bxg4 (10. ... Qb6 would be more circumspect) 11. Qxb7 Qe7 12. Qxa8 Qxe3+ 13. Be2 Qxf2+ 14. Kd2, Black's attack came to nothing.

9. h4-h5 (1) ...

No. 64

9. ... Ng8-h6!? (0)

The idea behind this innovation is to show that White's far advanced Pawns may become the object of an attack. At the same time, the Exchange at h6 would give Black good piece play.

Previously, 9. ... Qb6 was played here. For instance, the Belyavsky-Geller game (50th USSR Championship, 1983) continued 10. Rb1 Ngf6 11. f3 0-0 12. Bd3 c5 13. Nge2 Rac8 14. Kf1 cxd 15. exd, with White having the initiative.

10. Bf1-e2 (10) Nd7-b6 (3)
11. Ra1-c1 (12) Be7-d6 (28)

In order to make the position of his Knight secure, Karpov offers to exchange the black-squared Bishops but, as a result, White achieves a harmonious deployment of his forces.

The line 11. ... Nc4 12. b3 Nd6 would be more in the spirit of Black's original plan here, and this would seem to give him more chances for counterplay.

12. Ng1-h3 (7)	Bd6xf4 (0)
13. Nh3xf4 (0)	Be6-d7 (2)

White threatens 14. Nxe6 fxe 15. f4; therefore, Black avoids exchanging his Bishop and, at the same time, intends to play f7-f5.

14. Rh1-g1 (10)	g7-g5 (18)

14. ...f5 would certainly have been followed by 15. g5; but 14. ... Qg5 is worth considering here.

15. h5xg6 (10)	h7xg6 (0)

Black has succeeded in exchanging one of White's far advanced Pawns, but now he has to decide where he should place his King.

16. Ke1-d2? (0)	...

By this original move White enables his Queen to get to the K-side.

16. ...	Qd8-e7 (4)

Meanwhile, Black prepares for Q-side castling. The alternative is 16. ... Kf8 17. Rh1 Kg7 to keep his King near the h-file, which is to become an arena of further operations.

If, Black were to choose a different order of moves by playing first 16. ... g5 17. Nd3 Nc4+ 18. Kc2 Qe7, then after 19. b3 Nd6 20. Kb2 he would not be able to castle long, because White could capture the d5-Pawn with his Knight.

17. b2-b3 (10)	g6-g5 (8)
18. Nf4-d3 (0)	0-0-0 (5)
19. Rg1-h1 (11)	...

White's plan is to bring his Queen to g3 and

double his Rooks on the h-file. Black's subsequent play is essentially forced.

19. ...	f7-f6 (1)
20. Qd1-g1 (4)	Kh6-f7 (10)

20. ... Qd6 would be dangerous, because of 21. Nb5 Qb8 22. a4.

21. Qg1-g3 (1)	Qe7-d6 (3)

In cramped positions, simplifications usually facilitate the defender's task, but in this specific position the Exchange of Queens leads to an end game which is difficult for Black, his situation being confined to a passive defence. For this reason, many commentators suggest 21. ... Nd6 to mask the dangerous diagonal and to retain the Queens on the board, which would help to restrict White's initiative, because of the rather unstable position of his King on d2. Nevertheless, White's chances would even then be preferable.

22. Qg3xd6 (6)	Nf7xd6 (0)
23. f2-f3 (3)	...

No. 65

In the resulting complex end game, White has rich possibilities of activating his minor pieces. The White Bishop should be transferred to d3, the Knight to g3, and then White would threaten e3-e4. Black should carefully parry his opponent's threats, but he himself cannot undertake anything positive.

| 23. ... | Rd8-g8 (9) |
| 24. Nd3-c5 (8) | Kc8-d8 (5) |

An attempt at counterplay with 24. ... f5 could only result in the g5-Pawn becoming weak.

| 25. Be2-d3 (10) | Bd7-c8 (1) |
| 26. Nc3-e2 (2) | Nb6-a8 (7) |

In this, rather uncommon, way Black brings his b6-Knight into play.

27. Bd3-h7!? (2) ...

A typical manoeuvre. Interestingly, a similar device was employed, in a Ruy López position, by Karpov himself in order to seize possession of the a-file (Be3-a7! , etc.). In the present game, blocking the h-file with his Bishop, White intends to double his Rooks on it.

27. ...   Rg8-f8 (4)

The reply 27. ... Rg7 seems dangerous, because of 28. Bf5 and if 28. ... Rxh1 29. Rxh1 Nxf5, then 30. Rh8+ Kc7 31. gxf Nb6 32. Ng3, with a decisive advantage for White. However, after 28. ... Rgg8!?, the game would become much sharper.

28. Rh1-h6 (1) ...

Should the Rook be moved along the h-file to any other square, Black could answer with 28. ... f5.

28. ...	Na8-c7 (0)
29. Ne2-g3 (2)	Nd6-f7 (6)
30. Rh6-h2 (2)	...

Here 30. Rh5 Ne6 31. Nxe6+ Bxe6 32. Rch1 deserves serious consideration, since after 33. Bg6! White could seize the h-file.

30. ...	Nc7-e6 (0)
31. Nc5-d3 (0)	Ne6-g7 (0)
32. Rc1-h1 (2)	Kd8-e7 (1)
33. Nd3-f2 (1)	Rf8-d8 (3)

Black attempts to prevent e3-e4.

34. Bh7-f5 (5)   ...

Thus bringing about the Exchange of Rooks, whereupon White should at last be able to advance his centre Pawn.

34. ...	Rh8xh2 (8)
35. Rh1xh2 (0)	Ng7xf5 (0)
36. g4xf5 (0)	Rd8-h8 (1)
37. Rh2xh8 (0)	Nf7xh8 (0)
38. e3-e4 (0)	...

No. 66

If the Black Knight were placed on d6, then 38. e4 would be totally harmless, because of 38. ... b6 39. Ng4 dxe 40. fxe c5. As it is, this advance looks menacing.

| 38. ... | Nh8-f7 (1) |
| 39. Nf2-g4 (0) | Nf7-d6 (1) |

Otherwise, e4-e5 cannot be averted.

| 40. Ng4-e3 (3) | ... |

The last, control move, which was criticised by the commentators as an inexactitude, because the Knight on e3 prevents the White King from defending the Pawn on d4. However, the recommended 40. Nh6 could be met by the immediate 40. ... Kf8! (rather than by 40. ... dxe 41. fxe Kf8, in view of 42. e5 Kg7 43. exd Kxh6 44. Ke3, with a won end game); for instance, 41. e5 Kg7 42. exd Kxh6, and the d-Pawn would be cut off from White's other forces.

Possibly 40. Ke3 was White's best chance.

| 40. ... | d5xe4 (1) |
| 41. f3xe4 (3) | ... |

No. 67

Here the game is adjourned, and Karpov seals his 41st move.

The experts were unanimous in believing that, because of the threat of e4-e5, the Challenger had winning chances. However, only four more moves were played and the game was drawn.

| 41. ... | b7-b6! (19) |

Probably the strongest sealed move.

| 42. b3-b4 (1) | ... |

Why not the natural 42. e5! , Analysis has revealed that this advance could be countered by 42. ... Nb5 43. Kd3 (not, of course, 43. Nh5 Nxd4 44. Nxf6 Nxf5! 45. Nxf5 Bxf5 46. Ke3 c5 47. Kf3 Bb1) 43. ... Ba6 44. Ng4 Nc7+ 45. Ke4 Nd5, and Black would have good counter-chances. Of course, White would have retained the initiative even in that case, but, being two points ahead, Kasparov was unwilling to take the risk.

42. ...	Bc8-a6 (0)
43. Ne3-g4 (2)	Nd6-b5 (0)
44. Kd2-d3 (21)	Nb5-a3+ (2)

Game drawn.
Time: 2.55-2.48.

5 November 1985

GAME TWENTY-TWO

Queen's Gambit Declined

A. Karpov   G. Kasparov

This game was postponed by the World Champion who found himself in a critical situation. Winning this game was his only practical chance to save the title. And to achieve this, the utmost concentration and the most expedient plan of action were required.

The White pieces offered Karpov the option between burning his boats in order to strive for a hand-to-hand fight, in which much could depend on luck, and fighting a long, hard battle, in which the eventual success would depend on the depth of the respective strategic plans and the stronger will-power under the terrible strain of five hours of play. It is this uneasy, second course that Karpov decides to take.

And what about Kasparov? His task was also a difficult one, both in terms of game and psychological. On the one hand, being aware of Karpov's uncompromising attitude towards the game Kasparov had to get into the mood for a strenuous, relentless battle. On the other hand, the proximity of the long-cherished goal—he needed only one point more, for which two draws in the remaining three games would suffice—and the overpowering feeling of tremendous responsibility for each decision and for each move paralysed him and dictated an overcautious approach. This unfortunate state of his mind was sure to affect Kasparov's performance that night.

1. d2-d4 (0)	d7-d5 (1)
2. c2-c4 (0)	e7-e6 (1)
3. Kb1-c3 (0)	Bf8-e7 (1)
4. c4xd5 (0)	e6xd5 (0)
5. Bc1-f4 (0)	. . .

Remarkably, this strategically involved scheme of opening attracts the players' attention at a decisive moment of their mammoth contest. The stability of the central position betokens long manoeuvres with possibilities of active wing operations, which is entirely in line with Karpov's intention to use the colour of his pieces effectively and without too serious a risk.

5. . . .	Ng8-f6 (0)

Kasparov's patent. In the preceding game, Karpov preferred 5. . . . c6.

6. e2-e3 (0)	. . .

Not wishing to repeat the manoeuvre 6. Qc2 (see game 20), which proved inadequate.

6. . . .	0-0 (1)
7. Ng1-f3 (4)	. . .

7. Bd3, to prevent the activation of the Black Queen's Bishop, appears to be more natural here. However, in this case, White would have to reckon with transposition to the line 7. . . . c5! 8. dxc Bxc5, in which the White Bishop is better posted at e2. After 7. Nf3, the reply 7. . . . c5 is not as good as after 7. Bd3, because of 8. dxc Bxc5 9. Be2 Nc6 10. 0-0, and White would have a firm grip of the vital d4-square.

7. . . .	Bc8-f5 (2)

Of course, the tame 7. . . . c6 could be advantageously answered with 8. Bd3. (**No. 68**)

8. h2-h3!? (21)	. . .

This is perhaps the best method, when circumstances offer for starting double-edged complications. The thrust 8. Qb3 would be too risky here, because of 8. . . . Nc6 (and if 9. Qxb7, then 9. . . . Nb4), while the developing moves 8. Bd3 and 8. Be2 are too harmless. Furthermore, the attacking Pawn advance g2-g4,

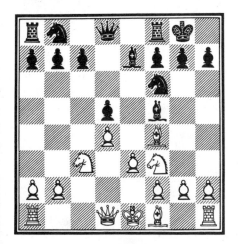

No. 68

intended by Karpov, is quite justified positionally. Indeed, one should remember that in the variation 5. ... c6 6. e3 Bf5 7. g4 Be6 8. h3, White launches active operations even before his forces are fully deployed and before it becomes clear whether Black castles short or long.

| 8. ... | c7-c6 (31) |

Judging from his long meditation, Kasparov played this move very unwillingly. His c-Pawn is usually to play the more active role of undermining White's position in the centre. However, in this particular position White could, after 8. ... c5 9. dxc Bxc5, offer to exchange the Bishops by 10. Bd3 and, in any case, Black would have his hands full, trying to protect his isolated d5-Pawn, and without having sufficient counterplay.

| 9. g2-g4 (7) | Bf5-g6 (18) |

Again, an uneasy decision, because of Black's rather wide choice of continuations.

One possibility would be 9. ... Be6 10. Bd3 c5 11. Kf1 Nc6 12. Kg2 Rc8, which could transpose to a position from the thirteenth game of the Merano Match (1981). This is playable, but not very attractive for Black.

Another possibility, 9. ... Be4, would be justified only after an impulsive Exchange at e4, whereas in the event of 10. g5 Nh5 (perhaps 10. ... Ne8 would be better) 11. Bxb8!? Rxb8 12. Rg1, Black's difficulties would still remain.

Finally, the line chosen by Kasparov also has its disadvantages.

| 10. Nf3-e5 (0) | Nf6-d7 (2) |

He would, of course, like to complete his development by 10. Nbd7, but then 11. h4 would be unpleasant.

| 11. Ne5xg6 (4) | f7xg6!? (0) |

An uncommon idea. After 11. ... hxg, Black would have to watch very carefully the possible advance of White's h-Pawn and, moreover, he would not have had any counterplay. As it is, the semi-open f-file is at his disposal.

| 12. Bf1-g2 (4) | ... |

Karpov played this move quite rapidly. However, the fianchettoed Bishop for a long time remains inactive at this square, and it is now easier for Black to solve his problems. 12. Bd3 would be more vigorous here.

| 12. ... | Nd7-b6 (4) |

Parrying the tactical threat of Nc3xd5 and preparing for the Exchange of the black-squared Bishops by Be7-d6.

121

| 13. 0-0 (4) | Kg8-h8 (17) |

A preventive, waiting move à la Petrosyan, whose implication seems to be psychological. Before deciding on the final placing of his pieces, Kasparov wishes to find out his opponent's strategic goal.

| 14. Nc3-e2 (7) | g6-g5 (4) |
| 15. Bf4-g3 (1) | Be7-d6 (1) |

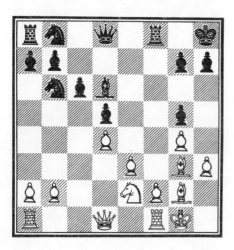

No. 69

16. Qd1-d3 (5)   ...

A somewhat unexpected decision. It would seem that Karpov intended to carry out the natural manoeuvre Ne2-c1-d3, with prospects for active operations in the centre or on the Q-side. Instead, he starts a far less obvious and much sharper plan. His choice was evidently motivated by the overall situation in the match, rather than by the requirements of the position.

| 16. ... | Nb8-a6 (4) |
| 17. b2-b3 (8) | ... |

Before launching the intended operation it would be useful to restrict the mobility of the Black Knight on b6.

17. ...   Qd8-e7 (4)

Why did not he play 17. ... Nc7!? at once? This tempo could come in handy. The line 17. ... Bxg3 18. Nxg3 Nc7 is also worth considering.

| 18. Bg3xd6 (8) | Qe7xd6 (0) |
| 19. f2-f4 (0) | ... |

Karpov starts executing his rather risky plan of advancing on the K-side. The game is now opened up, Black taking possession of the files "e" and "f".

19. ...	g5xf4 (15)
20. e3xf4 (0)	Ra8-e8 (2)
21. f4-f5 (9)	Na6-c7 (2)
22. Rf1-f2 (5)	...

A restrained move, suggesting that all is not well for White. Indeed, after 22. Nf4, Black has the unpleasant 22. ... g6!?, while after the attempt to consolidate by 22. Rae1, White would have to reckon with the pinning 22. ... Qe7.

22. ...   Nb6-d7?! (4)

In our opinion, it is at this moment that Kasparov loses the thread of his budding counterplay. He should have preferred either 22. ... Nc8, followed by 23. ... Qe7, or the immediate 22. ... Qe7, with excellent prospects in both cases.

23. g4-g5 (3)   ...

Of course! Why should he allow the Black Knight to go to f6 if it is rather awkwardly posted at d7?

23. ...	Qd6-e7	(5)
24. h3-h4 (8)	...	

The White Bishop will at last be able to come into play, as the h3-square is now accessible to it.

24. ...	Qe7-e3	(3)
25. Ra1-d1 (0)	Nc7-b5	(2)
26. Qd3xe3 (7)	Re8xe3	(0)

Both sides may be satisfied with the Exchange of Queens, because now Black may no longer fear White's attack on his King, while White has, in his turn, succeeded in neutralising, to some extent, Black's pressure along the e-file. Still, the situation remains rather sharp.

No. 70

27. Kg1-h2! (0) ...

A versatile manoeuvre. The White King will now be able to secure convenient posts for two White pieces: the Knight on g3 and the Bishop on h3. But who could have foretold that this is also the beginning of a victorious raid?

27. ... Nd7-b6 (6)

Admitting his inaccuracy on move twenty-two. Since the Knight on d7 is clearly uncomfortable (Black has to reckon with the threat of 28. Bh3 and 29. f6), Black has to lose valuable tempo to improve its position.

28. Ne2-g3 (6)	Nb6-c8	(2)
29. Ng3-f1!? (7)	...	

The Black Rook is too active to be left unattended.

29. ... Re3-e7 (1)

With time pressure approaching one would like to play "solidly"; therefore Kasparov probably disregards the vigorous, though debatable, 29. ... Rc3!?

30. Rd1-d3 (2) ...

It is evident that Karpov is now optimistic. Of course, the repetition of the position by 30. Ng3 Re3 does not suit him.

30. ...	Nc8-d6	(1)
31. Nf1-g3 (1)	Nd6-e4?!	(3)

Under severe time pressure Kasparov strives to force matters, which results in a drastic deterioration of his position. Meanwhile, he had at his disposal the excellent interposition 31. ... Re1, which would greatly enhance the strength of the move actually played. Black would then be able to continue 32. ... Ne4, even after 32. a4. It should be added that the modest 31. ... Kg8 could still have maintained the balance.

32. Bg2xe4 (1)	d5xe4	(0)
33. Rd3-e3 (0)	Nb5xd4	(3)

Here 33. . . . Nd6 deserves consideration.

34. Kh2-h3! (10) . . .

This move is not only strong, but also extremely unpleasant for Black, considering that he is hard pressed for time. Perhaps Kasparov expected 34. f6, but White does not have to force matters.

34. . . .	Re7-e5 (7)
35. Kh3-g4 (2)	. . .

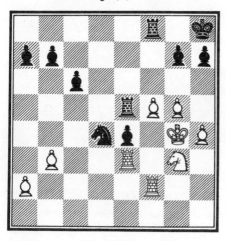

No. 71

35. . . .	h7-h5+ ? (2)

The decisive mistake. With the patient 35. . . . Kg8 36. Rf4 Rfe8, Black could still defend himself, because, after 37. Rexe4 (37. Rfxe4 is unplayable, because of 37. . . . Nxf5!) 37. . . . c5, it would be rather difficult for White to mount his pressure.

After Kasparov's move, however, there comes an unexpected, rapid denouement.

36. Kg4xh5 (1)	Nd4xf5 (0)
37. Rf2xf5 (0)	Rf8xf5 (0)
38. Ng3xf5 (0)	Re5xf5 (0)
39. Re3xe4 (0)	Kh8-h7 (0)
40. Re4-e7 (1)	b7-b5 (0)

40. . . . Rb5 would not help either, because of 41. a4.

41. Re7xa7 (1) b5-b4 (4)

Here the game is adjourned and Karpov seals his move 42. Kh5-g4(15), but the game is not resumed.

Black resigns, as he has no defence against the decisive h4-h5-h6.

Time: 2.32-2.33

7 November 1985

GAME TWENTY-THREE

Queen's Gambit Declined

G. Kasparov   A. Karpov

As a result of Karpov's victory in the twenty-second game, the situation in the match has become extremely sharp, Kasparov's lead being seriously endangered. And it is the psychological, rather than the chess, considerations that have begun to play the decisive role now.

Whose nerves will prove the stronger? Who will be cool and firm enough to play the last games with maximum concentration and purpose? And, last but not least, on whom will Caïssa smile? The penultimate game of the match failed to give exhaustive answers to these questions, but it again reminded us of Kasparov's impulsiveness and Karpov's self-control and persistence.

That night the contestants' tasks were quite definite. Kasparov, who has the White pieces for the last time in match, chooses a variation which could offer him both winning chances and a high degree of security. For a draw in this game, though delaying the attainment of his ultimate object, would not spoil his chances altogether.

Karpov's plans are even more definite: he has to hold his ground, thus transferring the decisive battle to the last game of the match.

All these considerations represent the leitmotiv of the events to follow. White indeed succeeds in gaining a lasting advantage, but the end of the game turns out to be highly intriguing.

1. d2-d4 (0)	d7-d5 (0)
2. c2-c4 (0)	e7-e6 (0)
3. Nb1-c3 (1)	Bf8-e7 (0)
4. Ng1-f3 (3)	. . .

In the twenty-first game, Kasparov preferred 4. cxd exd 5. Bf4. Now, somewhat unexpectedly, he comes back to an old variation but, as will soon become evident, with new arguments.

4. . . .	Ng8-f6 (0)
5. Bc1-g5 (0)	h7-h6 (3)
6. Bg5xf6 (1)	Be7xf6 (4)
7. e2-e3 (0)	. . .

He rejects 7. Qb3 (game 3), as well as 7.Qd2 (games 19 and 21 of the previous match).

7. . . .	0-0 (3)
8. Ra1-c1 (2)	. . .

'The new is the long-forgotten old." This outmoded plan seems to come as a surprise to Karpov, because from now on he thinks over his moves for quite a long time, but still fails to solve his opening problems. This is really astonishing, specially if we remember that Karpov is a leading exponent of the variation with the Exchange on f6, repeatedly employing it as both White and Black

(in particular, in the fourth game he played 8. Qc2, and in the 6th—8. Qd2).

8. . . .	c7-c6 (8)

The less orthodox treatment is 8. . . . Nc6, but Karpov is an adherent of classical formations.

9. Bf1-d3 (1)	Nb8-d7 (6)
10. 0-0 (1)	. . .

Another possibility is the Karlsbad Variation: 10. cxd exd (after 10. . . . cxd 11. 0-0 b6 12. e4!? dxe 13. Bxe4 Rb8 14. Nb5, White has the initiative— the Yusupov-Balashov game, 48th USSR Championship, 1980-81) 11. b4 Be7 12. b5, with the minority attack. The choice here is a matter of taste and preparation.

10. . . .	d5xc4 (9)
11. Bd3xc4 (1)	e6-e5 (0)

No. 72

125

This position has occurred in innumerable games, and two continuations have been tested in particular, 12. Ne4 and 12. Bb3, with Black finding convincing means to equalize in both cases:

1) 12. Ne4 exd 13. Nxf6+ Nxf6 14. Nxd4 (or 14. Qxd4 Qxd4 15. Nxd4 Re8 16. Rfd1 Bd7 17. Kf1 Kf8 18. a3 Re5 19. Be2 a5 20. Nf3 Rd5—Andersson-Spassky, Niksic, 1983) 14. ... Qe7 15. Qb3 Bg4 (15. ... c5 16. Ne2 b6 is also rather good) 16. f3 c5 17. Ne2 Bd7 18. a4 Qe8 19. Ra1 Rb8 20. e4 b5 21. axb Bxb5 22. Rxa7 Bxc4 23. Qxc4 Rxb2 (Vaganyan-Ivkov, Sochi, 1980);

2) 12. Bb3 exd 13. exd Re8 14. h3 (if 14. Qd2, then 14. ... Nf8!; or 14. Re1 Rxe1+ 15. Qxe1 Nf8!) 14. ... Nf8!.

14. ... Nb6 is worse, because of 15. Re1 Bf5 16. Rxe8+ Qxe8 17. Qd2 Qd7 18. Re1, and White would exert pressure—Gligorić-Hansen (Plovdiv, 1983) and Gavrikov-Belyavsky (Minsk, 1983).

15. d5 (15. Qd2 Be6!) 15. ... Bd7 (Black may also play 15. ... Bf5, or 15. ... cxd 16. Bxd5 Rb8, followed by 17. ... Be6) 16. Re1 Rxe1+ 17. Qxe1 cxd 18. Rd1 Bxc3 19. Qxc3 Be6 20. Bxd5 Rc8 21. Qb3, drawn (Ribli-Karpov, London, 1984).

In the light of the above variations, Kasparov's attempt to infuse new life into this well-known variation is all the more interesting.

12. h2-h3! (1)   ...

An apparently innocuous, but venomous move. Black is now in a peculiar position of *zugzwang* (12. ... Re8? 13. Qb3!), being practically forced to go over to the variation considered disadvantageous to him.

12. ...   e5xd4 (13)
13. e3xd4 (1)   Nd7-b6 (2)
14. Bc4-b3 (0)   Rf8-e8 (20)

Or 14. ... Bf5 15. Re1 Re8, which is equivalent to the text move.

15. Rf1-e1 (1)   Bc8-f5 (7)

In the event of 15. ... Rxe1+ 16. Qxe1 Nd5 (16. ... Bf5 17. Ne5!?) 17. Nxd5 cxd 18. Qb4, Black would be in serious difficulties.

16. Re1xe8+ (2) Qd8xe8 (0)
17. Qd1-d2 (0)   Qe8-d7 (10)
18. Rc1-e1 (1)   ...

No. 73

The position from the above-mentioned Gligorić-Hansen and Gavrikov-Belyavsky games has now been reached (by transposition). Black seems to have succeeded in solving the problem of his development, but his task is far from easy: he has to reckon with White's combined pressure along the a2-g diagonal and the e-file, the thrusts Qd2-f4 and Nf3-e5, and also, in the more distant future, the manoeuvre Nc3-e4.

We should also mention that, by now, Karpov has already used up one and a half hours on his clock, whereas Kasparov—only fifteen minutes!

18. ... Ra8-d8 (14)

In the event of 18. ... Re8 19. Rxe8+ Qxe8 20. Qf4 Be6 (20. ... Qd7? 21. Qb8+, or 20. ... Qc8 21. g4!?) 21. Bxe6 fxe (21. ... Qxe6 22. Qb8+) 22. Ne4, White's positional advantage would acquire menacing proportions.

Hansen played 18. ... Qd6 against Gligorić but, after 19. Ne5 Bxe5 (19. ... Nd5 20. g4!?) 20. Rxe5 Bg6 21. Qf4 Rd8 22. Ne2! Nd5 23. Qg3 Qb4 24. Bxd5 cxd 25. Qc3, he was doomed to defend himself in a difficult position.

19. Qd2-f4 (4) Nb6-d5 (9)

The opinion was expressed that Karpov should have complicated the game by 19. ... g5 20. Qg3 Bxd4. However, this recommendation is hardly well-founded, as White has many attractive retorts; for example, 21. Nxd4 Qxd4 22. Qf3 and, after 22. ... Qf4 (neither 22. ... Qd3 23. Rd1, nor 22. ... Qf6 23. g4, nor yet 22. ... Qc5 23. g4 Bg6 24. Qf6 Qd6 25. Re8+!, is playable and, after 22. ... Bg6, 23. Rd1 is decisive) 23. Qh5 Nd5 24. Nxd5 cxd 25. Qxh6, the threats of 26. Bxd5, 26. g3, and 26. Qf6 would make Black's position critical.

Belyavsky defended against Gavrikov by 19. ... Bg6 and, after 20. Qg3 Bh5 21. Ne4 Bxd4 22. Nxd4 Qxd4 23. Qh4 Bg6 24. Rd1 Qxd1+ 25. Bxd1 Rxd1+ 26. Kh2 Rd5 27. Qf4 Bxe4

28. Qxe4 Nd7 29. Qe8+ Nf8 30. Qb8 Rb5, managed to hold his own in an ending where he had a Rook, a Knight and a Pawn against the White Queen.

20. Nc3xd5 (5) c6xd5 (0)
21. Nf3-e5 (0) ...

The tempting 21. Rc1 would be met by the strong counterblow 21. ... g5.

21. ... Bf6xe5 (8)
22. Re1xe5 (5) Bf5-e6 (0)

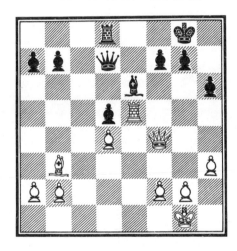

No. 74

As a result of all the previous play, a position has been reached which seems to have come from a reader in chess. In spite of the complete symmetry of the Pawn formation and the small number of the forces left, White clearly stands better. His pieces are free to manoeuvre and can be used for active operations on any part of the board, whereas Black, who has to protect his d5-Pawn, has no choice but to defend himself passively.

127

We should again stress that, for Karpov, serious time pressure is approaching: Karpov has already used up one hour and fifty-six minutes, whereas Kasparov—only half an hour!

23. Qf4-e3 (34)   Kg8-f8 (0)

These manoeuvres are logical. White strives to prevent f7-f6, which would drive his Rook away from an ideal position in the centre. Black, on the other hand, is preparing for this advance (the immediate 23. ... Re8 fails to 24. Bxd5!).

24. Qe3-d3 (10)   ...

The beginning of a long phase of manoeuvring, whose purpose is to find the most effective posts for his forces and to enable him to exploit his positional advantage. The enticing attempt to force matters, by 24. f4 Re8 25. Qf3 (25. Qc3!? is also interesting) 25. ... f6 26. f5!?, would not be preferable. After 26. ... Bf7 27. Rxe8+ Qxe8 (but not 27. ... Kxe8?, in view of 28. Qg3! Qxf5 29. Ba4+!) 28. Qf4 (if 28. Bxd5, then Black replies with 28. ... Bxd5 29. Qxd5 Qe3+ 30. Kh2 Qf4+ 31. 31. g3 Qf2+ 32. Qg2 Qxf5 33. Qxb7 Qf2+ 34. Qg2 Qxd4) 28. ... Kg8 29. Kf2 a6, White would have gained nothing.

24. ...   f7-f6 (6)
25. Re5-e1 (6)   Be6-f7 (4)

Such a gradual consolidation is Karpov's favourite defensive device. 25. ... Rc8, to set up control over the open c-file, also deserves attention here, although it would not change the assessment of the position as being favourable to White.

26. Qd3-c3 (4)   Qd7-d6 (2)

But 26. ... Rc8 is no longer playable, in view of 27. Qb4+ Kg8 28. Re7.

27. Re1-c1 (3)   Bf7-e8 (2)

Karpov is defending himself very carefully. He is now ready to meet the threat of the White Rook's penetration by Be8-c6. Here 27. ... Re8 would fail, to 28. Ba4.

Kasparov replies by transferring his Bishop to f3, intending a Q-side action.

28. Bb3-d1 (12)   a7-a6 (8)

His motto is prevention! In this situation, this is the best method. The attempt at activity by 28. ... Bd7 (with the idea of 29. ... Rc8) is refuted by 29. Qa5.

29. Bd1-f3 (3)   g7-g6 (2)

According to Razuvayev, this is a moot point. But to secure a shelter for his King, while he still can, is useful to Black.

30. h3-h4 (11)   ...

White is in no hurry either. Kasparov places his Pawns on the "right" black squares to give more scope to his Bishop.

30. ...   h6-h5 (1)
31. g2-g3 (5)   ...

In the event of 31. Qc7, Black could coolly ward off White's threat by 31. ... Rd7 (but not 31. ... Qxc7? 32. Rxc7 Bc6, which would be dangerous to him, because of 33. Be2! a5 34. Bd3); and 32. Qc8 (32. Qxd6 Rxd6 is harmless) would be met by 32. Qe7, with an elastic defensive set-up.

31. ...	Be8-f7 (2)
32. a2-a4 (6)	Rd8-d7 (1)
33. a4-a5 (2)	...

This, at any rate, is consistent, although 33. Qa5 is also attractive.

33. ...	Kf8-g7 (0)
34. Qc3-b3 (4)	Qd6-e6 (1)
35. Qb3-b4! (2)	Qe6-e8 (1)

In spite of his circumspect defence, Black has to retreat step by step. White threatens 36. Rc8, while the Exchange of Queens by 35. ... Qe7 36. Qxe7 Rxe7 would lead to a very difficult end game for Black.

36. Kg1-g2?! (3) ...

One can understand Kasparov's desire to refrain from taking any important decisions before the adjournment, but at this moment he could add to his positional advantage by 36. Bg2, with the vexing threat of 37. Bh3!.

36. ...	Qe8-d8 (1)
37. Rc1-c5? (2)	...

Kasparov's vigilance seems to have been lulled! At this square, the Rook loses its manoeuvrability and, for some time, will be out of play. Here 37. Rc3, or even 37. Kh2, would be better, for White would then retain the initiative.

37. ...	Qd8-e7 (0)
38. Qb4-c3 (1)	...

Again an inexactitude, the third in a row. He should perhaps have preferred 38. Qd2, to meet 38. ... g5 by 39. hxg fxg 40. Rc3, ensuring a harmonious co-ordination of his forces. In the event of 38.

... Rc7, he could respond with 39. b4 (39. ... Rxc5 40. bxc!, etc.).

Suddenly, the situation radically changes.

No. 75

38. ...   g6-g5! (0)

A powerful counter-blow, also entailing a great psychological effect! Just before the control time, the Black pieces, which have long been huddled in the back rows, have suddenly found scope, Black's play becoming dynamic. Now Kasparov urgently has to change his plans and get ready to repulse Black's attack. After having the initiative for such a long time this is not easy and surely is a disappointment to him.

39. Qc3-e3?! (1) ...

Otherwise, he would run the risk of being exposed to an attack, but after 39. hxg fxg 40. Kf1 g4 41. Bg2, White would perhaps have retained some winning chances.

39. ...	g5-g4 (1)
40. Bf3-d1 (2)	Qe7-e4+ (0)
41. Kg2-g1 (2)	

Having played this move (41. Kh2, incidentally, is more precise), Kasparov offers a draw, which is accepted by Karpov—after some hesitation. The position still has some life in it, but the players have perhaps had too much excitement in this game to wish to prolong the fight. The more so that, after the evident 41. ... Re7 42. Rc3 Bg6 43. Kh2, their chances would be roughly even. ~~what is if (41)...~~

Time: 2.23-2.33

Re7 (42) Rc3
Qb1 (43) Rc1
axb2!
x(43) Qd2 ~ects
(th)reat.

9 November 1985

GAME TWENTY-FOUR

Sicilian Defence

A. Karpov   G. Kasparov

By the final game of the match, the tension of the battle has reached its climax. After many months of the colossal contest between the world's strongest chess players, after forty-eight games of their first match and twenty-three of the second, the fate of the World Chess Title was to be decided in this single, last game.

Karpov had to win the game to retain the title, whereas Kasparov could be satisfied with a draw. But, to the delight of the spectators, his fighting spirit prevailed.

1. e2-e4 (0)   ...

"This move is an old favourite of mine," confessed Karpov. It may be easy for us, when analysing not only the game, but also the match as a whole, to question the expediency of this choice of opening for the decisive battle. Seven encounters of the present contest (and many of the previous) have shown that Karpov has failed to find a key to fit the lock of Kasparov's Sicilian fortress. Indeed, the Challenger has displayed a profound understanding of this opening. And the dry figures are even more convincing than so many words: the score +0−2=5 is catastrophic.

On the other hand, Karpov has achieved a positive score (+2−0=3) with the Queen's Gambit. So wasn't he wrong to have chosen the Sicilian for the decisive game?

1. ...   c7-c5 (0)

There could be no doubt that Kasparov would answer with this move. The following moves were played with an almost demonstrative rapidity.

2. Ng1-f3 (0)	d7-d6 (1)
3. d2-d4 (0)	c5xd4 (0)
4. Nf3xd4 (1)	Ng8-f6 (0)
5. Nb1-c3 (1)	a7-a6 (0)
6. Bf1-e2 (0)	e7-e6 (0)
7. 0-0 (1)	Bf8-e7 (0)
8. f2-f4 (0)	0-0 (1)
9. Kg1-h1 (0)	Qd8-c7 (0)
10. a2-a4 (1)	Nb8-c6 (0)
11. Bc1-e3 (0)	Rf8-e8 (0)
12. Be2-f3 (1)	Ra8-b8 (1)
13. Qd1-d2 (2)	Bc8-d7 (2)
14. Nd4-b3 (1)	b7-b6 (0)

No. 76

Thus far, nothing new. In the 18th game there followed 15. Bf2 Bc8 16. Bg3 Nd7 17. Rae1 Bb7 18. e5 Rbd8, with roughly level chances.

But still the question remains why Karpov decided to return to this variation. The point may well be that only a few days after the 18th game of the match, Sokolov demonstrated an original, bold treatment of this variation against Ribli (Candidates' Tournament, France, Montpellier, 1985). The Soviet Grandmaster here continued: 15. g4!? Bc8 16. g5 Nd7 17. Bg2 Na5 18. Qf2 Bf8? 19. Rad1 Nc4 20. Bc1 b5 21. axb axb 22. Rd3 g6 23. Rh3 Bg7 24. f5! Nce5 25. Qh4 Nf8 26. f6 Bh8 27. Nd4 b4 28. Nd1 Ba6 29. Re1 Rec8 30. Ne3 h5 31. Nf3 Nfd7. 32. Nd2 Kf8 33. Ndf1 b3 34. Ng3 Ke8 35. Nxh5! gxh 36. Qxh5 Ng6 37. Nf5! Bxf6 38. gxf exf 39. exf+ Nge5 40. Qh8+ Nf8 41. Qxf8+ !, and Black resigned.

Without a doubt, both Karpov and Kasparov would have scrutinised Sokolov's idea, an idea which is very much suited to a reckless attempt for a win.

In spite of the risk involved, Karpov has made up his mind.

15. g2-g4!? (0)	Bd7-c8 (1)
16. g4-g5 (0)	Nf6-d7 (1)
17. Qd2-f2! (1)	...

This indicates that the World Champion has carefully analysed the stem-game. Sokolov played 17. Bg2 first, but after 17. ... Na5 18. Qf2 Ribli could reply with 18. ... Nc4!, rather than 18. ... Bf8?, and gain a good game, because White's Bishop's forced retreat 19. Bc1 would have left his Rook on a1 out of play. After the move actually played by Karpov, this possibility is ruled out, because 17. ... Na5 would be followed by 18. Rad1, and after 18. ... Nc4 the retreat 19. Bc1 is quite convenient for White.

But Kasparov's team was also on the alert. . .

17. ...	Be7-f8 (17)
18. Bf3-g2 (1)	Bc8-b7 (0)

Grandmaster Timoshchenko commented: "Now that the game has already been played I can tell a small secret. We foresaw that Karpov would attempt to improve on Sokolov's plan, so we prepared a new plan of counterplay. After 18. ... Na5? there would have arisen a position from the game cited above. As it is, White's initiative is not so dangerous." One should add that, in the harmonious placement of Black's forces intended by Kasparov, the Knight on c6 is to play an active role in Black's counterplay—at b4.

19. Ra1-d1 (9)	g7-g6 (3)
20. Be3-c1 (44)	Rb8-c8 (26)

Kasparov said later that this move was a waste of time and 20. ... Nc5 is stronger here.

21. Rd1-d3 (7)	Nc6-b4 (11)
22. Rd3-h3 (0)	Bf8-g7 (2)

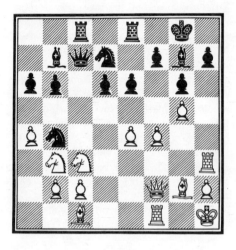

No. 77

23. Bc1-e3 (3)   ...

The apparently menacing 23. Qh4 could be parried by 23. ... Nf8, and 24. f5 would then be met by 24. ... exf 25. exf Bxg2+ 26. Kxg2 Qb7+ 27. Kg1 Bxc3 28. bxc Re4!. However, the immediate 23. f5 comes into serious consideration, as it appears to be the move that best meets the requirements of the position. In that case, the game could become complicated and double-edged, full of tactical possibilities for both sides.

For instance, 23. ... exf 24. exf gxf 25. Qh4 (if 25. Qxf5, then simply 25. ...Nf8) 25. ... Qc4! (25. ... Nxc2 is worse, in view of 26. Qxh7+ Kf8 27. Qxf5 Bxg2+ 28. Kxg2 Ne1+ 29. Kg1 Nc5 30. Nd5! Qd7 31. Qxd7 Nxd7 32. g6) 26. Qxh7+ (26. Qxc4 would, of course, have been followed by 26. ... Bxg2+ 27. Kxg2 Rxc4, while 26. Rf4—by 26. ... Bxg2+ 27. Kxg2 Qc6+ 28. Kg1 Nd5, with sufficient counterplay) 26. ... Kf8 27. Qxf5 Re5 28. Qf2 Bxg2+ 29. Kxg2 Re7!?, and in the resulting position, White has an extra pawn and attack. In the opinion of Kasparov, the right move would be 24. ... Ne5! (instead of 24. ... gf) with intricate complications. For instance, 25. f6 Bxg2 26. Kxg2 Qb7+ 27. Kg1 Bf8 28. Qh4 h5 29. Qxb4 Rc4 30. Na5 Qc8! 31. Nxc4 d5! , or 25. Qh4 Qc4 26. Qxh7 Kf8 27. Nd2 Bxg2 28. Kxg2 Qc6+ 29. Nf3 gf 30. Qxf5 Nd5! etc.

23. ...   Re8-e7! (28)

An original and highly useful preventive manoeuvre which, as Kasparov later admitted, was "the most difficult move in the game". The move indeed looks bizarre. But if one goes into it, then one can see that the move's purpose is logical and simple: the vulnerable f7-square is now reliably protected, thus securing the castled position of the Black King.

23. ... Bxc3? 24. bxc Qxc3 would certainly be erroneous here, because after 25. Bd4 Qxc2 26. Rxh7! e5 (26. ... Kxh7 27. Qh4+) 27. Qh4, the Black King would be mated.

24. Kh1-g1 (30)   ...

That Karpov thinks over this move for half an hour shows how hard it is for him to take the decision, primarily for psychological reasons. He has failed to launch a direct K-side attack and his task now is to find a better plan. Indeed, 24. Bd4 promises nothing tangible, in view of 24. ... e5 25. fxe Bxe5 (25.

... dxe 26. Be3 is worse) 26. Bxe5 dxe 27. Rf3 Nf8, while 24. f5?! would be met by 24. ... exf 25. exf Bxg2+ 26. Kxg2 (to 26. Qxg2 Black would simply respond with 26. ... gxf!) 26. ... Bxc3 27. bxc Qxc3, and White's position is in ruins.

We may venture to suppose that in his heart Karpov was not at all convinced of the correctness of his reckless K-side advance, unfortunately dictated by the situation in the match. Such reckless play is alien to his clear classical style. He himself has said: "Risky play in the style of chess musketeers is admired by adventure-seekers, but it is not to my liking. I try to appraise my chances soberly and not to play against my principles."

This time, however, fate has decided otherwise. . .

24. ...   Rc8-e8!? (15)

The Black pieces are excellently co-ordinated, and White's spatial advantage is probably only sufficient for maintaining the balance of the game.

25. Rf1-d1 (1)   f7-f5 (9)

A signal to counter-attack!

26. g5xf6 (2)   . . .

Here 26. Qd2, to put pressure on the d6-Pawn, looks attractive, but in reply to this move Kasparov has at his disposal a powerful counter-blow in the centre, 26. ... e5!, whereupon the Black pieces would suddenly become tremendously active.

26. ...   Nd7xf6!? (0)

Black could also have continued 26. ... Bxf6, but Kasparov, believing that his

forces are deployed well enough to start active operations, does not stop at sacrificing a Pawn.

27. Rh3-g3 (8)   . . .

This preventive manoeuvre is unnecessary. Moreover, it only plays into Black's hands. But after the immediate 27. Bxb6, White would have to reckon with the thrust 27. ... Ng4, forcing a sharp end game as a result of 28. Bxc7 Nxf2 29. Bxd6 Nxd1 30. Bxe7 Rxe7 (30. ... Nxc3 31. bxc Nxc2 is worse, because of 32. Bd6) 31. Nxd1 Nxc2. Although a Pawn behind, Black would have excellent chances for a draw after both 32. e5 Bxg2 33. Kxg2 g5! and 32. Rd3 Bh6! 33. Nc5 Bxf4 34. Bh3 Kf7 35. Bxe6+ Rxe6 36. Rd7+ Re7 37. Rxb7 Rxb7 38. Nxb7 (Lepeshkin).

True, in reply to 27. Bxb6, Kasparov intended to play 27. ... Qb8, followed by Re7-f7. And White would then have had a much wider choice of continuations than in the actual game (for instance, 28. a5 or 28. Kh1).

27. ...   Re7-f7 (5)

Now the attack against the f4-Pawn gains momentum.

28. Be3xb6 (1)   Qc7-b8 (0)
29. Bb6-e3 (8)   . . .

There is nothing better in sight.

29. ...   Nf6-h5 (2)
30. Rg3-g4 (5)   . . .

This is forced, because 30. Rf3 could have been followed by 30. ... Bxc3 31. bxc Na2!, and White's material losses would be unavoidable.

30. ...   Nh5-f6 (3)

No. 78

A dramatic moment! Karpov, always objective in assessing a position, was undoubtedly aware that the repetition of moves here by 31. Rg3 Nh5 would be justified from the point of view of the laws of chess. But the laws of the struggle dictated a different decision. A draw would mean the loss of all hope of saving the match. And, as Karpov later confessed, he would have refused Kasparov's offer of a draw at this moment.

And at the press conference after the match Kasparov also said quite sincerely: "It would be tempting to call the 24th game the best in the match. It is interesting as regards both its creative and sporting aspects. But Karpov spurned the opportunity of drawing the game by the three-time repetition of moves, thus violating the logic of the duel..."

"...violating the logic of chess, but not of the struggle," we should like to add.

31. Rg4-h4?! (5) ...

Here 31. Rg5 is also disadvantageous to White; for instance, 31. ... Bh6 32. Rg3 Nh5 33. Rf3 Ref8 34. Bh3 Bc8.

31. ...   g6-g5! (3)

An obvious, but very powerful blow. By sacrificing a second Pawn, Black gains a very strong initiative.

32. f4xg5 (0)   Nf6-g4! (0)

Perhaps Karpov pinned his hopes on the apparently attractive thrust 32. ... Nxe4? Indeed, in that case, after 33. Qxf7+! Kxf7 34. Nxe4, his pieces would have come to life. As it is, events take quite a different course.

33. Qf2-d2 (12) ...

At this juncture, the Queen sacrifice by 33. Qxf7+ Kxf7 34. Rxg4 would be hopeless, because of 34. ... Nxc2 35. Bf2 Ba8.

33. ...   Ng4xe3 (0)
34. Qd2xe3 (1)   Nb4xc2 (1)
35. Qe3-b6 (0)   ...

The White Queen may not leave the g1-a7 diagonal, in view of Black's terrible threat of 35. ... Qa7+.

(No. 79)
35. ...   Bb7-a8! (3)
36. Rd1xd6? (1) ...

A desperate attempt under severe time pressure. By giving up his inactive Knight on b3, White avoids exchanging the Queens, although it is Black who profits by this. The logic of the struggle again seems to prevail, for White's best chance 36. Qxb8 Rxb8 37. Bh3! Rxb3

134

No. 79

38. Bxe6, would allow him to hope only for a draw, as for example in the variation 38. ... Bd4+! 39. Kh1 Rxb2 40. Rf1 Bxc3 41. Rxf7 Nd4 42. Ra7+ (not, of course, 42. Bc4? d5!) 42. ... Nxe6 43. Rxa8+ Nf8 44. Rxa6 Be5.

Curiously, in the event of 40. Rf4 (instead of 40. Rf1) 40. ... Bxc3 41. Rxd6 Kf8! 42. Bxf7 (or 42. Rxf7+ Ke8 43. Rf4 Ne3!) 42. ... Ke7 43. Rxa6 Ne3! 44. h4, Black would have at his disposal not only the reliable 44. ... Bb7 45. Re6+ Kd7, but also the spectacular 44. ... Nf5!.

36. ...	Rf7-b7 (1)
37. Qb6xa6 (0)	Rb7-b3 (0)
38. Rd6xe6 (0)	...

White has obtained three Pawns for the lost piece, which is sufficient compensation, as far as material is concerned; but his position...

38. ...	Rb3xb2 (1)
39. Qa6-c4 (2)	Kg8-h8 (3)

For a draw (and victory in the match!),

39. ... Qa7+ 40. Kh1 Rxe6 41. Qxe6+ Qf7 42. Qc8+ Qf8 would be sufficient, but Kasparov strives to win the game.

> 40. e4-e5? (0)   ...

His resistance could be prolonged by 40. Rxe8+ Qxe8 41. Nd1, but after 41. ... Na3 42. Qd3 Ra2 43. Qh3 (43. Bf3 is a little more stubborn) 43. ... Bd4+ 44. Kh1 Ra1, Black's attack would decide the issue.

40. ...	Qb8-a7+ (1)
41. Kg1-h1 (0)	Ba8xg2+ (2)
42. Kh1xg2 (0)	Nc2-d4+ (1)

This check turns out to be the last of several thousand moves played in the seventy-two games. Karpov resigns.

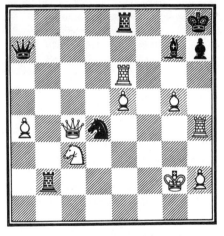

No. 80

The concluding position, reflecting the historical moment of a new king ascending to the chess throne. Garri Kasparov has become the thirteenth World Chess Champion.

The final score is 13:11 in favour of Kasparov.

Time: 2.33-2.25.

After the Match

Garri KASPAROV

(From a conversation with journalists
from *Sovietski Sport, Literaturnaya Gazeta* and *Nedelya,*
and with readers of *Komsomolskaya Pravda*)

Question. *You are the youngest ever world champion. What
are your feelings now?*

Answer. I am happy. But from the experience of the Candidates' matches, I know that after the first emotional fervour
there will be ordinary fatigue, like at the end of a hard day.
And this fatigue is redoubled after every match. If we count up:
159 days the first match went on for last year, plus 70 for the
one which has just finished. When are we to rest, and when can
we prepare for the next opponent? It is not easy, of course, to
live by the principle "I must", but without this clear, laconic
"I must", without gritting your teeth and putting all your energy
into something, you will never succeed.

Q. *Of your closest aides, who has helped the most to build
up your game and bring you such an impressive triumph?*

A. In my training camp, as it were, there are Alexander
Nikitin and Alexander Shakarov, who began teaching me
while I was still at school, the international chess master from
Alma-Ata Yevgeny Vladimirov, and there are Gennady Timoshchenko from Novosibirsk and Iosif Dorfman from Lvov, both of them
Grandmasters. All five of these men are exceptionally hardworking
and have such faith in my ability. I am grateful to them for having
come with me along the stony path to the throne of world chess.

Q. *What was the basis of your preparation for this second match?*

A. This time the preparation was both more complicated
and more straightforward. More complicated because there was
so little time. I had to renew my reserves of nervous energy.
We all understood that the nervous tension would be much
greater. We were all convinced that the fight would be of a
totally different nature and we would need to be prepared for
the widest variety of possible situations.

As for the purely theoretical work, we managed to work
through a whole mass of information and we evaluated it
correctly. We took a great deal into consideration. Our choice
of new openings was based on all this work. Let us take, for
example, the Nimzowitsch Defence, which was so successful

136

for us. It is incidentally, one of the cornerstones of Karpov's openings which we had not until now tested in our games. And using this opening he got, as we say, "minus three", he lost three games. That is the advantage of preparatory theoretical study! And I am convinced that it is possible to impose one's own play on a game only if one has had the best possible preparation and can create a sufficient number of surprises for one's opponent.

But the psychological preparation is no less important. When I won the first game, for example, I was quite taken aback: it was so unexpected. I had been losing in the match which was stopped in February, and here I was in front. Then I was in a good position at the adjournment of the second game. I was in a state of euphoria and didn't know what to do with myself. We had not predicted anything like that. And as it turned out, we had missed something here. And when I lost two games in a row, everything was back in perspective.

I have noticed in the past that I normally always win on the day after losing. A defeat seems to spur me on. But in the matches with Karpov this never happened. Besides which, I twice lost two games in a row to him. And that was when I realised that losing to an opponent like Karpov is simply new food for thought. But losing in the twenty-second game brought me back to my normal psychological condition. I settled down and finished the match not at all badly.

Q. *What do you think of Karpov's play in this match?*

A. Karpov is a whole epoch in chess. He has managed to stay at the top for more than ten years. He has raised the sporting significance of chess to quite a new level, and he has done a great deal to popularise our sport. He was an active World Champion, arousing interest in chess in all corners of the world. Many people did not understand the phenomenon of Karpov for a long time: and I could not make him out for a long time either.

As for his play in this match, I do not think he managed to come out in full force. It is my opinion that for a long time he had no opponent to make him play to the limit and show his full potential. And I also think that he did not draw the right conclusions from our first, unlimited, match. But in the second match he made it a true fight, he played open chess and did everything he could to win: he created as much as possible, even in the worst of positions, and he made use of all his opportunities in the best of positions.

His play was quite amazing, even when everyone thought his position in a game was beyond help. I must give him his due for his defensive efforts towards the end of the match when he was playing Black, and for his attacking power playing White.

But the decisive factor was how each player approached the second match, who had the richer store of ideas, and who had evaluated the first match the better.

In my opinion Karpov made a serious mistake in not drawing his conclusions from the final games of the first match, and in not properly assessing the facts at his disposal. We managed to understand Karpov's game, which is easier said than done, but it took us until the tenth game of the new match before we were sure that we had made the right preparation. We got the impression that Karpov had exaggerated his abilities when playing on "my" territory, and had underestimated the strong sides of my game.

Q. *The first match was stopped with the score at 5:3 in Karpov's favour. What do you think would have been the outcome if that match had continued?*

A. The question is unanswerable. I think any answer would be just so much hypothesis.

Q. *At what point in the second match did you think that you might become World Champion?*

A. The first time that I felt I might win was after the fifteenth game. It was the type of confidence which is sometimes lacking in contests between equals. That may be how I managed to win the sixteenth game. I believed I had a real chance of winning after the eighteenth game, and then I won the nineteenth. It is true, though, that my confidence was rocked a little towards the finish but, as they say, I managed to pull myself together.

Q. *What were your feelings before the last game?*

A. When there is only one game left, and that game is to decide whether or not you will be the World Champion, then you really must gather all your strength. I simply told myself that if I wanted to become World Champion, then I had to play as though it were the last game of my life. To the limit. And at the same time I had to play quite calmly. Otherwise it would not work out. I think I can say that it worked out for me.

Q. *And in the evening, when the match was over, what did you do?*

A. I analysed the twenty-fourth game. There were congratulations coming in by telephone, and an unending stream of questions to answer, though I probably didn't answer any of them intelligently.

Q. *What was it like to wake up the first morning as champion?*

A. Quite honestly it was hard to open my eyes. But I heard my mother's voice saying: "Good morning. It is your first day today."

Q. *Was it your favourite menu for breakfast?*

A. My menu during matches never changes. But no one makes *dolma* from vine leaves like my granny can.

Q. *Which do you think was your best game in the match?*

A. It is tempting to say the twenty-fourth was the best because it was the decider. But in that game my opponent was playing for a win, refusing to accept a peaceful draw, and that upset the logical development of the game. From a creative point of view, then, I would choose the sixteenth game. I took the lead after winning it and never looked back. But more importantly, it gave me a great deal of creative satisfaction: sacrificing the pawn on the eighth move has even been called Kasparov's Gambit.

Q. *Why, then, did you not use your innovation more often in the match?*

A. That, I'm afraid, must remain a tactical secret. But in the future, of course, I shall use it, since I was the one who devised it. For the time being I can only say that I did not use the Gambit for a third time because I did not wish to tempt fate.

Q. *What do you think of this match as a whole?*

A. We should, I think, look not just at the one match, but at the two of them, the full seventy-two games. This contest stands out as something special. The first half was unlimited, the second half was totally different. The proportion of games won and lost in the second match was much greater. And the tension was greater, too. It is not surprising: we had studied each other so thoroughly that we both had to find new ways to win. And the nature of the struggle itself was incomparable. In this second match we had no breathing spaces, no "customary" draws. We could both see the far shore, and we went for it in the open. And the basis of my victory? Probably that I sifted through the experience of the first match better, and drew more benefit from it. To a great extent, my success was predetermined by the better quality of my preparation, not just in the opening play but in the game in general.

Going back to the match as a whole, I can say that it has given us an enormous amount of new information, and a great many new ideas were brought forward. It has been said that the

basis of my winning games was in the opening phase. This is
probably true, but in the middle game and in the end game
I tried to play modern chess too.

Q. *Will anyone else be able to join in with the two of you in
the near future?*
A. Most probably we will have more matches in the future.
And they promise to be even more interesting because we are
getting to know more and more sides of each other's play. It
is inevitable that we will have to discover still more new ways
of winning.

Q. *Can we return to the Tchaikovsky Hall, where the
audiences saw one or other of you leave the stage from time to
time and go into the wings? What did you do in the wings?*
A. There were two rest-rooms there: the larger one for whoever
was playing White, the other for Black. Sometimes, when the
position in the game allowed it, it was good to have a rest or
simply to be alone. If you think about it, we faced one another
for three hundred and twenty-five hours in the two matches put
together.

There were two monitors in the rooms. One showed the player
still at the board, and the other showed the board itself. Tea and
coffee were brought to the room if required, and there was choc-
olate available too if we wanted it. We could relax there, while
still keeping an eye on the game in progress.

Q. *How did you go about analysing the games in the
overnight breaks?*
A. The adjourned games cancelled out all natural patterns of
living. And the excitement, with no time to sleep! The position
in the game was the only thing that mattered. Basically the
whole team would gather together, ready to set to work. We
split up into groups of two or three, and then we were away.
We reached the best analysis in the ninth game. The position
looked good at first. But then we realised it was better for
Karpov. I lay awake in bed until five in the morning and went
through, move by move, more or less everything that turned up
on the board after the resumption. In the morning I dictated
the full analysis.

Q. *Before adjourning the nineteenth and twentieth games
you opened the secret of your final moves. Why was this?*
A. Everything was so obvious that there was no point in hiding
them.

Q. *What is your best form of relaxation: books, the theatre, music, football, jogging?*

A. All at once, as far as possible. How could I get by without books or music? And what could be better than a good run, or a game of football for toning yourself up and helping you to look on the bright side of things? But of course, during the match I only allowed myself football of the television variety. I gave up running because it would have been too heavy a load. But I did play badminton!

Besides which I also read the newspapers (only missing out the match reports), and I read a book...

Q. *Only one book in the whole seventy days of the match?*

A. But it has seven hundred pages. It is a work by Johann Gottfried von Herder, *Ideen zur Philosophie der Geschichte der Menschheit,* published eight years ago by Nauka Publishers. I began reading it in Baku before the match.

There is a widely held opinion that chess players have a mathematical bent. But this does not apply to me. Thanks to chess I have developed an interest in the humanities. History, philosophy and art interest me no less, if not more, than chess. Although chess is very similar to life, the one cannot replace the other. Deepening your understanding of this ancient game can help you to find your style more quickly, and to find your own means of self-expression.

Q. *To what extent are you interested in history? Surely your involvement in chess hampers this interest?*

A. Chess has greatly developed my capacity for synthesis and analysis. And this same capacity helps me to study history. I have never studied it scientifically, as such, but I see no reason why I should not take it up seriously one day. There will come a time, I think, when I shall have exhausted my creative potential in chess, my resources will no longer carry the effect I would like, and my ideas will not come as quickly as they ought; then my task will be to at least maintain my level of play. And then perhaps I will be in a position to realise my accumulated knowledge in another field. I am optimistic about this.

Q. *A traditional question: what is chess, how does the number one chess player see the game?*

A. It is not really possible to say what the essence of chess is. And this is perhaps the fascination of the game. Chess is an ancient game, it started out as a light entertainment, a game to play over a cup of coffee, and it has become an art which attracts millions of people all over the world. The game's accessability and, at the same time, a certain mysterious aura about it, attract ever new devotees, calling on them to perfect both their own game and chess as a whole.

If you recall, the traditional definition of chess is that of a harmonious fusion of sport, science and art. And it is not at all easy to add anything to that. Whether the champion likes it or not, one of these component concepts is more a part of him than the others. Botvinnik, for example, excelled in the scientific aspect. Karpov fully developed the sporting side of chess which had previously, as it were, remained in the shadows. I have the universal approach. Chess for me is a battle and a sport. But I feel that chess is more in evidence as a fusion of science and art.

I am always trying to extend my knowledge of chess, working hard at adding to my store of chess ideas. And this allows me to create a greater number of positions, so as to find my way more easily. This requires thinking far ahead, as well as speed and initiative. My game itself is built on the most general rules of chess and on the particulars of a given position.

Q. *What do you see as the role of chess in the modern world?*
A. Its role has grown considerably in the last ten or fifteen years. And at all levels. This is particularly noticeable in the contest for the world title. Public interest in chess depends on the top players. After Fischer, Karpov became an active champion, and he was always in the public eye. It is not at all surprising that my battle with Karpov brought a new wave of interest in chess both here and abroad. And many people expected a clash of new creative trends, a clash which would be an impetus for a further development of the game.

This ancient game will undoubtedly spread even more widely in the future. Such is the effect of its wisdom, such its power. I am firmly convinced that time is on its side.

Q. *How do you see the further development of chess?*
A. I think the best outlook is arrived at by joining together Tal's beautiful style and the strictly rational approach of Karpov. I personally am in favour of elegant, inspired chess, something close to art and giving the game's devotees a truly aesthetic pleasure. In this sense, I think, the World Title Match has been decisive for the leading style of play. It is the same, incidentally, as in football. You may remember, the Dutch national team had a series of brilliant victories, and at once everyone started playing "total football". Isn't that how it happens? Whole trains move forward thanks to locomotives.

Q. *What has chess given you, and what have you given chess?*

A. Chess is the core of my life. But it is not its only meaning. Through chess, as Alekhine used to say, you can form your character. But chess cannot develop anything in a person which he does not already have. It can only develop the seeds which are sown in him. I am grateful to chess most of all because it has helped me to understand myself more clearly and to choose my path in life. And not only in chess. If I had not made the choice I did, and if I had not worked myself to the limit, I could hardly have achieved as much as I have in my twenty-two years.

If it is true that the champion widens people's notions of chess, then I too have probably managed to do something in this line. And I am happy if I have opened up a new concept of the great depth of the game. And perhaps, thanks to me and following in my footsteps, players from the younger generation will enter the top level of chess.

Q. *In so many sports it is the general rule that the younger athletes win the honours. Are chess players getting younger? You yourself have reached the top at the age of only twenty-two.*

F. Twenty-two, in terms of chess, is really quite young. More experienced players have a more refined understanding of positional nuances, and a better perception of their opponent's psychology. But the opportunities for the younger generation are a lot higher than it would seem at first sight. Let us take, for example, the six best players in the world: I am twenty-two, Sokolov the same, and Yusupov is only three years older. So the odds are clearly on the side of players under twenty-five. Why? Sokolov, of course, has less experience than, say, Tal. But Sokolov has a mass of other advantages, basically his fanatical belief in his own ability, very much like a steam train brushing aside everything in its path.

Q. *Will the trend towards youth really continue, and are we likely to see an even younger world champion?*

A. There is a limit to everything. In chess, twenty is probably the cut-off point. I cannot see anyone taking the world title before that age.

Q. *Did you ever take part in the youth competitions for the* Komsomolskaya Pravda *prizes?*

A. I have played in them four times. And on the whole, I think they are very necessary. They are perhaps one of the best traditions of Soviet chess. Young people learn directly from Grandmasters, and can see them play. Seeing a real live Grandmaster sitting next to you is a great thrill for a novice. I can vouch for that from my own childhood. It was a moment I shall never forget: Mikhail Tal himself shook me by the hand!

Later, when I became a Grandmaster myself, I felt it was my moral duty to continue playing for the team I had played for as a boy. I think these competitions would be even more interesting if all the leading chess players took part in them. We have a great many young Grandmasters, and each one of them could be the leader of a youth team. Five of the six team captains in the last tournament in Irkutsk, all of them Grandmasters, had entered these same competitions as boys.

I have heard of an excellent idea of organising a youth tournament between the socialist countries. We must see this idea realised.

Q. *We know you attended Mikhail Botvinnik's chess school. But seven years ago the school stopped operations...*

A. I think schools like that are absolutely indispensable. I myself was a pupil at one not so long ago and had to sit for chess study sessions. Matches were played between them, and we had our homework to do just like in a normal school. Botvinnik personally looked through my games, gave advice and made recommendations. I got lot of benefit from learning this way. Many of our leading players have attended this school.

In the coming months Botvinnik's school will start work again. At the moment the idea is for it to be a correspondence school of teacher and pupil—Botvinnik and Kasparov. We will be carrying on a most useful tradition of Soviet chess.

Q. *Have you ever played against a computer?*

A. I once had an exhibition match of simultaneous games in Hamburg. Four major electronics firms put up eight machines each. In order not to offend anyone, I won all the games, 32:0.

Q. *What advice would you give to young people just beginning to take an interest in chess?*

A. I would like to say, first of all, that I am still quite young myself. And I really have insufficient experience to teach others. In my opinion the most important thing is having the right attitude to yourself. You must not be afraid of hard work. You need to have a goal to aim for. It is also important that you do not let yourself weaken.

Q. *Can you arrange all the World Champions in order of their ability and strength?*

A. That is difficult. Each one of them brought something of his own into the game. To single out one of them would mean upsetting the natural flow of history. It is fairly meaningless to discuss how Capablanca, for example, would play today if he was to be transported here in some magical time machine.

Q. *Are you attracted by the creative talents of any World Champion in particular?*
A. As a boy I used to love the games played by Alexander Alekhine. I tried to copy him in a lot of ways. When I was at Botvinnik's school I imitated his scientific approach to chess and his match preparation programme.

Q. *Imagine for a moment that Robert Fischer reappeared in the chess arena and that he challenged you to a match.*
A. A match with Robert Fischer would be a splendid opportunity to test any player's ability, even a world champion's. But only on condition that Fischer would play the way he played in 1972.

Q. *When you are out for a win, which route do you prefer to take to reach you victory—the most delicate and refined, or the shortest?*
A. I think chess, by its very nature, is such a harmonious game that the shortest route to victory is also very often the most delicate and refined. That is, delicacy and finesse accompany brevity, and brevity, if you like, is the friend of delicacy and finesse.

Q. *I wonder if you could describe your feelings when you are under time pressure.*
A. My consciousness is no longer in control of my actions. Everything is in the realm of the subconscious, when my fingers are all I have to make my moves with and there is no time to make decisions. That is, control has gone beyond the realm of feelings, of something I can remember and talk about later. I simply rely on my fingers.

Q. *And is there a difference, for you, between playing under time pressure and blitz play?*
A. These are two quite different things. When there is time pressure your whole game is at stake; a man has lived in the game, it was part of his life. And then in a matter of seconds he has to decide the fate of a five-hour struggle. But blitz play is a totally different matter. The responsibility just isn't there,

I might add, by the way, that a person who plays blitz very well, may easily lose his head under time pressure.

Q. *Do you like blitz play yourself?*
A. I liked it when I was a boy. Now I seldom play it.

Q. *Do you play blind chess?*
A. Blind chess can be quite harmful. But I did try it once abroad. I was playing against ten opponents of about master level. And we played to time. In one game I made an elementary error, but I won 9:1 overall.

Q. *We know you enjoy football. What does Kasparov the chess player think of Kasparov the footballer?*
A. There's a certain amount of humorous scepticism involved, but people who know something about football do say that he has ball-sense, ball-control, and even the ability to play a one-two, round the defender and score. I have supported Moscow Spartak for a long time. The team may unexpectedly win or unexpectedly lose, but whatever happens their play will be emotional, entertaining and truly artistic; and I think it is just these very qualities which have been lacking recently in chess.

Q. *Do you have a football idol?*
A. Yes, Lev Ivanovich Yashin. And I have an ice-hockey idol as well, Vladislav Tretyak.

Q. *And do you have a favourite chess piece?*
A. Every chess piece is a favourite if you use it well. But as a boy I had a secret weakness for the Bishop, I liked it for the way it could attack from a distance. I even had an unusual game with a friend of mine, Rostik Korsunsky, who was about seven years older than me. I played with only Bishops; that is, all my pieces moved only like Bishops; and he played with only Knights. I won the game. The Bishop really is a useful piece to have. And in general, if you think about it, any piece is useful if it attacks successfully.

Q. *What do you think of chess matches between men and women?*
A. Twenty-five years ago the men had to give the women a considerable head-start in a game. Now the women's game is stronger than it was, but they still cannot compete on even terms. I think that chess is the type of game which belongs entirely to men. In a contest like chess one is trying to assert

oneself, to prove the supremacy of one's own ego. Women have a different psychology.

Q. *And when will the new chess king find himself a queen?*
A. I don't think it will be soon. Finding the right "move" in this is no easier than becoming World Champion.

Q. *Do you not regret that chess deprives you of a lot of other things in life? Does it never seem that a lot may have passed by you?*
A. Just the opposite; chess has given me too much. The rhythm which it has put into my life has allowed me to achieve more than I could have in any other way. And the circle which I joined at an early age certainly helped me to grow up and widen my horizons. And the great number of hurdles, which I have had to overcome in the sport, have helped develop a certain versatility of thought. For most children time simply slips through their fingers, but time is not infinite and it is a pity to waste it. We can lose a lot in our childhood years. But my time was co-ordinated and satiated; a great deal of self-discipline was demanded of me. And I think this stopped me from wasting my time, developed and enriched my whole life.

Anatoly KARPOV
(From an interview with a TASS correspondent)

Looking back at this match, I have to say that I am dissatisfied with myself, both from a creative and a sporting point of view. Kasparov was particularly well-prepared. If we compare the current match with the last one, we can see that he raised himself up one step (or half a step), and I fell accordingly. Therefore the difference between us was now greater.

My best form came between the second and eleventh games. This form disappeared with an unbelievable blunder in the eleventh. Nonetheless, I am pleased with one thing: that even after the upset in the eleventh game I kept up the fight and was able to take it to the last hurdle. And I even got close to levelling the score and so retaining the title. I had my chances in that twenty-fourth game, but...

A draw in that game—of course—was no good at all; it meant losing the match. Draw it or lose it, it was all the same to me. And I will tell you that even if Kasparov himself had suggested that I sign the peace treaty in that game, I would still have refused.

I think the best games of the match were the fifth, a Ruy López Defence which I won playing Black, and the sixteenth, a Sicilian Defence which Kasparov won, also playing Black.

About the quality of the chess: except for the fourth game, where I managed to set up a fine positional manoeuvre and secure the win, there were mistakes in all the games. But, as recompense, we did have some very interesting drawn games.

On the whole, the match was hard-fought and interesting. It demonstrated the advantage of a match with a predetermined maximum number of games, rather than the open-endedness of the first match.

On the 16th of November in Lucerne the Soviet national team will play in the first ever men's team World Championships. It will be a very interesting competition, with immensely strong opposition. It should be a fascinating contest.

I have again been given the honour of being the Soviet team-captain, and will play on the first board.

Many people are perhaps surprised that I am taking part in this event so soon after such a difficult match as this has been. But it seems better to me to throw off this defeat in new battles, rather than lock myself away, tormented by memories of the chances I missed.[1]

FLORENCIO CAMPOMANES
(From an interview with a correspondent of *Sovietski Sport*)

Question. *What is your general impression of the match? Has it become a mile-stone in modern chess?*

Answer. Certainly, yes. In practically every game played you will find something which enriches chess theory and practice. Both players surprised us time and time again with their self-possession and determination, their masterly technique and theoretical innovations, their psychological firmness and sporting spirit. These remarkable Grandmasters of the modern game have given us many chess masterpieces. And most importantly—the match itself, which was not decided until the very last game.

Q. *Do you consider it the logical outcome that the younger man should have won?*

A. I consider it logical that the match should have been won by a representative of Soviet chess, which is highly regarded

[1]The Soviet team won this championship, Karpov himself winning three and drawing four of the seven games he played.—*Ed.*

around the world. And of course since 1948, with the exception of a three-year gap, the world champion has always been a Soviet player.

Q. *Do you like the way Kasparov plays, his chess style?*

A. The active and, I would say, explosive manner in which he plays cannot fail to please true devotees of chess. I had the pleasure of watching the reaction of the audiences in the hall as Kasparov made his moves. There were moments when he literally set the hall alight with his energetic manoeuvres. I am certain that the new champion will be an active player, and will give his followers much enjoyment.

Q. *Where do you see the strengths and weaknesses of the Champion?*

A. His thorough preparation of the opening play, his confidence when playing with a large number of pieces on the board, constantly and persistently striving for the initiative, not being afraid to take risks—this is where he is exceptionally strong. His weakness, perhaps, is the fact that he is insufficiently sure of himself in simple situations, with few pieces on the board.

Q. *What do you think was the deciding factor in this contest?*

A. My greatest impression was the Champion's attitude to the game of chess. He is a talented and hard-working pupil of his teachers. His ability to quickly and effectively learn lessons from his defeats is staggering. The experience of the first match helped him in the second—that is beyond question. The deciding factor, in my opinion, was his preparation of the opening play. The Champion is well-versed in the theoretical side of this, and sets a good example to all young chess players who dream of great victories.

Q. *And your opinion of Karpov's play?*

A. Mentioning the new champion, we must also give credit to his opponent. This was a match of worthy opponents, two players without equal in the world. Karpov gave us a series of glittering games. He is very probably blaming himself now for his missed opportunities and his choice of openings. But can *we* blame him for anything? Without Karpov, the match would not have been the glittering event that it was.

Q. *What would you say of the match organisation?*

A. On behalf of the International Chess Federation I would like to express my gratitude to the organisers, the two participants, their aides, all devotees of this ancient game, and to everyone who helped to make the match a success.

Q. *What is your opinion of the Moscow chess audiences?*

A. I must admit that I have never met more educated audiences. And I repeat: I had the pleasure of watching the hall—watching its intellectual and emotional participation. Kasparov and Karpov delighted everyone move after move. The audience reacted to each strong or, indeed, weak move as though it were an audience of chess masters; or, at the very least, of future masters. The spectators applauded the winner of each game, no matter on whose side their sympathies lay. And the players need this applause for their self-confidence, no less than actors, for example, need it. I will go further and say that Soviet chess fans are as impressive a phenomenon as the phenomenon of Soviet chess itself. The thirteenth and youngest World Champion—indeed, all Soviet chess lovers can be justly proud!

Q. *Which of the games did you like the most?*

A. The twenty-third. It was drawn, but it was a grandiose draw, in which the conflict held everyone in suspense from beginning to end, in which both players demonstrated models of play in attack and in defence.

Q. *The new World Champion said in an interview with match reporters: "I hope, in the current situation, that there will be no more unlimited matches." What is your opinion on this subject?*

A. I share the hopes of the World Champion, and I believe that there will be no repetition of the chess marathon which Karpov and Kasparov had to endure; it has taken 229 days in all, playing the 72 matches to decide the current champion. It is now more obvious than ever that stopping the unlimited contest after forty-eight games was the optimum decision. It halted the competition, gave the players the chance to take a rest, and afforded us the opportunity to reconsider chess duels at the highest level.

All members of FIDE are happy that this episode is now behind us and that we have now proclaimed the victor of the contest. The aim of FIDE is, of course, to find the best chess player in the world. And you know what a complex and sometimes agonising process that can be. We acted then, and we are acting now, in the interests of chess players and chess as a whole. And I am grateful to the Soviet Chess Federation for its support of FIDE.

In Retrospect
Moscow 1984-85

FIDE

GAME ONE

Sicilian Defence

A. Karpov	G. Kasparov
1. e2-e4	c7-c5
2. Ng1-f3	e7-e6
3. d2-d4	c5xd4
4. Nf3xd4	Ng8-f6
5. Nb1-c3	d7-d6
6. g2-g4	...

The Keres Attack, initiated by this move, is undoubtedly the most ambitious and dangerous line White can take in reply to the Scheveningen Variation.

6. ...	h7-h6
7. h2-h4	...

For a long time White preferred 7. g5 hxg 8. Bxg5, but Black had found a reliable defence. This may be illustrated by the Karpov-Andersson game (Skara, 1980): 8. ... Nc6 9.Qd2 Qb6 10. Nb3 a6 11. 0-0-0 Bd7 12. h4 Qc7 13. f4 Be7 14. Be2 0-0-0 15. h5 Kb8 16. Kb1 Bc8

7. ...	Nb8-c6
8. Rh1-g1	h6-h5!?

Other possibilities, e.g. 8. ... Nxd4 9.Qxd4 Nd7, 8. ... a6, 8. ... g6, or 8. ... d5 would leave less opportunity for Black to equalize and gain counterplay (A. Gipslis).

9. g4xh5	...

It is exactly because of this reply, as the monograph *Sicilian Defence. Scheve-*

ningen Variation by Kasparov and Nikitin, points out that Black's eighth move does not solve all the problems posed by White. In this position, White also repeatedly tried 9. g5 Ng4 10. Be2 Qb6 11. Bxg4, whereupon Black replied 11. ... hxg4, or 11. ... Nxd4, with varying success (M. Taimanov).

9. ...	Nf6xh5
10. Bc1-g5	Nh5-f6

In the stem-game Vasyukov-Larsen (Manila, 1974), Black answered 10. ... Qc7, but after 11. Qd2 a6 12. 0-0-0 Nxd4 13. Qxd4 Bd7 14. Kb1 Rc8 15. Be2 b5 16. Rge1! Qc5 17. Qd2 Nf6 18. a3 Qc7 19. f4 Larsen failed to neutralize White's initiative.

11. Qd1-d2	...

If 11. h5, then, as A. Gipslis indicates, White should consider the replies 11. ... Qb6!?, or 11. ... e5 12. Nb3 Be7 13. Be2 Be6, as occurred in the Nunn-Adorján game (Biel, 1983).

11. ...	Qd8-b6
12. Nd4-b3	Bc8-d7
13. 0-0-0	a7-a6
14. Rg1-g3	Qb6-c7
15. Bf1-g2	...

(No. 81)

15. ...	Bf8-e7

Thus far, the contestants have repeated the Glek-Sokolov game (Moscow Championship, 1983), which proceeded as follows: 15. ... Nh7? (if 15. ... 0-0-0, then 16. Nd5!) 16. Be3 (16. Nd5!? is also interesting) 16. ... Ne5 17. Bd4 Nc4 18. Qe2 Nf6 19. f4 Rxh4 20. Nd5! Nxd5 21. exd e5 22. fxe dxe 23. d6! with a dangerous attack. The new move

No. 81

played by Kasparov consolidates Black's position.

| 16. f2-f4 | 0-0-0 |
| 17. Qd2-f2 | ... |

The apparently tempting 17. Nd5?! would fail against 17. ... exd 18. exd Nxd5! 19. Bxd5 f6, while after 17. Rd3 (or 17. Ne2 Nh5!) White should consider both 17. ... Nb4, and 17. ... Nh5!? 18. Bxe7 Nxe7 19. Rxd6 Bc6. Incidentally, on the previous move the manoeuvre 16. ... Nh5 (instead of 16. ... 0-0-0) would have been disastrous for Black after 17. Rd3 f6? 18. e5! (M. Taimanov).

| 17. ... | Kc8-b8 |
| 18. f4-f5!? | ... |

Karpov's intentions are obvious: he wishes to create a weak Black Pawn on e6; put pressure on it and, should this Pawn advance to e5, occupy the vitally important square d5 himself. Yet the price to pay for the execution of this plan is high: Black may now get an excellent post on e5 for his Knight, and Kasparov avails himself of this opportunity at once. White should perhaps have preferred 18. a3 followed by Rg3-d3 (E. Gufeld).

| 18. ... | Nc6-e5 |
| 19. Bg2-h3 | Ne5-c4!? |

This move caused a heated debate in the press room. Many recognized exponents of the Scheveningen Variation preferred 19. ... Rc8. The thrust 20. Nd4 would then be parried by 20. ... Qb6. Possibly, 19. ... Rc8 seemed unattractive to Kasparov because of 20. Be3 threatening 21. Bb6 or 21. Na5 (A. Gipslis).

| ·20. Nb3-d2! | ... |

The only move! White does not miss the opportunity to trade his idle Knight for the actively placed Black invader on c4. After 20. Nd4, Black has a most unpleasant retort 20. ... Qb6 (E. Gufeld).

20. ...	Nc4xd2
21. Rd1xd2	Rd8-c8
22. f5xe6	Bd7xe6!

This is better than 22. ... fxe. Exchanging the light-squared Bishops simplifies Black's defensive task. Indeed, Black can easily protect the e6-square, while the co-ordination of his forces is now much facilitated (A. Suetin).

| 23. Bh3xe6 | f7xe6 |
| 24. Qf2-g1 | ... |

Maybe White should prefer 24. Qe2 or 24. Qg2, but the World Champion is already pressed for time.

No. 82

24. ...   Qc7-a5

At this moment Black has a hidden, paradoxical possibility 24. ... Bf8!? with the idea of transferring the Knight via f6 and d7 to e5 or c5.

25. Qg1-d4!   ...

The centralisation of one's pieces is almost always a guarantee of safety. At the same time, White, in his turn, threatens with 26. Be3, simultaneously attacking squares a7 and g7 (M. Taimanov).

25. ...   Qa5-c5
26. Qd4-d3   ...

After 26. Qxc5 Rxc5 27. Be3 Black could answer 27. ... Rc7, or even 27. ... Rxc3!? 28. bxc Nxe4 29. Rxg7 Bf8.

26. ...   Qc5-c4
27. Qd3-e3.   Kb8-a8

The simple 27. ... Qc5 would probably have forced a draw (E. Gufeld).

28. a2-a3   Qc4-c6

The reply 28. ... Rc6!? deserves consideration.

29. e4-e5   d6xe5

At this juncture, Kasparov spent nearly all his remaining time considering an interesting positional piece sacrifice: 29. ... d5!? 30. exf gxf 31. Bf4 Rxh4.

30. Qe3xe5   Kh8-d8
31. Rg3-d3   Rd8xd3
32. Rd2xd3   Qc6-h1+
33. Nc3-d1   ...

If 33. Rd1, then 33. ... Qc6, with the threat of 34. ... Bxa3; or 33. ... Qh3, intending 34. ... Qf5.

33. ...   Qh1-g2
34. Rd3-d2   Qg2-c6
35. Rd2-e2   ...

It seems that bringing the White Knight via f2 to d3 would have meant Kasparov remaining on the alert (M. Taimanov).

No. 83

The Pawn on e6 is practically the only weakness Black has, and this can be readily defended. Moreover, Kasparov finds an effective retort (A. Gipslis).

| 35. ... | Be7-d6! |
| 36. Qe5-c3 | ... |

Not, of course, 36. Qxe6?, because of 36. ... Re8.

| 36. ... | Qc6-d7 |

Game drawn. *It 34)Rd3-c3,*
Time: 2. 28-2.25 *white had a very fine chance to win.*

12 and 13 September 1984

GAME TWO

Queen's Indian Defence

G. Kasparov	A. Karpov
1. d2-d4	Ng8-f6
2. c2-c4	e7-e6
3. Ng1-f3	b7-b6
4. g2-g3	Bc8-b7
5. Bf1-g2	Bf8-e7
6. 0-0	0-0
7. d4-d5! ?	e6xd5
8. Nf3-h4	...

Polugayevsky's patent. Before he introduced this innovation, 8. Nd4 was played, but after 8. ... Bc6, Black had every opportunity for a successful defence (Yu. Razuvayev).

| 8. ... | c7-c6 |
| 9. c4xd5 | Nf6xd5 |

The answer 9. ... cxd5 has been played

less frequently. The representative line is 10. Nc3 Na6 11. Nf5 Nc7 12. Bf4 Bc5 13. Rc1 Bc6 14. a3 a5 15. Na4, and White has only a slight advantage.

| 10. Nh4-f5 | Nd5-c7 |

The idea 10. ... Bc5 would be less effective. In the twelfth game of the Polugayevsky-Korchnoi match in Buenos Aires, 1980, White responded 11. e4 Ne7 12. Nxg7! Kxg7 13. b4! Bxb4 14. Qd4+, with a winning attack.

| 11. Nb1-c3 | d7-d5 |

Karpov avoids repeating his game against I. Timman (Tilburg, 1983) which continued 11. ... Ne8 12. Bf4 Na6 13. Qd2 d5 14. e4 Nac7 15. Rad1 Bf6 16. exd Nxd5 17. Nxd5 cxd 18. Ne3 Nc7 19. Bxc7 Qxc7. The game equalized and the opponents agreed to draw.

| 12. e2-e4 | Be7-f6 |
| 13. Bc1-f4 | ... |

In the Kasparov-Marjanović game (1980 Olympic Team Tournament, Valletta, Malta), White continued 13. exd cxd 14. Bf4 Nba6 15. Re1, and won in a spectacular manner as follows: 15. ... Qd7? 16. Bh3 Kh8 (16. ... Qd8 would be more stubborn) 17. Ne4! Bxb2 18. Ng5 Qc6 19. Ne7 Qf6 20. Nxh7! Qd4 21. Qh5 g6 22. Qh4 Bxa1 23. Nf6+, and Black resigned. But it was soon found that after 15. Re1, Black could have reliably defended himself by 15. ... Nc5!

| 13. ... | Bb7-c8 |

It would be dangerous to play 13. ... d4, in view of 14. e5 dxc3, 15.

Qg4!?, while after 13. ... Nd7 14. Re1 d4, White has, apart from 15. Nxd4, the strong reply 15. e5! (D. Dzhanoev).

14. g3-g4!　　　Nb8-a6

After 14. ... Bxf5 15. gxf d4 16. Ne2 Re8 17. Ng3, White's King-side initiative associated with Qd1-g4 and Ng3-h5 would be quite dangerous (A. Suetin).

15. Ra1-c1　　　...

Preventing the manoeuvre 15. ... Nc5. ... which is refuted by 16. Bxc7 Qxc7. 17. exd, with the threat of b2-b4!, White aims at the weak squares c6 and c7 in the enemy camp and also supports his Knight on c3 (I. Dorfman)

15. ...　　　　Bc8-d7

The alternative 15. ... Bxf5 16. gxf Bg5! (not of course 16. ... dxe?! 17. Bxe4) 17. Bxc7 (unclear is 17. Qg4!? Bxf4 18. Qxf4 dxe 19. Rfd1 Nd5) 17. ... Nxc7 18. f4 Be7.

16. Qd1-d2　　　Na6-c5

No. 84

17. e4-e5!?　　　...

Kasparov relies on a King-side attack, although he has at his disposal another continuation, equally tempting but more restrained: 17. Bxc7 (or 17. exd Nxd5!) 17. ... Qc7 18. exd a5 (or 18. ... Bxf5 19. gxf Rad8·20. b4) 19. Ne4.

17. ...　　　　Bf6-e7
18. Nf5xe7+　　　...

An interesting possibility would be 18. Bg3; for instance, 18. ... Re8 19. Nxe7+ Qxe7 20. f4! Bxg4 21. f5, with a strong initiative.

18. ...　　　　Qd8xe7
19. Bf4-g5　　　Qe7-e6
20. h2-h3　　　Qe6-g6!
21. f2-f4　　　...

In the event of 21. Be7, Black could reply either 21. ... Qd3, or 21. ... h5, with good counterplay.

21. ...　　　　f7-f6!

Black has thus neutralized the advance of White's Pawns. Now 22. Bh4 would be countered by 22. ... f5!

22. e5xf6　　　g7xf6
23. Bg5-h4　　　f6-f5
　　　(No. 85)
24. b2-b4?　　　...

By playing 24. gxf! followed by Bf1-f3-g3 White would have retained the initiative owing to the weakness of the black squares in the enemy camp and the exposed position of the Black King (I. Dorfman).

24. ...　　　　f5xg4!

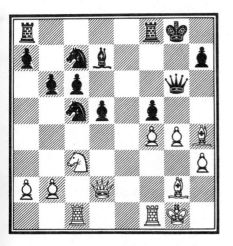

No. 85

Karpov's intentions are clear: the variation 25. bxc gxh 26. Rf2 hxg 27.Rxg2 Bg4, followed by h7-h5 would lead to his indisputable advantage.

25. h3xg4	Nc5-d3
26. Rf1-f3!	...

Kasparov finds a hidden possibility: by sacrificing the Exchange he greatly complicates the situation on the board (Yu. Razuvayev).

26. ...	Nd3xc1
27. f4-f5	Qg6-g7
28. Qd2xc1	Ra8-e8

The attempt to bring the Black Knight into active operations by 28. ... Ne8 is worth considering.

29. Qc1-d2	d5-d4
30. Nc3-e2	Nc7-d5

To 30. ... Re4 (unclear is 30. ... c5, 31. bxc bxc 32. Ng3, followed by 33. Nh5) White has the strong reply 31.

Nf4 Nd5 (if 31. ... Qh6, then 32. Qf2) 32. Nh5 Qf7 33. Rg3.

31. Ne2xd4	Kg8-h8

Probably, Black does not like 31. ... Re4, because of 32. f6 Qg6 33. Nf5 (A. Suetin).

From this moment on the opponents are under severe time pressure.

32. g4-g5	Re8-e4
33. Bh4-f2	Qg7-e5
34. Rf3-g3	Re4-f4
35. f5-f6	Bd7-e8

No. 86

36 b4-b5?!   ...

The Challenger ought to have preferred 36. Nf3, and there would still have been everything to fight for (I. Dorfman).

36. ...	c6-c5
37. Nd4-c6	Qe5-a1+
38. Bg2-f1	...

It would perhaps be better to play 38. Kh2 here (Yu. Razuvayev).

38. ...	Rf4-f5
39. g5-g6?!	Be8xg6
40. Rg1xg6	Rf5xf6?

Both opponents could run out of time any moment now, and only this may account for Karpov's missing the decisive 40. ... Nxf6, or 40. ... Rxf2! 41. Kxf2 (41. Qxf2 hxg) 41. ... Nxf6.

| 41. Rg6xf6 | ... |

The sealed move and the only one possible: to 41. Rg2, Black has the strong reply 41. ... Nf4.

| 41. ... | Qa1xf6 |

White's task would be more complex after 41. ... Nxf6 (if 41. ... Rg8+ 42. Kh2 Nxf6, then 43. Be1!) 42. Qe1! Qxa2 43. Qc3. It seems that with precise defence White could save himself; for instance, 43. ... Qg8+ 44. Bg2 Qg7 45. Bg3 Ng4 46. Qxg7+ Kxg7. 47. Bh3 (or 47. Bb8 at once) 47. ... Ne3 48. Bb8 (I. Dorfman).

| 42. Qd2-e1! | ... |

This is a clear way of drawing. White intends to strengthen his position by 43. Bg3, threatening Bg3-e5!

42. ...	Rf8-g8+
43. Kg1-h2	Qf6-f4+
44. Bf2-g3	Rg8xg3
45. Qe1xg3	Qf4xf1
46. Qg3-b8+	Kh8-g7
47. Qb8-g3+	

Because of the variation 47. ... Kf7 48. Nd8+! Kf8 (or 48. ... Ke8 49. Qg8+ Qf8 50. Qxd5) 49. Qd6+ Ne7 50. Ne6+ Kf7 51. Ng5+ Ke8 52. Qb8+,

and perpetual check, the opponents agreed to draw.

Time: 2.53-2.48

17 September 1984

GAME THREE

Sicilian Defence

| A. Karpov | G. Kasparov |

1. e2-e4	c7-c5
2. Ng1-f3	e7-e6
3. d2-d4	c5xd4
4. Nf3xd4	Nb8-c6

Although the Challenger could be satisfied with the outcome of the opening adopted in the first game of the match he now chooses an order of moves which precludes the Keres Attack. Yet White may respond to it with another ambitious line to exert pressure on the centre (L. Polugayevsky).

| 5. Nd4-b5 | d7-d6 |
| 6. c2-c4 | Ng8-f6 |

In the case of 6. ... a6 7. N5c3, the other White Knight can rapidly come into play via d2, e.g. 7. ... Nf6 8. Be2 Be7 9. 0-0 0-0 10. Be3 b6 11. Nd2, with better chances for White.

7. Nb1-c3	a7-a6
8. Nb5-a3	Bf8-e7
9. Bf1-e2	0-0
10. 0-0	b7-b6
11. Bc1-e3	Bc8-b7

Previously, Kasparov successfully adopted 11. ... Ne5, to parry the thrust 12

Qb3 by 12. ... Ned7, and after 13. Rfd1
Qc7, 14. f3 Bb7, he achieved a harmonious arrangement of his forces.

12. Qd1-b3   ...

Initiating the plan which has more than
once resulted in convincing wins for the
world champion.

No. 87

12. ...   Nc6-a5?!

One cannot help wondering that there
are so many untrodden paths remaining
in chess theory. The old 12. ... Nd7,
followed by Nd7-c5 has up to now been
considered compulsory (L. Polugayevsky).

13. Qb3xb6   ...

Karpov has shrewdly assessed that the
ending which must now result is far
from safe for Black (S. Makarychev).

After 13. Qc2 Rc8, the White Queen
would be "X-rayed" by the Black Rook,
e.g. 14. Rfd1 b5! , etc. (E. Gufeld).

13. ...	Nf6xe4
14. Nc3xe4	Bb7xe4
15. Qb6xd8	Be7xd8
16. Ra1-d1!	...

By taking his Rook away from a1 Karpov
has rendered harmless the threat of
Bd8-f6. He now intends playing Na3-
b1-c3. White's Pawn configuration on the
Queen's side is more stable and elastic
than Black's. Moreover, Black's Pawns at
d6 and a6 are rather weak (A. Suetin).

16. ...   d6-d5?!

Having pondered over the position for
fifty minutes, Kasparov rejects the
rational 16. ... Nb7 17. Nb1 Bf6 in
favour of a dubious pawn sacrifice
(E. Gufeld).

The line that suggests itself at this
juncture is 16. ... Be7, followed by
Rf8-c8. White's game would then, of
course, be more promising, but Black's
position would still by quite solid
(L. Polugayevsky).

| 17. f2-f3 | Be4-f5 |
| 18. c4xd5 | ... |

The continuation 18. g4 Bg6 19. cxd
exd 20. Rxd5, is erroneous because of
20. ... Re8 21. Kf2? Bh4+.

| 18. ... | e6xd5 |
| 19. Rd1xd5 | Bf5-e6 |

Little would be changed by 19. ... Re8
20. Kf2 Be6, (E. Gufeld, A. Suetin). Yet
L. Polugayevsky and S. Makarychev are
of the opinion that Black should have
preferred 19. ... Re8, as the Rook would
then have escaped the attack of the White
Bishops and would have been placed on
the open e-file with a gain of tempo.

20. Rd5-d6! ...

If White had played 20. Rd2 the idea behind Black's last move would have been fully justified, e.g. 20. ... Be7!, (20. ... Bxa2? 21. b4!) 21. Ra1 (21. Bb6 Bb4) 21. ... Bxa3 22. bxa Nc4, and the game would probably end in a draw.

No. 88

20. ... **Be6xa2?**

After 20. ... Be7! (if 20. ... Bf6, then 21. b4 Be7 22. Rb6) 21. Rxa6 Rxa6 22. Bxa6 Rb8 23. Bd4 Nc6 24. Bc3 Bc5+ 25. Kh1 Bxa2, it would not be so easy for White to promote his extra Pawn (L. Polugayevsky).

21. Rd6xa6	Ra8-b8
22. Be3-c5	Rf8-e8
23. Be2-b5!	Re8-e6

To 23. ... Rxb5 (or 23. ... Re5 24. Bd6!) 24. Nxb5 Bc4, White could respond with either 25. Nd6 Bxf1 26. Kxf1 or 25. Rd1 Bxb5 26. Rxd8! Rxd8 27. Rxa5, retaining all his winning chances.

24. b2-b4 **Na5-b7**

Neither 24. ... Nb3 25. Rxe6 fxe, nor 24. ... Rxa6 25. Bxa6 Nb3 26. Re1!, threatening 27. Re8 mate, would be satisfactory for Black.

25. Bc5-f2	Bd8-e7
26. Na3-c2!	Ba2-d5
27. Rf1-d1	Bd5-b3

No. 89

28. Rd1-d7! **Rb8-d8**

Black could not save himself by 28. ... Bxc2 either, because of 29. Rxe6 fxe 30. Rxe7 Nd6 (or 30. ... Nd8 31. Bf1) 31. Bd7 Rxb4? 32. Bc5 Rb1+ 33. Kf2.

29. Ra6xe6	Rd8xd7
30. Re6-e1!	Rd7-c7
31. Bf2-b6.	

Black resigns, because after 31. ... Rxc2 32. Rxe7 Nd6 33. Bc5, he will lose a piece.

Time: 2.10-2.22

КАРПОВ КАСПАРОВ

The tense struggle
begins in the opening
phase of the game

The players' arrival.
Ten minutes to wait
before the game

A general view of the hall
where the match was
played

Drawing lots. In the
second match it was
Anatoly Karpov's turn
to begin as Black

КАРПОВ   К.

КАРПОВ

Black (Kasparov) seems
to be having difficulties
in this game

Time pressure. Referee Mikenas watches the clocks carefully

The players agree to call it a draw

A referee's work. Bottom:
A game being adjourned

КАРПОВ КАСПАРОВ

The audience in rapt
attention

The move has been made
but the doubts linger

Masters and Grandmasters in the press-centre analyse the changing positions

The twenty-fourth and
deciding game: Karpov
thinks over his last move,
but doesn't make it;
he is the first to congratulate the new World
Champion. Referee
Malchev attempts to
quieten the enthusiastic
audience

A change of champion

After the match

Surrounded by autograph hunters

His first press conference as World Champion: Kasparov answered journalists' questions for fully two hours

The president of FIDE
proclaims Kasparov
World Champion

On the summit of
Olympus

GAME FOUR

Queen's Indian Defence

G. Kasparov	A. Karpov
1. d2-d4	Ng8-f6
2. c2-c4	e7-e6
3. Ng1-f3	b7-b6
4. g2-g3	Bc8-a6

The World Champion selects the well-known line which both parties have followed on numerous occasions in the past.

5. b2-b3	Bf8-b4+
6. Bc1-d2	Bb4-e7
7. Bf1-g2	...

The line beginning 7. Nc3! ? has also been played and if Black replies 7. ... c6, then 8. e4 d5 9. e5 Ne4 10. Bd3 Nxc3 11. Bxc3, resulting in a complicated game.

7. ...	Ba6-b7
8. Nb1-c3	d7-d5
9. c4xd5	e6xd5
10. 0-0	0-0
11. Bd2-f4	Nb8-a6
12. Qd1-c2	c7-c5

A popular approach, which has been successfully employed by Karpov for a decade or so. The distinguishing feature of this position is the White Pawn which has advanced to b3. Many experts believe that it would be more advanageous for White to keep his Pawn on b2 (the White Queen will be able to go to b3 or a4 and the black squares a3 and c3 will not be weakened); but the Pawn on b3 has its positive side too: Black's counterplay with c5-c4 is now impeded, while the White Queen may conveniently be placed on b2 (M. Najdorf).

13. Rf1-d1	Qd8-c8
14. Bf4-e5	...

This manoeuvre was introduces into master play by A. Yusupov. White intends to increase his pressure on d5 and also keeps an eye on Black's h7-Pawn (Yu. Razuvayev).

14. ...	Rf8-d8
15. Ra1-c1	...

The attack 15. Ng5 would be refuted by 15. ... Nb4 16. Qb1 h6 17. Bxf6 Bxf6 18. Qh7+ Kf8 19. Nf3 cxd, and the White Knight on c3 is endangered. But the move 16. Ng5 is a real threat.

15. ...	Nf6-e4

A step in Black's strategy.

16. Qc2-b2	...

The continuation 16. Nxe4 dxe17. Nd2 would fail against 17. ... e3! 18. fxe Bxg2 19. Kxg2 Qb7+, followed by f7-f6 and Black would have the advantage. But 16. dxc is worth considering.

16. ...	Qc8-e6
(No. 90)	
17. Nc3-b5! ?	

The grandmasters in the press room preferred 17. dxc; for instance, 17 ... bxc (or 17. ... Bxc5 18. Bd4!) 18. Nxe4 dxe 19. Nd2 Bg5 (or 19. ... f6 20. Bc3 Nb4 21. Nc4) 20. e3 f6 21. Bc3 Nb4 22. Bxb4 cxb 23. h4 Bh6 24. Nc4.

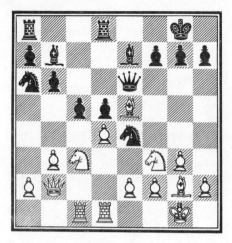

No. 90

instance, 26. Rxd8 Rxd8 27. Qc4 Qxc4 28. Rxc4 Nb4, with an ending slightly inferior for Black, but still tenable.

24. Ne5-c6!	Nb4xc6
25. b5xc6	Qe8xc6
26. Bf4-g5	a7-a5

If 26. ... Be7 27. Bxf6 Bxf6, Black would have to reckon with both 28. Qd3! ?, and 28. e4! ?

| 27. Bg5xf6 | Qc6xf6 |
| 28. Bg2xd5 | Ra8-a7 |

After 28. ... Rab8 29. Qe4 Rb4 30. Bc4 Rd4 31. Qa8, White's game would also be better (R. Vaganyan).

| 17. ... | Be7-f8 |
| 18. Be5-f4 | Qe6-e8! ? |

The routine 18. ... h6 also seems satisfactory (Yu. Razuvayev).

| 19. a2-a4 | ... |

This move is perhaps too committing. After 19. Nc3, White's game would be slightly better (I. Dorfman).

19. ...	Bb7-c6
20. d4xc5	b6xc5
21. Nf3-e5	Bc6xb5
22. a4xb5	Na6-b4!

After 22. ... Qxb5 23. Rxd5 Rxd5 24. Bxe4 White would win the Pawn back and seize the initiative.

| 23. Qb2-b1! | Ne4-f6?! |

Another possibility is 23. ... Qxb5 24. Bxe4 dxe 25. Qxe4 Na2! , which seems to offer more safety for Black; for

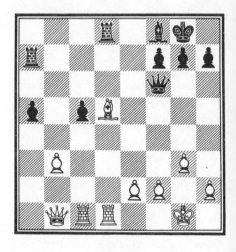

No. 91

29. Rc1-c4?!   ...

Having built a position with his good Bishop against Karpov's bad one (such positions are commonly referred to as "won as a matter of technique"), Kasparov demurs. 29. Rd3! , followed by doubling the Rooks along the d-file would be more vigorous.

29. ...	Qf6-b6

But not 29. ... Rad7, because of 30. Rf4, and White would have a dangerous initiative (Ye. Vasyukov).

30. Qb1-c2	Ra7-d7
31. e2-e4	Kg8-h8!

Karpov is getting ready to undermine the White Pawn on e4 with f7-f5, thereby depriving the White Bishop on d5 of its support and rendering the White Pawns relatively immobile. More importantly, however, Black would get rid of his weakness on f7 (Yu. Razuvayev).

32. Kg1-g2	...

The alternative 32. Rd3! is stronger (I. Dorfman).

32. ...	f7-f5
33. f2-f3	g7-g6
34. Rc4-c3	Qb6-c7
35. Rc3-d3	...

Doubling the Rooks along the d-file at this stage is no longer effective.

35. ...	f5xe4
36. f3xe4	Bf8-g7
37. Bd1-c1	Rd8-c8
38. Rd3-f3	Qc7-e5
39. Rc1-f1	Qe5-d6
40. Qc2-e2	Rd7-a7
41. Qe2-e3	...
(No. 92)	
41. ...	Qd6-e5

The sealed move. White's position is still more promising but in the adjourn-

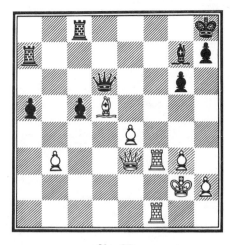

No. 92

ment analysis Kasparov failed to find a way of building up his initiative.

42. Rf1-f2	...

White could attempt to render the game sharper by 42. h4! ? Now the curious variation 42. ... a4 43. bxa Rxa4 44. Rf7 Ra1. 45. R1f3 Rb8 46. Qxc5 Rb2+ 47. Rf2 Rg1+ 48. Kxg1 Qxg3+ 49. Kf1 Qh3+ would lead to a draw (S. Makarychev).

42. ...	a5-a4!
43. b3xa4	Ra7xa4
44. Rf3-f7	Ra4-b4

With the idea of simplifying the game by 45. ... Rb2.
    Game drawn.
    Time: 2.54-2.39

GAME FIVE

Sicilian Defence

A. Karpov   G. Kasparov

1. e2-e4   c7-c5
2. Ng1-f3   d7-d6
3. d2-d4   c5xd4
4. Nf3xd4   Ng8-f6
5. Nb1-c3   a7-a6
6. Bf1-e2   e7-e6
7. 0-0   Bf8-e7
8. f2-f4   0-0
9. Kg1-h1   Qd8-c7
10. Be2-f3   Nb8-c6
11. a2-a4   Rf8-e8
12. Bc1-e3   Ra8-b8

No. 93

13. Rf1-e1   Bc8-d7
14. Qd1-d3   Nc6xd4
15. Be3xd4   e6-e5
16. Bd4-a7   Rb8-c8
17. Ba7-e3   Qc7-c4

White has prevented the liberating b7-b5, but now Black has a chance of reaching equality.

18. a4-a5   h7-h6
19. h2-h3   Be7-f8
20. Be3-d2   Qc4-d4
21. Bd2-e3   Qd4-b4

Now 22. Bd2 can again be answered by 22. ... Qd4.

Game drawn.

Time: 1.35-1.53

GAME SIX

Queen's Indian Defence

G. Kasparov   A. Karpov

1. d2-d4   Ng8-f6
2. c2-c4   e7-e6
3. Ng1-f3   b7-b6
4. g2-g3   Bc8-a6
5. b2-b3   Bf8-b4+
6. Bc1-d2   Bb4-e7
7. Bf1-g2   0-0

This time Karpov does not take the pressure off the White Pawn on c4 by playing 7. ... Bb7, as he did in the fourth game.

8. 0-0   d7-d5
9. Nf3-e5   ...

In the event of 9. Bc3 Nbd7 10. Ne5 Bb7 11. Nd2, Black would strike in the centre with 11. ... c5! , with a rather convenient game.

9. ...	c7-c6
10. Bd2-c3	Nf6-d7

The Gheorghiu-Karpov game (25th Olympic Team Tournament, Lucerne, 1982) continued: 10. ... Bb7 11. Nd2 Na6 12. e3 c5 13. Qe2 Rc8 14. Rfd1 Rc7 15. e4 cxd 16. Bxd4 dxc 17. Ndxc4 Qa8, with a good game for Black. By playing 12. e4 c5 13. exd exd 14. Re1! , as will occur in the sixteenth game, White could pose more problems for his opponent.

11. Ne5xd7	Nb8xd7
12. Nb1-d2	Ra8-c8

In the Torre-Seirawan game (1982 Toluca Interzonal Tournament), after 12. ... Rb8?! 13. e4 b5 14. Re1 dxc 15. bxc Nb6 16. cxb cxb 17. Rc1 b4 18. Ba1 Rc8 19. Nb3 Bc4 20. d5! , White took the early initiative. 12. ... f5! ?, which impedes the standard breakthrough e2-e4, is worth considering (A. Yusupov).

13. e2-e4 ...

A vigorous continuation. After 13. Re1, Black could succeed in getting a rather good game with either 13. ... f5 or 13. ... c5.

13. ... b6-b5

A consistent reply. Now White cannot play c4-c5 because of the threat of b5-b4! And he must therefore sacrifice the c-Pawn in order to be able to struggle for the initiative.

14. Rf1-e1	d5xc4
15. b3xc4	...

No. 94

15. ... Nd7-b6?!

It would be better to accept the sacrificed Pawn. After 15. ...bxc 16. Qa4 Bb5 17. Qc2 Nf6 18. a4 Ba6, or 17. ... Qc7 (17. ... Ba3! ?) 18. a4 Ba6 19. Rad1 e5, there would arise a complicated position with chances for both sides.

16. c4xb5?! ...

The commentators are unanimous in believing that 16. c5! would lead to some advantage for White. For instance, 16. ... Na4 17. Qc2 e5 (otherwise 18. e5!) 18. Nf3 Nxc3 19. Qxc3 exd 20. Nxd4, followed by 21. Rad1; or 16. ... b4 17. Bb2 Nc4 18. Nxc4 Bxc4 19. Qc2 Bb5 20. a3 bxa 21. Rxa3 Qd7 (21. ... a5 22. Qc3!) 22. f4.

16. ...	c6xb5
17. Ra1-c1	Be7-a3

In contrast to the situation in the above-mentioned Torra-Seirawan game, the

Black Queen's Rook is now where it should be. In A. Denker's opinion, 17. ... b4 18. Ba1 Rxc1 19. Qxc1 Qd7 would be simpler. On the other hand, after 20. Nb3 Na4 (or 20. ... Rc8 21. Nc5!) 21. d5 Rc8 22. Qf4, A. Yusupov adds, the game would be very sharp indeed.

18. Rc1-c2	Nb6-a4
19. Bc3-a1	Rc8xc2
20. Qd1xc2	Qd8-a5?!

Putting his Queen on this square, Black runs the risk of losing tempo. The correct continuation is 20. ... Qe7!, preventing d4-d5 and preparing for the occupation of the c-file by his Rook (A. Yusupov).

21. Qc2-d1!	...

To keep out of harm's way, the White Queen retreats from the c-file. From the square it now occupies, the Queen protects the Rook on e1 to the great relief of the Knight, which may be conveniently placed on b3 for the time being. The move in the text also contains a better hidden motif—the support of the orthodox breakthrough d4-d5. The White Queen may do it either from its present position on the d-file or, should the opportunity present itself, from g4 (E. Gufeld).

21. ...	Rf8-c8?

Black should have played 21. ... Bb2 22. Nb3 Qb4, or 21. ... Nb2 22. Nb3 Qc3.

22. Nd2-b3	Qa5-b4
23. d4-d5!	e6xd5

After 23. ... Nc3, White could answer 24. Bxc3 Qxc3 25. dxe fxe 26. Bh3, giving him a potent attack.

24. e4xd5	Na4-c3
25. Qd1-d4!	Qb4xd4
26. Nb3xd4	Nc3xa2

Understanding that the White d-Pawn will be hard to stop, Karpov snatches a Pawn, "just in case". The situation is now extremely complicated.

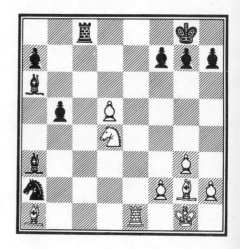

No. 95

27. Nd4-c6?!	...

The commentators in the press room considered 27. Nf5! to be the strongest continuation, as Black would have difficulty in warding off White's threats. For instance,

1) 27. ... Rc1 (27. ...g6? 28. d6 gxf 29. d7, or 27. ... Bf8? 28. d6 Rd8 29. Bc6 Bc8 30. Ne7+) 28. Rxc1 Bxc1 29. d6 Bg5 30. h4, and then 30. ... Bd8 31. Ne7+ Kf8 32. Nc6 Ke8 33. Bh3! , or 30. ... Bc8 31. hxg Bxf5 32. Bc6 Kf8 33. Bd4 (or 33. Bxb5) 33. ...

Nb4 34. Bxb5, putting White in a winning position;

2) 27. ... Bb4 28. Re2 Nc1 29. Re4, and then 29. ... Nd3 30. Bf1 Bf8 31. Ne7+ Bxe7 32. Rxe7 b4 33. d6 Kf8 (33. ... Bb5 34. d7!) 34. Re3! Nc5 35. Bd4 Bxf1 36. Bxc5 Rxc5 37. d7, or 29. ... Bf8 30. d6 b4 (both 30. ... Nd3 31. d7 Rd8 32. Re8 Rxd7 33. Bxg7, and 30. ... Rd8 31. Ne7+ Bxe7 are bad, if 31. ... Kh8, then 32. Nc6! ; 32. dxe Re8 33. Re3, threatening 34. Bc6) 31. Nh6+! gxh 32. Rg4+ Bg7 33. Rxg7+ Kf8 34. Bd5 Ne2+ 35. Kg2 Nc3 36. Rxf7+ Kg8 37. Bxc3 bxc 38. Rxa7+ Kf8 39. Rxa6 c2 40. d7 c1Q 41. dxcQ+ Qxc8 42. Ra8, and the fight would be over (A. Yusupov).

27. ...   Ba3-c5!

To 27. ... Bd6, White can reply strongly with 28. Be5! Re8 (and 28. ... Bxe5 29. Rxe5 is just as bad for Black) 29. Ra1 Bxe5 30. Rxa2 Bb7 31. Rxa7 Bxc6 32. dxc Kf8 33. Bh3! Re7 34. Bd7. Now 28. Bd4 allows Black to defend himself by 28. ... Bxd4 29. Nxd4 Rc1 (E. Geller).

28. Bg2-h3?   ...

What is it—a miscalculation or sheer mental fatigue? In the variation 28. Ne7+ Bxe7 29. Rxe7 b4 (29. ... Rc1+ 30. Bf1 Kf8 is bad because of 31. Rxa7 Rxa1 32. Rxa6 b4 33. d6, and then Kg1-g2) 30. Bb2, followed by 31. Rxa7, White would have a great advantage in a position with equal forces.
According to A. Yusupov, after 30. h4 it would also be hard for Black to defend his position, e.g., 30. ... Nc3 ? 31. d6 Bb5! 32. Rxa7 Rd8 (32. ... Kf8? 33. Rb7! , or 32. ... Rb8 33. d7 Rd8 34. Bh3) 33. Rb7 Be8 34. Rxb4 Nb5 35.

Be5, and White would have the advantage.

28. ...   Rc8-a8
29. Ba1-d4   ...

This was mapped out on the previous move; yet after the exchange of the Bishops Black will be able to stop the d-Pawn.

29. ...   Bc5xd4
30. Nc6xd4   Kg8-f8!
31. d5-d6   ...

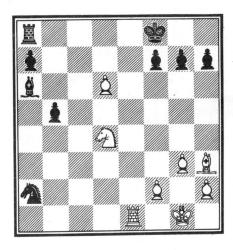

No. 96

31. ...   Na2-c3!

In spite of the growing time pressure, Karpov refuses to accept a draw, which could be reached by 31. ... Rd8 32. d7 Bb7 33. Nxb5 Bc6.

32. Nd4-c6?   ...

White ought to have forced a draw by 32. Bg2 (32. Re5?!) 32. ... Rd8 (or

167

32. ... Re8 33. Ra1) 33. Bc6 Bc8 34.
Nxb5 (A. Yusupov).

32. ...	Ba6-b7
33. Bh3-g2	Ra8-e8!

Just in time! The tempting 33. ... b4?
would allow White to compose a small
endgame study: 34. d7 b3 35. Nb8! !
Rxb8 36. Bxb7 b2 37. Bc8, winning
(A. Denker).

34. Nc6-e5?!   ...

Better would be 34. Ra1 Bxc6 35.
Bxc6 Re6! (35. ... Rd8 36. Re1!)
36. Rxa7 (or 36. d7 Ke7 37. Bf3) 36. ...
Rxd6 37. Bd7, and White would have
a chance to save himself.

34. ...	f7-f6!
35. d6-d7	...

After 35. Nd7+ Kf7 36. Ra1 (36. Rxe8
Kxe8 would be no better) 36. ... Bxg2
37. Kxg2 Ke6, Black would have a decisive material advantage. 35. Bxb7 would
not save White either, because of 35. ...
Rxe5 36. Ra1 b4 37. Rxa7 b3.

35. ...	Re8-d8
36. Bg2xb7	f6xe5
37. Bb7-c6	Kf8-e7?

A time-trouble move. After 37. ... e4!
38. Ra1 Ke7! 39. Rxa7 Kd6 40. Ra6
Kc7 41. Kf1 b4, White would not be
able to stop the Black b-Pawn.

38. Bc6xb5!   Nc3xb5! ?

Black could also play 38. ... Kd6 39.
Bd3 Rxd7! 40. Bxh7 a5 to advantage
(A. Yusupov).

39. Re1xe5+	Ke7xd7
40. Re5xb5	Kd7-c6

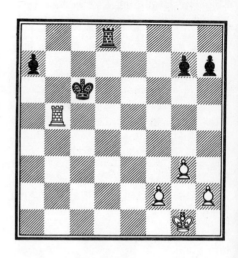

No. 97

41. Rb5-h5   ...

Now 41. Re5! ? is worth considering.
If 41. ... Ra8, then 42. Re6+ Kc5 43.
Re7 a5 44. Rxg7, capturing both Black
Pawns on the K-side.

41. ...	h7-h6
42. Rh5-e5	Rd8-a8

The sealed move. The World Champion
places his Rook according to the time-
honoured rule—behind the passed Pawn.
42. ... Rd5 could also be considered.

43. Re5-a5   ...

White would be lost after 43. Re6+
(43. Re7 a5 44. Rxg7 a4 is equally bad)
43. ... Kc5 44. Rg6 a5 45. Rxg7 a4 46.
Rc7+ Kb4 47. Rb7+, because of 47. ...
Ka5! 48. g4 a3 49. Rb1 a2 50. Ra1

Kb4 51. f4 Kb3 52. Kf2 (or 52. g5 hxg 53. fxg Ra5! 54. h4 Ra4) 52. ... Kb2 53. Rxa2+ Rxa2 54. Ke3 Kc3 55. h4 Rh2 56. h5 Rh4 57. g5 Rxh5 58. g6 Rh4! 59. f5 Rg4.

| 43. ... | Kc6-b6 |
| 44. Ra5-a2 | ... |

By playing 44. Ra1, White could set an interesting trap. After 44. ... a5 45. Kf1 a4 46. Ke2 a3 47. Kd3 Kc5 48. Kc3 (or 48. Kc2 Kc4!) 48. ... a2 49. Kb2 Kb4 50. f4! h5 51. Rxa2 Rxa2+ 52. Kxa2 Kc3 53. f5!, the Pawn ending would most likely give a draw, e.g. 53. ... Kd3 54. Kb3 Ke4 55. Kc4 Kxf5 56. Kd4 Kg4 57. Ke5 Kh3 58. Kf5 Kxh2 59. Kg6 Kxg3 60. Kxh5. Instead of 48. ... a2, the correct line would be 48. ... Kd5! 49. Kb3 a2 50. Kb2 Ke4 51. Re1+ Kf3, with a won endgame (A. Yusupov).

| 44. ... | a7-a5 |
| 45. Kg1-f1 | a5-a4 |

45. ... Re8 is also possible.

46. Kf1-e2	Kb6-c5
47. Ke2-d2	a4-a3
48. Kd2-c1	Kc5-d4
49. f2-f4	...

As the commentators pointed out, neither 49. Kb1 Rb8+ 50. Ka1 Rb2 51. Rxa3 Rxf2 52. Ra6 Rf6! 53. Ra7 g5, nor 49. Rd2+ Kc3 50. Rc2+ Kb3, threatening 51. ... a2, nor 49. h4 Ke4 50. Kb1 Kf3 51. Rc2 a2+ 52. Ka1 Ra7, followed by Kf3-g2, would save White.

49. ...	Kd4-e4
50. Kc1-b1	Ra8-b8+
51. Kb1-a1	Rb8-b2

| 52. Ra2xa3 | Rb2xh2 |
| 53. Ka1-b1 | Rh2-d2 |

With the threat of 54. ... Rd3.

| 54. Ra3-a6 | ... |

If the Black Pawn had been on h7, White could have saved himself by 54. Ra7! As it is, Black would answer 54. Ra7 with the simple g5.

| 54. ... | Ke4-f5 |
| 55. Ra6-a7 | ... |

Now the retreat 55. Ra3 would, according to A. Denker, be a last-ditch attempt to resist.

| 55. ... | g7-g5 |
| 56. Ra7-a6 | ... |

No. 98

| 56. ... | g5-g4! |

The line 56. ... Rh2 57. Kc1 Kg4 is unclear because of 58. Rg6! Rh5 59.

Kd2 Kxg3 60. Ke3! g4 61. Ke4, and White would have a good chance of a draw (A. Yusupov).

57. Ra6xh6   ...

After 57. Ra3, 57. ... Rf2 would serve his purpose. The Black g4-Pawn decides the issue.

57. ...   Rd2-g2
58. Rh6-h5+   ...

Both 58. Rh8 Rxg3 59. Rf8+ Ke4 60. f5 Rf2 61. f6 Rf4, and 58. Kc1 Rxg3 59. Kd2 Rf3 60. Ke2 would be bad for White because of 60. ... Kxf4 61. Rf6+ Kg3, winning.

58. ...   Kf5-e4
59. f4-f5   Rg2-f2
60. Kb1-c1   ...

Or 60. Rg5 Kf3 61. f6 Kxg3 62. Rg6 Rf4, and the g-Pawn will queen.

60. ...   Ke4-f3
61. Kc1-d1   ...

Now 61. f6 would be more stubborn. After 61. ... Kxg3 62. Rh6 Kg2! 63. Kd1 g3 64. Rg6 (or 64. Ke1 Kg1 65. Rg6 g2 66. Rh6 Rf5 67. Ke2 Re5+ 68. Kf3 Kf1 69. Rg6 Re6!) 64. ... Rf5 65. Ke2 Re5+ 66. Kd3 Kf3 67. Kd4 (67. f7 Rf5 68. Rg7 Rf4!) 67. ... Rh5! ! 68. f7 Rf5 69. Rg7 g2, White would be in sugzwang: 70. Kd3 is met by 70. ... Rf4, and 70. Kc4 by 70. ... Kf2 (S. Dolmatov).

61. ...   Kf3xg3
62. Kd1-e1   Kg3-g2
63. Rh5-g5   g4-g3
64. Rg5-h5   ...

If 64. Kd1, then 64. ... Kh3! 65. Ke1 Kh4, winning.

64. ...   Rf2-f4
65. Ke1-e2   Rf4-e4+
66. Ke2-d3   Kg2-f3
67. Rh5-h1   g3-g2
68. Rh1-h3+   Kf3-g4
69. Rh3-h8   Re4-f4
70. Kd3-e2   Rf4xf5

White resigns, as he has to give up his Rook for the Black g-Pawn.

One of the most dramatic and hard-fought games of the match!

Time: 3. 19-3.43.

---

28 September 1984

GAME SEVEN

Queen's Gambit Declined
Tarrasch Defence

A. Karpov   G. Kasparov

1. d2-d4   d7-d5
2. c2-c4   e7-e6
3. Ng1-f3   c7-c5
4. c4xd5   e6xd5
5. g2-g3   Ng8-f6
6. Bf1-g2   Bf8-e7
7. 0-0   0-0
8. Nb1-c3   Nb8-c6
9. Bc1-g5   c5xd4
10. Nf3xd4   h7-h6
11. Bg5-e3   Rf8-e8

This is a popular variation of the Tarrasch Defence—Kasparov's main weapon in his Candidates' matches. His opponents adopted 12. Qa4, 12. Qc2, and 12. a3. In this encounter, the World Champion has chosen a relatively rare line, interest in which has increased quite recently.

12. Qd1-b3	Nc6-a5
13. Qb3-c2	Bc8-g4
14. Nd4-f5	...

The continuation 14. h3 Bh5 15. Rad1 Rc8 16. g4 Bg6 17. Nf5, analysed by the Yugoslav Encyclopedia of Chess Openings, would be less dangerous to Black.

| 14. ... | Ra8-c8 |

In the Portisch-Chandler game (Amsterdam, 1984) after 14. ... Bb4 15. Bd4! Bxc3 16. Bxc3 (16. bxc! ? is also interesting) 16. ... Rxe2 17. Qd3 Re8 18. Ne3 Be6 19. Qb5 b5 20. Rad1, White had active play for the lost Pawn. According to Portisch, Black should have defended himself by 20. ... Rc8; for instance, 21. Bxa5 (21. Nxd5? Nxd5 22. Bxd5 Rc5) 21. ... bxa 22. Nxd5 Nxd5 23. Bxd5 Qb6.

| 15. Nf5xe7+ | ... |

This exchange, though strategically advantageous, is still premature. In the ninth game, Karpov will demonstrate a better plan—15. Bd4! (S. Makarychev).

| 15. ... | Re8xe7 |

At this juncture, 15. ... Qxe7 16. Bd4 Ne4 is worth considering, to answer 17. Bf3 with 17. ... Bf5.

| 16. Ra1-d1 | ... |

After 16. Bd4?! , Black would seize the initiative by 16. ... Ne4! Now Black leaves his d5-Pawn unprotected and prepares for Re7xe3 or Na5-c4.

| 16. ... | Qd8-e8 |

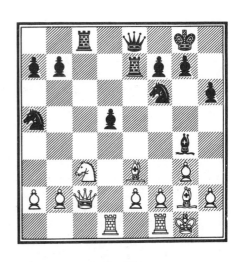

No. 99

| 17. h2-h3 | ... |

Should White play 17. Bxd5 at once, Black could respond with 17. ... Bh3 18. Bg2 Bxg2 19. Kxg2 Rxe3! 20. fxe Nc4, or 17. ... Nxd5 18. Rxd5 Bh3 19. Rfd1 Rxe3! 20. fxe Nc4, with compensation for the lost Exchange.

17. ...	Bg4-h5
18. Bg2xd5	Bh5-g6
19. Qc2-c1	Nf6xd5
20. Rd1xd5	Na5-c4
21. Be3-d4	Re7-c7

The attempt 21. ... Rxe2? would be refuted in fine style: 22. Nxe2 Qxe2 23. Re1 Qf3 24. Rc5! Rxc5 25. Re8+ Rh7 26. Rh8+! Kxh8 27. Qxh6+, and 28. Qxg7 mate. After 21. ... Rd7 22. Rd1, or 21. ... b5 22. Rxb5 Qd7 23. Qf4 Qxh3 24. b3 (or 24. Rb8! ?— S. Makarychev) 24. ... Nb6 25. a4, White has the advantage.

22. b2-b3   ...

Many commentators are of the opinion that 22. Qf4 would give White more chance, even though Black could well count on equalizing the game after 22. ... f6 (if 22. ... a6, then 23. e4; the variation 22. ... Qe6 23. g4 f6 has also been suggested) 23. b3 Nb6 24. Bxb6 Rxc3 25. Bxa7 Qxe2.

22. ...	Nc4-b6
23. Rd5-e5	Qe8-d7
24. Qc1-e3	f7-f6!
25. Re5-c5	Rc7xc5
26. Bd4xc5	Qd7xh3
27. Rf1-d1	...

White would have gained nothing by 27. Bxb6 axb 28. Nd5, because of 28. ... Re8; for instance, 29. Nf4 Rxe3 30. Nxh3 Re7, with a roughly even ending.

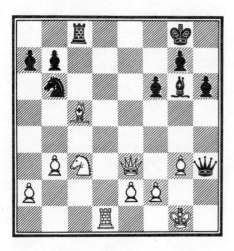

No. 100

27. ...   h6-h5?!

A time-trouble move. Having success-

fully won back the Pawn, Kasparov had at his disposal several reliable continuations; for instance, 27. ... Kh7 (S. Makarychev), 27. ... Re8 (E. Gufeld), 27. ... Be8 28. Bxb6 Bc6, or 27. ... Bf7 28. Bd6 Qe6 (D. Bronstein, E. Geller). The move actually played has only weakened the Black King's protection.

28. Rd1-d4   Nb6-d7

Not, of course, 28. ... Rxc5?, in view of 29. Rd8+ followed by 30. Qxc5.

29. Bc5-d6   ...

29. Bxa7? would be a mistake because of 29. ... Ne5! , with a strong threat of 30. ... Ng4.

29. ...   Bg6-f7

After 29. ... Nb8 (intending 30. ... Nc6) White could continue 30. Rh4 Qd7 31. Bxb8 Rxb8 32. Qxa7 and thus win a Pawn (Ye. Vasyukov).

30. Nc3-d5	Bf7xd5
31. Rd4xd5	a7-a6
32. Bd6-f4	Nd7-f8
33. Qe3-d3	Qh3-g4

In the event of 33. ... h4?, White could respond with 34. Rf5! threatening 35. Qd5+ followed by 36. Rh5+, and Black's position would be very bad (S. Makarychev).

34. f2-f3	Qg4-g6
35. Kg1-f2	...
(No. 101)	
35. ...	Rc8-c2?

This is a time-trouble move again, and a terrible blunder because now Black

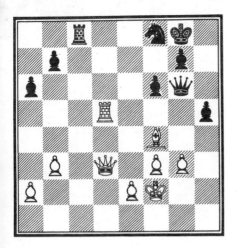

No. 101

Kasparov resigns without resuming play, the score now being 3:0 to Karpov. Time: 2.29-2.34

3 October 1984

GAME EIGHT

Catalan Opening

G. Kasparov	A. Karpov
1. d2-d4	Ng8-f6
2. c2-c4	e7-e6
3. g2-g3	d7-d5
4. Bf1-g2	Bf8-e7
5. Ng1-f3	0-0
6. 0-0	d5xc4
7. Qd1-c2	a7-a6
8. Qc2xc4	b7-b5
9. Qc4-c2	Bc8-b7
10. Bc1-d2	Bb7-e4
11. Qc2-c1	...

simply loses the game, whereas after 35. ... Qxd3 36. Rxd3 Kf7, or 36. ... Rc2, the Challenger would still have a good chance of a draw (E. Gufeld).

36. Qd3-e3!	Rc2-c8
37. Qe3-e7	b7-b5

The defence 37. ... Qf7 38. Qxf7+ Kxf7 39. Rxh5 g5 would be stouter, but after 40. Bd6! White should still win.

38. Rd5-d8	Rc8xd8
39. Qe7xd8	Qg6-f7

The variation 39. ... Kf7 40. Qd5+ would hardly be better for Black. In any event, he would inevitably lose several Pawns.

40. Bf4-d6	g7-g5
41. Qd8-a8	Kg8-g7
42. Qa8xa6	

This move was sealed.

No. 102

11. ...   Be4-b7

An innovation which has enabled Black to quickly equalize the game.

12. Bd2-e3	Nf6-d5
13. Nb-c3	Nb8-d7
14. Rf1-d1	Ra8-c8
15. Nc3xd5	Bb7xd5
16. Nf3-e1	c7-c6
17. Ne1-d3	Qd8-b6
18. Qc1-c3	b5-b4
19. Qc3-d2	a6-a5
20. Rd1-c1	

Game drawn.
Time: 1.30-1.25

GAME NINE

Queen's Gambit Declined
Tarrasch Defence

A. Karpov	G. Kasparov
1. d2-d4	d7-d5
2. c2-c4	e7-e6
3. Ng1-f3	c7-c5
4. c4xd5	e6xd5
5. g2-g3	Ng8-f6
6. Bf1-g2	Bf8-e7
7. 0-0	0-0
8. Nb1-c3	Nb8-c6
9. Bc1-g5	c5xd4
10. Nf3xd4	h7-h6
11. Bg5-e3	Rf8-e8
12. Qd1-b3	Nc6-a5
13. Qb3-c2	Bc8-g4
14. Nd4-f5	Ra8-c8

(No. 103)

15. Be3-d4!   ...

This is stronger than 15. Nxe7+, as in the seventh game.

No. 103

15. ...   Be7-c5

No reasonable alternative can be suggested; for instance, 15. ... Qd7 is met by 16. Ne3 Be6 17. Rfd1, with the threat of 18. Bxf6 (A. Mikhalchishin).

16. Bd4xc5   ...

But not 16. Rad1? because of 16. ... Bxe2! 17. Nxe2 Bxd4.

16. ...   Rc8xc5
17. Nf5-e3!   ...

White increases his pressure on the Black d5-Pawn; he does not fear 17. ... d4, in view of 18. Rad1. If White were to play 17. Nd4 (17. b4? Bxf5), Black could keep the game level by playing 17. ... Ne4.

17. ...   Bg4-e6
18. Ra1-d1   ...

The advance 18. b4? is erroneous because

of 18. ... Rc8 19. ba d4, or 19. ... Qxa5, but now White threatens to play b2-b4.

| 18. ... | Qd8-c8 |

White would have met 18. ... Nc4 (or 18. ... Nc6) by 19. Nexd5! Nxd5 20. e4.

| 19. Qc2-a4 | ... |

Also interesting is 19. Qb1 Rd8 20. Rd3, and 20. ... d4 fails against 21. Rfd1 Nc6 22. Bxc6 (A. Mikhalchishin).

| 19. ... | Re8-d8 |
| 20. Rd1-d3 | ... |

Karpov is executing a clear strategical plan which involves doubling his Rooks on the d-file against the d5-Pawn, thereby tying down his opponent's forces (Ye. Vasyukov).

| 20. ... | a7-a6 |
| 21. Rf1-d1 | ... |

The alternative 21. Qd1, recommended by S. Dolmatov and I. Dorfman, also comes into consideration. The idea behind it is to meet 21. ... Nc4 with 22. Nexd5 Nxd5 23. Nxd5 Bxd5 24. Bxd5 Nxb2 25. Bxf7+ Kxf7 26. Rxd8 Nxd1 27. Rxc8 Rxc8 28. Rxd1, with an extra Pawn in a Rook and Pawn ending. Consequently, Black would have to respond 21. ... Qc6, followed by b7-b5, as suggested by A. Mikhalchishin.

| 21. ... | Na5-c4 |
| 22. Ne3xc4 | ... |

Now 22. Nexd5 Nxd5 23. Nxd5 Bxd5 24. Bxd5 would have led, after 24. ... Rdxd5! 25. Rxd5 Rxd5 26. Rxd5

Nb6 27. Qd4 Nxd5 28. Qxd5 Qc1+ 29. Kg2 Qxb2, to a level Queen and Pawn ending.

| 22. ... | Rc5xc4 |

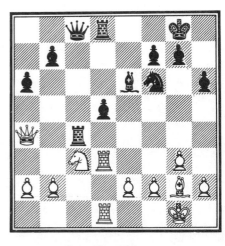

No. 104

| 23. Qa4-a5 | ... |

The variation 23. Qb3!? d4 24. Qxb7 Qxb7 25. Bxb7 Rb8 26. Bxa6 dxc 27. Bxc4, recommended by A. Yusupov, is unsatisfactory because of 27. ... c2 28. Rd8+ Ne8! For instance, 29. Rc1 (or 29. Bxe6 Rxd8!) 29. ... Rxd8 30. Rxc2 Bxc4 31. Rxc4 Rd2, and Black would win a piece (Ye. Vasyukov).

And yet 23. Qb3 is playable because 23. ... d4 would fail against the simple 24. Qb6! , and 24. ... Nd7 would be met with 25. Rxd4 (A. Mikhalchishin).

| 23. ... | Rc4-c5 |

Now 23. ... Rd7 (23. ... d4? 24. Bxb7) would have been more precise, as 24. Nxd5? is to be avoided in view of 24. ... Bxd5 25. Bxd5 Rc5.

175

| 24. Qa5-b6 | Rd8-d7 |
| 25. Rd3-d4 | ... |

The preliminary 25. h3, or 25. e3, is worth considering (A. Mikhalchishin).

| 25. ... | Qc8-c7 |
| 26. Qb6xc7 | Rd7xc7 |

Black has exchanged the Queens, taking advantage of the fact that the capture of the d5-Pawn would give nothing to White: 27. Nxd5 Nxd5 28. Bxd5 Bxd5 29. Rxd5 Rxd5 30. Rxd5 Rc2 31. Rd8+ Kh7 32. Rd7 Rxb2 33. Rxf7 Rxe2, and a draw would not be far off.

27. h2-h3 ...

Many commentators suggest 27. e3 to pursue the same plan as in the game but without losing time to advance the h-Pawn. But after 27. e3 g6 (or 27. ... Rc4! ?—R. Vaganyan) 28. a3 Kg7, White would gain nothing, as A. Mikhalchishin believes, by playing 29. Nxd5 Nxd5 30. Bxd5 Bxd5 31. Rxd5 Rxd5 32. Rxd5, because of 32. ... Rc2 33. b4 Ra2 34. Rd3 b5, and it would be very hard for White to exploit his extra Pawn.

27. ...	h6-h5
28. a2-a3	g7-g6
29. e2-e3	Kg8-g7

Black has indirectly protected his Pawn (30. Nxd5 Nxd5 31. Bxd5 Bxh3, or, should the capture occur one move later, 31. Nxd5 Nxd5 32. Bxd5 Rxd4 33. Rxd4 Bxd5 34. Rxd5 Rc2) and yet it would perhaps have been better for him to march his King to the centre at once (A. Gipslis).

30. Kg1-h2 ...

Also deserving consideration was the plan which T. Petrosyan adopted in similar positions: 30. Bf1, followed by f2-f3 and g3-g4, whereupon the White King would make his way to g3 (A. Mikhalchishin).

30. ...	Rc5-c4
31. Bg2-f3	b7-b5
32. Kh2-g2	Rc7-c5
33. Rd4xc4	Rc5xc4

An interesting possibility is 33. ... bxc4, whereas the natural 33. ... dxc4 would prove unsuccessful because of 34. Rd6 a5 35. Rb6 Bd7? 36. Rxf6! Kxf6 37. Ne4+.

| 34. Rd1-d4 | Kg7-f8 |
| 35. Bf3-e2 | Rc4xd4 |

After 35. ... Rc5! ?, followed by Nf6-e4 Black's defence would not be difficult.

| 36. e3xd4 | Kf8-e7 |

The active 36. ... Ne4! was the preference of those gathered in the press room; e.g., 37. Na2 Nd6 38. Nb4 a5 39. Nc6 Nc4!, maintaining the balance.

| 37. Nc3-a2 | Be6-c8 |

In the case of 37. ... Kd6 38. Nb4 a5?, Black would have lost a Pawn after 39. Na2! Bd7 40. Nc3 b4 41. axb axb 42. Na2 b3 43. Nc1 Ba4 44. Bd1 (A. Yusupov).

38. Na2-b4	Ke7-d6
39. f2-f3	Nf6-g8
40. h3-h4	Ng8-h6
41. Kg2-f2	Nh6-f5
42. Nb4-c2	...

With the Rooks off the board, the pawn configuration has somewhat changed and White no longer controls the d4-square. Yet he has retained a small advantage— owing to Black's idle Bishop (Ye. Vasyukov).

| 42. ... | f7-f6 |

The sealed move. If 42. ... Ng7, then 43. g4 f6 44. Bd3 g5 45. Bg6! hxg4 46. h5, and the h-Pawn is very dangerous (A. Mikhalchishin). But 42. ... Bd7 would perhaps be safer.

43. Be2-d3	g6-g5
44. Bd3xf5	Bc8xf5
45. Nc2-e3	Bf5-b1

The correct move here is 45. ... Ke6! For instance, 46. b4 Bg6 47. g4 hxg 48. hxg gxf 49. gxf Be4! 50. Ng4 Kf7 51. Kg3 Ke6 52. Ne5 Kxf6 53. Nd7+ Kf5 54. Nc5 f2! 55. Kxf2 Kf4 56. Nxa6 Bd3! 57. Nc5 Bc4! , reaching a rare position of mutual zugzwang; a draw, with White to move. Of course, rather than play 46. b4 at once, White could have marched his King to c3, thereby forcing Black's reply a6-a5; then White would play b2-b4 to fix the Black Pawn on b5 and return to the plan indicated above. But still the outcome would be uncertain (A. Mikhalchishin).

| 46. b2-b4 | ... |

(No. 105)

| 46. ... | g5xh4? |

Counting only upon the mechanical recapture 47. gxh4, whereupon Black would reply 47. ... Bg6, making his position impenetrable. But he should have played 46. ... Bg6 at once.

No. 105

| 47. Ne3-g2! | ... |

By sacrificing a Pawn, White captures the h4-square, and his King will now be able to penetrate Black's position on the King's side (Ye. Vasyukov).

47. ...	h4xg3+
48. Kf2xg3	Kd6-e6
49. Ng2-f4+	Ke6-f5
50. Nf4xh5	Kf5-e6
51. Nh5-f4+	Ke6-d6
52. Kg3-g4	Bb1-c2
53. Kg4-h5	Bc2-d1
54. Kh5-g6	Kd6-e7

If 54. ... Bxf3 55. Kxf6, Black, for whom a Pawn ending would be hopeless, would sooner or later have to give up the d5-Pawn.

| 55. Nf4xd5+ | Ke7-e6 |

E. Geller and A. Mikhalchishin indicate that after 55. .. Kd6 56. Nxf6 Bxf3, the ending would not be so easily won by White.

56. Nd5-c7+   Ke6-d7

Another possibility is 56. ... Kd6, and
after 57. Ne8+ Ke7 58. Nxf6 Bxf3, or
57. Nxa6 Bxf3 58. Kxf6 Kd5, the outcome is still uncertain.

57. Nc7xa6   Bd1xf3
58. Kg6xf6   Kd7-d6
59. Kf6-f5   Kd6-d5
60. Kf5-f4   ...

Here it is the tempo which enables
White to protect his d4-Pawn.

60. ...   Bf3-h1
61. Kf4-e3   Kd5-c4
62. Na6-c5   Bh1-c6

The alternative 62. ... Bg2 would be
answered 63. Nd3 Kb3 64. Nf4 Bb7
65. Kd3 Kxa3 66. Kc3, followed by
67. d5 to win.

63. Nc5-d3   Bc6-g2

A curious idea would be to play 63. ...
Be8 64. Ne5+ Kd5, in the hope of
holding the game despite the absence of
two Pawns.

64. Nd3-e5+   Kc4-c3

The reply 64. ... Kd5 also deserves
consideration.

65. Ne5-g6   Kc3-c4
66. Ng6-e7   ...
    (No. 106)
66. ...   Bg2-b7?

Now Black should lose because of
zugzwang. On 66. .. Kb3, White would
win by playing 67. d5 Kxa3 68. d6
Bh3 69. Nd5.

No. 106

A. Gipslis and A. Mikhalchishin are of
the opinion that Black could resist more
stubbornly after 66. ... Bh1! 67. Nc8
(not 67. d5? Bxd5 with a draw) 67. ...
Kd5. In spite of his two extra Pawns,
White will not win easily and even if he
plays a3-a4 there is no clear victory in
sight.

67. Ne7-f5   Bb7-g2

Even now White would have more
problems to solve after 67. ... Kd5.

68. Nf5-d6+   Kc4-b3
69. Nd6xb5   Kb3-a4
70. Nb5-d6

Black resigns.
Time: 3.25-3.55

GAME TEN

Queen's Indian Defence

G. Kasparov	A. Karpov
1. d2-d4	Ng8-f6
2. c2-c4	e7-e6
3. Ng1-f3	b7-b6
4. Nb1-c3	Bc8-b7
5. a2-a3	d7-d5
6. c4xd5	Nf6xd5
7. e2-e3	Nb8-d7
8. Bf1-d3	...

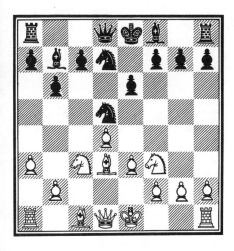

No. 107

8. ...	Nd5-f6

A new plan of defence, by which Black will soon obtain a convenient position.

9. e3-e4	c7-c5
10. d4-d5	e6xd5
11. e4xd5	Bf8-d6
12. 0-0	0-0

13. Bc1-g5	Qd8-c7!
14. Bd3-f5	a7-a6
15. Qd1-d2	

Game drawn.
Time: 1.03-1.10

10 October 1984

GAME ELEVEN

English Opening

A. Karpov	G. Kasparov
1. Ng1-f3	Ng8-f6
2. c2-c4	b7-b6
3. g2-g3	c7-c5
4. Bf1-g2	Bc8-b7
5. 0-0	g7-g6

Previously, Kasparov preferred to build up the hedgehog formation by playing 5. ... e6. His game against Karpov at the Match-Tournament of USSR Teams (Moscow, 1981), for instance, continued: 6. Nc3 Be7 7. d4 cxd 8. Qxd4 d6 9. Bg5 a6 10. Bxf6 Bxf6 11. Qf4 0-0 12. Rfd1 Be7 13. Ne4 Bxe4 14. Qxe4 Ra7 15. Nd4 Qc8, with a draw on move 41.

6. b2-b3	...

Another plan later tested in games 13 and 20, would be to play 6. Nc3 Bg7 7. d4 cxd 8. Nxd4 Bxg2 9. Kxg2.

6. ...	Bf8-g7
7. Bc1-b2	0-0
8. e2-e3	...

The line 8. Nc3, and then, for example, 8. ... d5 9. Nxd5 Nxd5 10. Bxg7 Kxg7 11. cxd Qxd5 12. d4 cxd 13. Qxd4+

Qxd4 14. Nxd4 Bxg2 15. Kxg2, was popular for a long time. But in the Mikhalchishin-Schüssler game (Copenhagen, 1979) Black easily held the endgame balanced after 15. ... Rc8 16. Rac1 Na6 17. Rfd1 Nb4 18. a3 Na2! 19. Rxc8 Rxc8 20. Rd2 Nc1.

In reply to 8. Nc3, 8. ... Na6 is also interesting. After 9. d4 d5 10. Ne5 (10. cxd Nxd5 11. e3 Nxc3 12. Bxc3 Rc8 is quite harmless, as in the Timman-Larsen game, Bugojno, 1978) 10. ... e6 11. cxd exd 12. dxc Nxc5! 13. Nf3 (13. Rc1 d4!) 13. ... Rfe8 (13. ... Nfe4! ?) 14. Nb5 a6 15. Nbd4 b5 16. Rc1 Qb6 (Chekhov-Zaichik, 50th USSR Championship Semifinal, 1982), Black would have excellent prospects.

8. ...	e7-e6
9. d2-d4	Qd8-e7
10. Nb1-c3	Nb8-a6
11. Qd1-e2	d7-d5
12. Rf1-d1	Rf8-d8
13. Ra1-c1	...

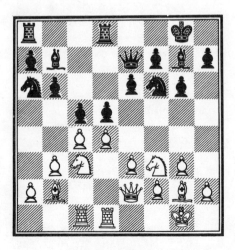

No. 108

13. ...   d5xc4

In the press room many preferred 13. ... Ne4. But, according to A. Mikhalchishin, this could be met with 14. cxd exd 15. a3 Rac8 16. Nb5.

| 14. b3xc4 | Ra8-c8 |
| 15. Nc3-b5 | ... |

Here 15. d5 exd 16. cxd Nb4 17. e4 is inferior in view of 17. ... Nfxd5! (S. Makarychev).

| 15. ... | Bb7-e4 |
| 16. a2-a3! | ... |

Confining the scope of the Black Knight on a6. Black is now forced to bring the Knight to the centre using a different route.

| 16. ... | Na6-b8 |

To 16. ... cxd 17. exd Nb8, White could respond with 18. a4! , threatening 19. Ba3

| 17. d4xc5 | b6xc5 |

After 17. ... Rxd1+ 18. Rxd1 Rxc5, White could win a Pawn by playing 19. Nxa7 Qxa7 20. Rd8+ Bf8 21. Bxf6, or continue 19. a4! , to transfer the Bishop to the a3-f8 diagonal (A. Gipslis).

18. Bb2-e5	Nf6-e8
19. Be5xg7	Kg8xg7
20. Nf3-e5	Be4xg2
21. Kg1xg2	f7-f6

Black might also have played 21. ... a6 22. Nc3 Nc6 23. Nxc6 Rxc6, but after 24. Ne4 White would retain some pressure (A. Suetin).

22. Ne5-d3	Nb8-c6
23. Nb5-c3	Ne8-d6
24. Nc3-a4	...

Not, of course, 24. Nxc5, in view of 24. ... Ne5!

No. 109

| 24. ... | Nc6-e5! ? |

Kasparov did not like the passive 24. ... Nb7; accordingly, he had to agree to the weakening of Black's Pawn structure.

| 25. Nd3xe5 | f6xe5 |
| 26. Na4-c3 | ... |

Those gathered in the press room also considered 26. Rb1 to prevent Black from checking on b7.

| 26. ... | Qe7-b7+ |
| 27. Qe2-f3 | ... |

The commentators had different assessments of the alternative 27. Kg1! ?. According to A. Gipslis, Black could

well respond to this with 27. ... Qb3, and after 28. Qg4 Qxc4 29. Qxc4 Nxc4 30. Ne4 Rxd1+! 31. Rxd1 Rc7, White would not have any real chance of winning. A. Mikhalchishin believed that a stronger continuation would be 28. a4! Qxc4 29. Qxc4 Nxc4 30. Rxd8 Rxd8 31. Ne4, giving a better endgame. Instead of 27. ... Qb3, he recommended 27. ... h5 with counterplay.

| 27. ... | Qb7xf3+ |
| 28. Kg2xf3 | Rc8-b8 |

The line 28. ... Nxc4 29. Rxd8 Rxd8 30. Ne4 Nxa3 31. Rxc5 would be in White's favour (A. Mikhalchishin).

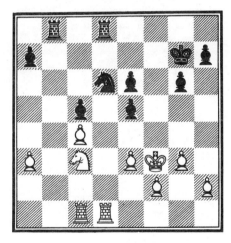

No. 110

| 29. Rc1-b1 | ... |

Throwing away a slight advantage, which could still be retained by 29. Ke2 or 29. Kg2.

| 29. ... | e5-e4+! |
| 30. Kf3-e2 | Rb8xb1 |

181

31. Rd1xb1	Kg7-f6
32. Rb1-d1	Kf6-e5
33. Nc3-b5	Rd8-d7!

33. ... a6 would be bad because of 34. Na7.

34. g3-g4	h7-h6
35. a3-a4	a7-a6
36. Nb5xd6	Rd7xd6
37. Rd1-b1	Rd6-d3
38. f2-f4+	Ke5-f6
39. Rb1-b6	Rd3-c3
40. Rb6xa6	Rc3-c2+
41. Ke2-d1	Rc2xh2

Black's last move was sealed.

The next day the World Champion offers a draw which the Challenger accepts without resuming play.

Time: 2.23-2.47

12 October 1984

GAME TWELVE

Queen's Gambit Declined

G. Kasparov	A. Karpov
1. d2-d4	Ng8-f6
2. c2-c4	e7-e6
3. Ng1-f3	d7-d5
4. Nb1-c3	Bf8-e7
5. Bc1-g5	h7-h6
6. Bg5-h4	0-0
7. e2-e3	b7-b6
8. Bf1-e2	Bc8-b7
9. Bh4xf6	Be7xf6
10. c4xd5	e6xd5
11. b2-b4	...
(No. 111)	
11. ...	c7-c5
12. b4xc5	b6xc5

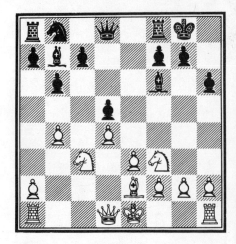

No. 111

13. Ra1-b1	Bb7-c6
14. 0-0	Nb8-d7
15. Be2-b5	Qd8-c7
16. Qd1-d2	Rf8-d8
17. Rf1-c1	Ra8-b8
18. Bb5xc6	Rb8xb1
19. Nc3xb1	Qc7xc6
20. d4xc5	Nd7xc5
21. Qd2-c2	

After 21. ... Be7 22. Nd4 Qa6 23. Nf5 (or 23. Nd2) 23. ... Bf8, the game would be about equal.

Game drawn.

Time: 1.15-1.02

15 October 1984

GAME THIRTEEN

English Opening

A. Karpov	G. Kasparov
1. Ng1-f3	Ng8-f6
2. c2-c4	b7-b6

3. g2-g3	c7-c5
4. Bf1-g2	Nc8-b7
5. 0-0	g7-g6
6. Nb1-c3	Bf8-g7
7. d2-d4	c5xd4
8. Nf3xd4	Bb7xg2
9. Kg1xg2	0-0
10. e2-e4	Qd8-c7

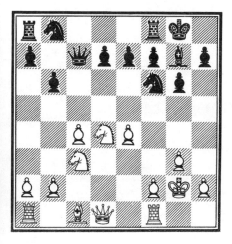

No. 112

This is a well-known opening position, in which 11. Be3 Qxc4 12. Rc1 merely leads to the repetition of moves after 12. ... Nc6 13. Ncb5 Qxa2 14. Ra1 Qc4 15. Rc1 (Ftáčnik-Adorján, Jevik, 1983).

On the other hand, in the Chekhov-Psakhis game (Irkutsk, 1983), White gained a slight advantage by 11. Qe2 Nc6 12. Nc2 a6 13. Bg5 b5?! 14. Rad1 bxc 15. Ne3! Qb7 16. Nxc4, but instead of 13. ... b5 Black should have played the more precise 13. ... Qb7! , indicated by V. Chekhov.

Karpov takes a line in which Black can fight for equality by launching a small combination.

11. b2-b3	Nf6xe4! ?
12. Nc3xe4	Qc7-e5
13. Qd1-f3	Qe5xd4
14. Bc1-a3	...

The variation 14. Be3 Qe5 15. Rad1 Qc7 16. Bf4 Qc6 (Kharitonov-Gavrikov, Jurmala, 1983) is advantageous to Black, but 14. Rb1! ? (see Game 20) is of interest.

14. ...	Nb8-c6
15. Ra1-d1	Qd4-e5
16. Rd1xd7	Qe5-a5!

The Keene-Adorján game (Plovdiv, 1983) continued: 16. ... Rad8 17. Rfd1 Rxd7 18. Rxd7 Rd8, and at this stage White could gain some advantage by 19. Nd6! (R. Keene).

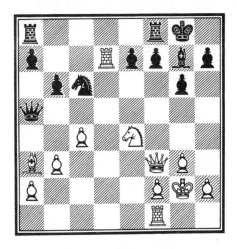

No. 113

17. Ba3xe7! ...

Karpov pondered over this Exchange sacrifice for over fifty minutes. After

183

17. b4 Nxb4 18. Rxe7 Nc2 (or 18. ...
Nc6), Black would have no problems.

17. ...	Nc6-e5
18. Qf3-d1!	...

Those gathered in the press room mainly
considered 18. Rd5, which could be met
with 18. ... Nxf3 19. Rxa5 Rfe8 20.
Rd5 Nxh2!, or 20. Ra6 Nxh2 21. Kxh2
Rxe7 22. Nd6 Rd8 23. Nb5 Rdd7, with
a probable draw.

18. ...	Ne5xd7
19. Qd1xd7	...

No. 114

19. ...	Qa5xa2!

The opponents apparently saw that the
attempt to retain an extra Exchange by
playing 19. ... Rfb8 could be repulsed
by 20. a4! Qe5 21. Re1 with a clear
advantage for White. Kasparov, however,
has found a clear-cut method of equalizing (I. Dorfman).

20. Be7xf8	Ra8xf8
21. Rf1-e1	Qa2xb3
22. Ne4-d6	Qb3-c3
23. Re1-e7	Qc3-f6
24. Nd6-e4	Qf6-d4
25. Qd7xd4	Bg7xd4
26. Re7-d7	Bd4-g7
27. Rd7xa7	h7-h6
28. Ra7-b7	Bg7-d4
29. Rb7-d7	Bd4-g7
30. h2-h4	f7-f5
31. Ne4-d2	Rf8-f6
32. Rd7-c7	Rf6-e6
33. Nd2-f3	Bg7-f6

Game drawn.
Time: 2.00-2.08

GAME FOURTEEN

Queen's Indian Defence

G. Kasparov	A. Karpov
1. d2-d4	Ng8-f6
2. c2-c4	e7-e6
3. Ng1-f3	b7-b6
4. g2-g3	Bc8-a6
5. b2-b3	Bf8-b4+
6. Bc1-d2	Bb4-e7
7. Bf1-g2	0-0
8. 0-0	d7-d5
(No. 115)	
9. c4xd5	Nf6xd5
10. Nb1-c3	Nb8-d7
11. Nc3xd5	e6xd5
12. Ra1-c1	c7-c5
13. d4xc5	b6xc5
14. Nf3-e1	Nd7-b6
15. a2-a4	Ra8-c8
16. a4-a5	

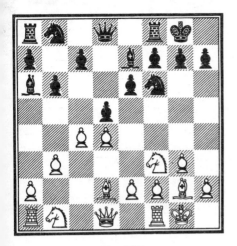

No. 115

After 16. ... Na8, Black's hanging Pawns on c5 and d5 are somewhat weak, but this is compensated for by the weakness of White's Pawns on the Queen's side.

Game drawn.

Time: 0.56-0.38

19 and 20 October 1984

GAME FIFTEEN

Queen's Indian Defence

A. Karpov	G. Kasparov
1. Ng1-f3	Ng8-f6
2. c2-c4	b7-b6
3. d2-d4	e7-e6
4. g2-g3	Bc8-a6

A surprise! The Challenger has added to his opening repertoire the line previously adopted with success by the World Champion.

5. b2-b3	Bf8-b4+
6. Bc1-d2	Bb4-e7
7. Bf1-g2	0-0
8. 0-0	d7-d5
9. c4xd5	...

This Exchange supersedes the equally interesting 9. Ne5, as played in the sixth game.

9. ...	Nf6xd5
10. Nb1-c3	Nb8-d7
11. Nc3xd5	e6xd5
12. Ra1-c1	Rf8-e8

The preceding game of the match went: 12. ... c5 13. dxc (13. Be3! ?) 13. ... bxc 14. Ne1 Nb6, and now the variation 15. Nd3 Rc8 16. Bh3 Rc7 17. Bf4 Bd6 18. Qd2 would have maintained the tension so desirable to White.

No. 116

13. Rc1-c2!   ...

Initiating a new plan. White intends a harmonious regrouping of his forces to

185

exert pressure along the c- and d-files (M. Taimanov).

13. ...	c7-c5
14. Rf1-e1	...

The alternative 14. Be3 deserves consideration, and after 14. ... Bb7?! White could continue 15. Qc1 Rc8 16. Rd1, saving important tempo, while after 14. ... Nf6 15. Re1 Black would no longer have the plan of counterplay which he actually uses in this game. The game could have continued 15. ... Ne4 16. dxc bxc 17. Nd2, with good prospects for White (Gavrikov-Sokolov, 52nd USSR Championship, 1985).

14. ...	Ba6-b7
15. Bd2-e3	a7-a5!

By opening the a-file and creating a weakness on b3, Black gains sufficient counterplay.

16. Qd1-c1	a5-a4
17. Re1-d1	...

After 17. Bh3 Black could continue 17. ... axb 18. axb cxd 19. Nxd4 Ba3! ? 20. Qd2 Nc5, with a sharp game (M. Taimanov).

17. ...	a4xb3
18. a2xb3	Be7-f6
19. Nf3-e1	...

A solid, safe continuation. The reckless 19. Bh3 cxd 20. Bxd7 Qxd7 21. Rc7 Qg4 22. Bxd4 Rxe2 23. Bxf6 Qxf3 24. Bd4 Ba6 would give the initiative to Black who would threaten with the unpleasant h7-h5-h4 (R. Vaganyan).

19. ...	h7-h6

The line 19. ... cxd 20. Bxd4 Bxd4 21. Rxd4 Nc5 is tempting, as it gives counter-chances (S. Makarychev).

20. Bg2-f3	Qd8-e7
21. Qc1-d2	...

White would gain nothing by playing 21. dxc, because of 21. ... Ra1 22. Qd2 Rxd1 23. Qxd1 Nxc5 24. Bxd5 Rd8 25. Rd2 Rxd5! 26. Rxd5 Qe4, or 24. Bxc5 bxc 25. Bxd5 Rd8 26. e4 Bxd5 27. exd Bxd4.

21. ...	Ra8-a3! ?

The game becomes sharper. Other possibilities deserving consideration are 21. ... cxd 22. Bxd4 Nc5 (M. Taimanov), or 21. ... Red8 (A. Mikhalchishin).

22. Rd1-b1	...

No. 117

22. ...	Re8-d8

Many commentators preferred 22. ... Rea8! , giving, after 23. dxc Nxc5, the following variations:

1)24. Qb4 (or 24. Bf4) 24. ... Ra1 25. Rcc1 d4! ;

2) 24. Bxc5 bxc 25. Bxd5 Rd8 26. e4 Bxd5 27. exd Bd4;

3) 24. Bxd5. Then there may follow:

a)24. ... Rd8 25. Qb4 Bxd5 26. Bxc5 (not 26. Qxa3? Qe4!) 26. ... bxc 27. Qxa3 Qe4 28. f3 Qe3+ 29. Kh1 Be4! ? (A. Gipslis);

b) 24. ... Ne4 25. Bxe4 (25. Qd3? Bxd5 26. Qxd5 Nc3) 25. ... Qxe4 26. f3 Qe6 (M. Taimanov).

In all these cases, Black would have active play. As it is, White takes advantage of the unprotected position of the Black Rook on a3.

23. d4xc5	Nd7xc5

After 23. ... bxc White could play 24. Bxd5, and after 23. ... d4?! 24. Bxd4 Ne5 a good continuation would be 25. Bxb7 Qxb7 (or 25. ... Rxd4 26. Qc1! ?) 26. Qc1!

24. Qd2-b4!	...

The line 24. Bxc5 bxc 25. Nd3 (if 25. Qc1, then 25. ... Rda8!) was much debated in the press room. Black could then solve all his problems by 25. ... Bg5! 26. Qd1 (26. Qe1 c4! 27. bxc dxc 28. Rxb7 cxd! 29. Rxe7 dxc is worse) 26. ... c4! 27. bxc dxc 28. Rxb7 Qe6 29. h4 Bf6.

24 ...	d5-d4!

(No. 118)

25. Be3xd4!	...

On 25. Qxa3 there could follow 25. ... dxe, threatening 26. ... exf+. White would

No. 118

have to play 26. Qc1, but then the terrible blow 26. ... Bd4! would make the position of the White King very dangerous (A. Mikhalchishin).

25. ...	Ra3xb3!

White would have the advantage after 25. ... Bxd4 26. Qxa3 Bxf2+ 27. Kxf2 Ne4+ (or 27. ... Nd3+ 28. Nxd3 Qxa3 29. Bxb7, but not 27. ... Bxf3? 28. Kxf3!) 28. Bxe4 Qxa3 29. Bxb7.

26. Rb1xb3	Rd8xd4
27. Qb4xb6	Nc5xb3
28. Rc2-c7	Rd4-d7

More accurate is 28. ... Rb4! 29. Rxe7 Rxb6 30. Rxb7 Rxb7 31. Bxb7, with an ending similar to that in the actual game (M. Taimanov).

29. Rc7xb7	...

With the Queens on the board (after 29. Rxd7 Qxd7 30. Qxb3) White would

have more chance to exploit his extra
Pawn.

Black could not then play 30. ... Qd2,
in view of 31. Qxb7 Qxe1+ 32. Kg2
followed by 33. Bd5 (S. Makarychev).

29. ...	Rd7xb7
30. Qb6xb7	Nb3-d4

In time-trouble Kasparov misses 30. ...
Qb7, and Karpov in turn lets slip his
last opportunity to get the better of it:
31. Qc8+ Kh7 32. Qc4.

31. Kg1-f1	Qe7xb7
32. Bf3xb7	Nd4-f5

No. 119

Now an extra Pawn is by no means a
guarantee of White's success. Three
factors are in favour of the defender:
all Pawns are on the same wing, there
are opposite-coloured Bishops on the
board and, finally, the queening square
of the White h-Pawn is not controlled
by the White Bishop (M. Taimanov).

In the fight that follows Kasparov
succeeds in building an impenetrable
position and repulsing Karpov's persistent attempts to win.

33. Ne1-d3	Bf6-c3
34. e2-e3	g7-g5
35. g3-g4	...

White should perhaps have tried 35.
e4 Nd6 36. Bd5 followed by f2-f4,
intending e4-e5 (A. Mikhalchishin).

35. ...	Nf5-d6
36. Bb7-f3	Kg8-g7
37. Kf1-e2	Kg7-f6
38. h2-h3	Kf6-e7
39. Bf3-d5	Ke7-f6
40. Nd3-c5	Kf6-e7
41. Nc5-a4	Bc3-a5

The sealed move.

42. Na4-c5	Ba5-b6
43. Nc5-a6	Bb6-a5
44. Na6-b8	Ba5-c3
45. Nb8-c6+	Ke7-d7
46. Ke2-d3	Bc3-e1
47. Nc6-e5+	Kd7-e7
48. Kd3-e2	Be1-c3
49. Ne5-f3	Bc3-a5
50. Bd5-b3	Ba5-b6
51. Nf3-e5	Bb6-c5
52. Ke2-d3	Bc5-b6
53. Bb3-d5	Bb6-c5
54. Kd3-c3	Ke7-e8
55. Kc3-b3	Ke8-e7
56. Kb3-a4	Bc5-b6
57. Ka4-b4	Ke7-e8
58. Ne5-c6	Ke8-d7
59. Kb4-c3	Kd7-e8
60. Kc3-d3	Bb6-c5
61. Kd3-e2	Ke8-f8
62. Ke2-f3	Bc5-a3
63. Bd5-b3	Ba3-c5

64. Nc6-e5	Kf8-e7	3. Ng1-f3	b7-b6
65. Ne5-d3	Bc5-b6	4. g2-g3	Bc8-a6
66. Nd3-b4	Bb6-c5	5. b2-b3	Bf8-b4+
67. Nb4-d5+	Ke7-f8	6. Bc1-d2	Bb4-e7
68. Bb3-c2	Bc5-a7	7. Bf1-g2	c7-c6
69. h3-h4	Kf8-g7		
70. h4-h5	Ba7-c5		
71. Kf3-e2	Nd6-c4		
72. Bc2-f5	Bc4-b6		
73. Nd5-c3	Bc5-b4		
74. Nc3-b5	Kg7-f6		
75. Bf5-c2	Nb6-c4		
76. Nb5-d4	Bb4-c5		
77. Nd4-f5	Nc4-d6		
78. Nf5-g3	Kf6-e5		
79. Ng3-f1	Bc5-b4		
80. Nf1-h2	Ke5-f6		
81. Bc2-b3	Bb4-c5		
82. Nh2-f3	Bc5-b6		
83. Ke2-d3	Bb6-c5		
84. Bb3-c2	Kf6-e6		
85. Nf3-g1	Ke6-e5		
86. Ng1-e2	Bc5-b6		
87. Bc2-b3	Bb6-c5		
88. Ne2-c3	Ke5-f6		
89. Nc3-d5+	Kf6-e6		
90. f2-f4!	g5xf4!		
91. g4-g5	f4xe3		
92. g5xh6	e3-e2!		
93. Nd5-f4+	Ke6-e7		

In the fourth game, Black's choice fell upon 7. ... Bb7, while in the sixth, fourteenth, and fifteenth games, on 7. ... 0-0.

8. Bd2-c3	d7-d5
9. Nb1-d2	Ba6-b7

The reply 9. ... Nbd7, as will occur in game 18, is also worth considering.

10. Nf3-e5	0-0
11. e2-e4	Nb8-a6
12. 0-0	c6-c5
13. e4xd5	e6xd5

Game drawn.
Time: 4.25-5.37

22 October 1984

GAME SIXTEEN

Queen's Indian Defence

G. Kasparov	A. Karpov

1. d2-d4	Ng8-f6
2. c2-c4	e7-e6

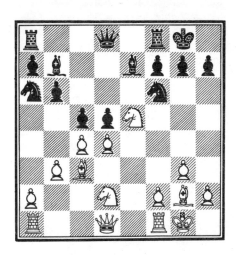

No. 120

14. Rf1-e1	...

In the Torre-Karpov game (Tilburg, 1982), after 14. Ng4 Qd7! 15. Ne5

Qc8 16. Re1 dxc 17. Ndxc4 Bxg2 18. Kxg2 cxd 19. Bxd4 Bd8, Black obtained good counterplay.

14. ...	c5xd4
15. Bc3xd4	Na6-c5
16. Ne5-g4	d5xc4
17. Nd2xc4	...

The line 17. Nxf6+ Bxf6 18. Bxc5 (or 18. Bxf6 Qxf6 19. Bxb7 Rad8!) 18. ... bxc 19. Bxb7 Bxa1 20. Bxa8 Bc3 21. bxc Bxd2 (Torre-Adorján, Wijk aan Zee, 1984) would very likely lead to a draw, while 17. Bxc5 Bxc5 18. Bxb7 can be parried by 18. ... Nxg4 (A. Adorjan).

17. ...	Bb7xg2
18. Kg1xg2	...

Many commentators indicated an interesting Exchange sacrifice: 18. Rxe7! ? Qxe7 19. Nxf6+ gxf 20. Qg4+ Kh8 21. Qf4 Nd7 22. Kxg2, and White keeps the initiative.

18. ...	Nf6xg4

Another method of fighting for equality is by playing 18. ... Ne6 19. Bxf6 Bxf6 20. Qxd8 Bxd8 (it is not so certain, A. Adorján believes, that 20. ... Raxd8 21. Nxf6+ gxf is bad for Black), but after 21. Rad1 Black has to defend himself very carefully in the ensuing endgame (Torre-Sokolov, USSR vs Rest of the World Match, London, 1984).

19. Qd1xg4	Be7-f6
20. Ra1-d1	...
(No. 121)	
20. ...	Bf6xd4

Another possibility is 20. ... h5! ? 21.

No. 121

Bxf6 hxg 22. Bxd8 Rfxd8, and Black has a fair chance of a draw; for instance, 23. Ne3 Nd3 24. Re2 Ne5; 23. Ne5 f5; or 23. Rxd8+ Rxd8 24. Re7 Rd7 25. Rxd7 Nxd7 26. Ne3 Ne5.

21. Rd1xd4	Qd8-c7

After 21. ... Qf6 22. Nd6, Black's position is far from pleasant, because White's lead in development is quite telling (A. Adorján).

22. Nc4-d6	Nc5-e6?

An oversight probably caused, as A. Adorján believes, by the strain experienced by the players in the present encounter and throughout the whole match. Black should have played 22. ... Rad8. **(No. 122)**

23. Re1xe6!	h7-h5

Of course, Black could not be happy witһ 23. ... fxe 24. Qxe6+ Kh8 25. Rc4

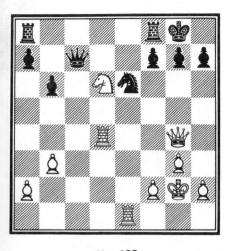

No. 122

No. 123

Rf6 (25. ... Qd8 26. Nf7+) 26. Qxf6
Qxc4 27. Qf3.

24. Qg4-e4	f7xe6	
25. Qe4xe6+	Kg8-h7	
26. Rd4-d5?	...	

Kasparov reciprocates, and his blunder
can be explained only by the enormous
tension. White had a tempting alternative 26. Ne4! ?, but it would be simpler
to play 26. Rc4! Qd8 27. Qd5 (or 27.
Qe4+) 27. ... g6 28. Qb7+ Kg8 29. Rc7
Qf6 30. Qd5+ Kh8 31. Nf7+, winning.

26. ...	g7-g6	
27. Nd6-e4	Ra8-d8	
28. Ne4-g5+	Kh7-g7	
29. Qe6-e4	Rf8-e8	
(No. 123)		
30. Qe4-d4+?	...	

A miscalculation by which the Challenger
lets slip his last winning chance. He could
still hope to exploit his extra Pawn in
the Rook and Pawn ending that would

arise from the line 30. Ne6+ Rxe6 31.
Qd4+ Re5! 32. Qxe5+! (but not 32.
Rxd8 Qc6+! , leading to a draw) 32. ...
Qxe5 33. Rxe5 Kf6 34. Re2.

30. ...	Kg7-g8	
31. Rd5xd8	Re8xd8	
32. Qd4-f6	Rd8-d6	
33. Qf6-f4	Qc7-c6+	
34. Kg2-h3	Qc6-d7+	
35. Kh3-g2	Qd7-c6+	
36. Kg2-h3	Qc6-d7+	

The game would probably also be drawn
after 36. ... Qd5 37. Ne4 Qe6+ 38. Kg2,
or after 36. ... Rf6 37. Qb8+ Rf8 38.
Qxa7 Qc8+ 39. Kg2 Qa8+ 40. Qxa8
Rxa8 41. a4 Rd8 42. Nf3.

37. Kh3-g2.
Game drawn.
Time: 2.11-2.19

GAME SEVENTEEN

Queen's Gambit Declined

A. Karpov	G. Kasparov
1. Ng1-f3	d7-d5
2. d2-d4	Ng8-f6
3. c2-c4	e7-e6
4. Nb1-c3	Bf8-e7
5. Bc1-g5	h7-h6
6. Bg5-h4	0-0
7. e2-e3	b7-b6
8. Bf1-e2	Bc8-b7
9. 0-0	Nb8-d7
10. Ra1-c1	c7-c5

18. Be2-d3	a5xb4
19. a3xb4	Be7xb4
20. Bd3xe4	Bd5xe4
21. Qd1-d4	Be4xf3
22. Qd4xb4	Bf3-e2

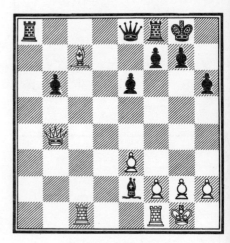

No. 125

After 23. Rfe1 Qb5 24. Qxb5 Bxb5 25. Bxb6, it would be pointless to prolong the game.

Game drawn.

Time: 1.28-1.01

No. 124

11. Bh4-g3	a7-a6
12. c4xd5	Nf6xd5
13. Nc3xd5	Bb7xd5
14. d4xc5	Nd7xc5
15. b2-b4	Nc5-e4
16. Bg3-c7	Qd8-e8
17. a2-a3	a6-a5!

GAME EIGHTEEN

Queen's Indian Defence

G. Kasparov	A. Karpov
1. d2-d4	Ng8-f6
2. c2-c4	e7-e6
3. Ng1-f3	b7-b6
4. g2-g3	Bc8-a6
5. b2-b3	Bf8-b4+

192

6. Bc1-d2	Bb4-e7
7. Bf1-g2	c7-c6
8. Bd2-c3	d7-d5
9. Nb1-d2	Nb8-d7
10. 0-0	0-0
11. Rf1-e1	c6-c5
12. e2-e4	d5xe4
13. Nd2xe4	...

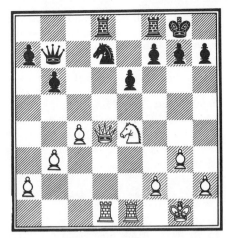

No. 127

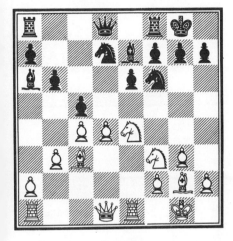

No. 126

13. ...	Ba6-b7!

A clear way of equalizing the game.

14. Nf3-g5	c5xd4
15. Bc3xd4	Qd8-c7
16. Ne4xf6+	Be7xf6
17. Bg2xb7	Qc7xb7
18. Ng5-e4	Bf6xd4
19. Qd1xd4	Ra8-d8
20. Ra1-d1	...
(No. 127)	
20. ...	Qb7-a8
21. Qd4-c3	Nd7-b8
22. Ne4-f6+	

Game drawn.
Time: 1.58-1.03

29 October 1984

GAME NINETEEN

Queen's Gambit Declined

A. Karpov	G. Kasparov
1. Ng1-f3	d7-d5
2. d2-d4	Ng8-f6
3. c2-c4	e7-e6
4. Nb1-c3	Bf8-e7
5. Bc1-g5	h7-h6
6. Bg5xf6	Be7xf6
7. Qd1-d2! ?	...

The beginning of a new and fruitful line in the dispute between the Champion and the Challenger over openings. The variation with the Exchange on f6 will more than once occur in the encounters to follow.

The line 7. e3 0-0 8. Qd2 (or 8. Qc2) is more frequently played. The idea behind 7. Qd2 is that, should an opportunity arise, White may play e2-e4 in one move (A. Mikhalchishin).

| 7. ... | Nb8-c6 |

In the variation 7. ... b6 (if 7. ... 0-0, or 7. ... c6, then 8. e4!) 8. 0-0-0! Bb7 9. cxd exd 10. Kb1 Nd7 11. e3 Nf8 12. Ne5 a6 13. f4, White has the advantage.

| 8. e2-e3 | 0-0 |
| 9. Ra1-c1 | ... |

To 9. 0-0-0, Black may reply 9. ... dxc 10. Bxc4 e5 11. d5 Na5 or, as A. Mikhalchishin recommended, 11. ... Ne7 followed by Ne7-f5-d6 and b7-b5.

| 9. ... | a7-a6 |

An important move in Black's defensive plan. Kasparov is not in a hurry to play d5xc4, followed by the undermining e6-e5, because 10. cxd exd is not dangerous for him (see, for example, the Lerner-Geller game, 50th USSR Championship, 1983).

10. Bf1-e2	d5xc4
11. Be2xc4	e6-e5
12. d4-d5	Nc6-a7

The alternative 12. ... Ne7 would seem more natural, but in his game against Gheorgadze (Hannover, 1984) the World Champion gained the advantage by 13. Ne4 Nf5 14. Be2 (14. Bb3! ?) 14. ... Nd6 15. Nxf6+ Qxf6 16. 0-0 e4 17. Nd4 Re8 18. Rxc7 Qg5 19. Rfc1 Bh3 20. Bf1 Bg4 21. Qb4!

No. 128

| 13. Qd2-c2! | ... |

This is an improvement upon the move played in the stem-game Lerner-Vaganyan (50th USSR Championship, 1983) where, after 13. Ne4 (or 13. Be2 Bf5!) Black continued 13. ... Bf5 14. Nc5?! b6! 15. Nxa6 c5! 16. dxc Nxc6 17. Bb5 e4 18. Qxd8 Rfxd8, and developed a dangerous initiative.

| 13. ... | Na7-b5! ? |

After prolonged thought Kasparov comes to a decision which is in harmony with his chess creed: when the opportunity offers he prefers to cut the Gordian knot rather than untie it. After the cautious 13. ... Bd7, the game might have proceeded as follows: 14. Bd3 (if 14. Ne4, then 14. ... Bf5!) 14. ... Nb5 15. Ne4 Nd6 16. Qxc7 Rc8 17. Qxd8 Bxc1+ 18. Kd2 Bxd8 19. Rxc1 Nxe4+ 20. Bxe4, and Black hardly has compensation for the lost Pawn (M. Tal).

14. Nc3xb5   ...

Eingorn, in his game against Lputyan (52nd USSR Championship, 1985), tried 14. Bxb5 axb 15. a3 (15. Nxb5?! c6 16. dxc bxc 17. Nc3 Ba6 is not good for White) 15. ... c5! ? (15. ... c6 is also rather good) 16. Nxb5 b6 17. e4 Ba6 18. a4 Qd7 19. 0-0 Bxb5 20. axb Qxb5 21. Ra1, with a slight advantage to White.

14. ...   a6xb5
15. Bc4-b3   ...

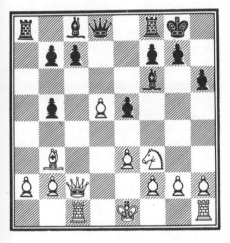

No. 129

15. ...   e5-e4! ?

In the same spirit as on move thirteen Black tries to play actively, whatever the costs (M. Tal).

After 15. ... Bg4 16. Nd2! Rc8 (16. ... c5 17. dxc bxc 18. 0-0 c5 19. f3! is in White's favour, according to M. Tal) 17. Qd3 Bd7 (17. ... c6 18. d6!) 18. Ne4, White would retain a small advantage (Chernin-Lputyan, 52nd USSR Championship, 1985).

16. Nf3-d4   ...

A more complicated situation would arise after 16. Qxe4 Bxb2 17. Rc2 Ba3 18. 0-0 Bd6 (or 18. ... Re8 19. Qd3?! c5! , as indicated by A. Chernin) 19. Nd4 Bd7 20. Qd3 Qe8 (Chernin-A. Petrosyan, 52nd USSR Championship, 1985).

16. ...   Bf6xd4
17. e3xd4   e7-c6

Getting rid of his weak Pawn, Kasparov move by move frustrates the World Champion's attempts to maintain the pressure.

18. d5xc6   Qd8xd4
19. 0-0   ...

Now 19. c7 would be wrong because of 19. ... Bd7! , followed by 20. ... Bc6.

19. ...   b7xc6
20. Qc2xc6   Bc8-d7

Black could also play 20. ... Ra7; for instance, 21. Rfd1 (not 21. Qxb5? Ba6, nor 21. Qc3 Qxc3 22. Rxc3 b4!) 21. ... Qxb2 22. Qxb5 Be6, with a probable draw.

21. Qc6-d5   Qd4xd5
22. Bb3xd5   Ra8-a6!
23. Rf1-d1   ...

The commentators also examined the variations 23. a3 b4! 24. axb Rb8 25. Rfd1 Be6 26. Bxe4 Rab6, and 23. Rc5 Rc8 (M. Tal indicated the alternative 23. ... Be6 24. Bxe6 fxe! 25. a3 Rf5) 24. Rxc8+ Bxc8 25. Rc1 Be6 26. Bxe6 fxe 27. a3 Rd6, and in both cases the game would have been drawn.

23. ...	Bd7-e6

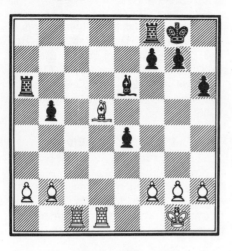

No. 130

24. a2-a3	...

White could hardly make headway by playing 24. Bxe6 Rxe6 25. Rd4 e3 26. f3 Ra8 27. a3 Ra4, and Black would have nothing to fear (M. Tal).

24. ...	Be6xd5
25. Rd1xd5	Rf8-b8

A. Mikhalchishin pointed out the possibility 25. ... b4! ? 26. axb Rb8 27. Rd4 Ra2 28. Rb1 f5, followed by 29. ... Ra4 to win back the Pawn.

26. Rd5-d4	Ra6-a4
27. Rc1-d1	Rb8-c8
28. Kg1-f1	Rc8-c2
29. Rd4-d2	Rc2xd2
30. Rd1xd2	Ra4-c4
31. Kf1-e2	b5-b4
32. Ke2-d1	...

Because of his passed Pawn on the other wing, White still retains a slightly superior

game. After 32. a4 b3 33. Ke3 Rxa4 34. Rd8+ Kh7 35. Rb8 f5 36. Rxb3 Kg6, Black's task would be even simpler (M. Tal).

32. ...	b4xa3
33. b2xa3	Rc4-a4
34. Rd2-a2	f7-f5!

Black hastens to counterplay.

35. Kd1-c2	f5-f4
36. Kc2-b3	Ra4-d4
37. Ra2-a1	...

Setting a trap. After 37. a4 e3 38. fxe fxe 39. a5 (or 39. Kc3 e2) 39. ... Rd3+, the game would rapidly end in a draw.

No. 131

37. ...	Kg8-f7

After 37. ... e3? there would follow 38. Kc3 Rd8 39. fxe fxe 40. Ra2! Kf7 41. Re2 Ra8 42. Kb4 Rb8+ 43. Kc4, and Black would lose his e3-Pawn without winning White's a-Pawn. According to

196

A. Mikhalchishin, Black could also draw by 37. ... Rd2.

38. a3-a4	e4-e3
39. Kb3-c3	Rd4-d8
40. f2xe3	f4xe3
41. Ra1-e1	Rd8-a8
42. Kc3-b3	Ra8-b8+

A. Yusupov pointed out that Black could also have played 42. ... Re8 43. Kc4 (or 43. Re2 Re4 44. a5 Kf6 45. a6 Re6) 43. ... Re4+ 44. Kb5 e2 45. a5 Re5+.

| 43. Kb3-c2 | Rb8-e8 |
| 44. Re1-f1+ | ... |

The sealed move.

Without resumption the players agree to draw.

Time: 2.14-2.46

31 October 1984

GAME TWENTY

English Opening

G. Kasparov	A. Karpov
1. Ng1-f3	Ng8-f6
2. c2-c4	b7-b6
3. g2-g3	c7-c5
4. Bf1-g2	Bc8-b7
5. 0-0	g7-g6
6. Nb1-c3	Bf8-g7
7. d2-d4	c5xd4
8. Nf3xd4	Bb7xg2
9. Kg1xg2	0-0
10. e2-e4	Qd8-c7
11. b2-b3	Nf6xe4
12. Nc3xe4	Qc7-e5
13. Qd1-f3	Qe5xd4

No. 132

| 14. Ra1-b1 | Qd4-e5 |
| 15. Bc1-f4 | |

The double-edged position that would arise from 15. ... Qe6 16. Nf6+ Bxf6 17. Qxa8 Nc6 18. Qb7 (Shabalov-Kenghis, Riga, 1983) promises Black sufficient counterplay for the Exchange he has sacrificed (for instance, 18. ... g5 19. Rbe1 Qf5, followed by g5-g4).

Game drawn.

Time: 0.34-1.03

2 November 1984

GAME TWENTY-ONE

Queen's Gambit Declined

A. Karpov	G. Kasparov
1. Ng1-f3	d7-d5
2. d2-d4	Ng8-f6
3. c2-c4	e7-e6
4. Nb1-c3	Bf8-e7

5. Bc1-g5	h7-h6
6. Bg5xf6	Be7xf6
7. Qd1-d2	d5xc4!

An improvement over the nineteenth game. Black intends to undermine the centre with c7-c5.

| 8. e2-e4 | c7-c5 |
| 9. d4-d5 | ... |

According to A. Mikhalchishin, 9. e5 could be answered with 9. ... cxd 10. exf dxc 11. Qxd8+ Kxd8 12. fxg Rg8 13. Bxc4 Rxg7, with a good game for Black.

| 9. ... | e6xd5 |
| 10. e4-e5 | ... |

After 10. Nxd5 Nc6, Black has a free development.

No. 133

| 10. ... | Bf6-g5! |

Not, of course, 10. ... d4?, because of 11. exf dxc 12. Qe3+ Be6 13. fxg Rg8 14. Qxc3, while 10. ... Be7 could be countered with 11. Nxd5, and White would have a promising game. But after the move in the text White should recapture on d5 with his Queen, because after 11. Nxg5 hxg 12. Nxd5, Black has a strong retort 12. ... Rh4! , threatening 13. ... Rd4.

| 11. Qd2xd5 | Nb8-c6 |
| 12. Bf1xc4 | ... |

But not 12. Qxc5 Be6 13. Bxc4?, in view of 13. ... Be7 14. Qb5 a6 15. Qxb7 Na5, and Black would win a piece.

| 12. ... | 0-0 |
| 13. 0-0 | ... |

On 13. Qxc5, Black would have a rather annoying retort 13. ... Bg4! If 13. Qe4, then 13. ... Re8, and Black would again have counterplay, threatening to win the Pawn on e5.

| 13. ... | Qd8xd5 |
| 14. Bc4xd5 | ... |

14. Nxd5 would be worse in view of 14. ... Be6, with the threat of Nc6-a5

14. ...	Nc6-b4!
(No. 134)	
15. Nf3xg5	...

The Ubilava-Dorfman game (52nd USSR Championship, Semifinal, 1984), played after this game, proceeded as follows: 15. Be4 (if 15. Bc4, then 15. ... Bf5!) 15. ... f5! 16. Bd5+ (16. exf Bxf6! , or 16. Bb1 Be6) 16. ... Nxd5 17. Nxd5 Bd8! 18. Rfd1 Re8 19. Rac1 b6 20. b4 cxb 21. Nxb4 Bb7 22. Nc6 Bg5!

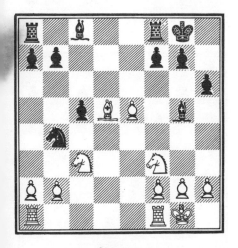

No. 134

23. Nxg5 hxg 24. Rd7 Bxc6 25. Rxc6 Rad8, and the game was soon drawn.

15. ...	Nb4xd5

On 15. ... hxg 16. Be4! would be strong (16. ... f5 17. exf!).

16. Nc3xd5	h6xg5
17. f2-f4!	...

Many commentators are of the opinion that this is the clearest way of keeping the game balanced, whereas after 17. Rfd1 Be6 18. Nc7 Rad8, Black would seize the initiative.

17. ...	g5xf4
18. Rf1xf4	...

Another possibility, also deserving consideration, is 18. Ne7+ Kh7 19. Rxf4 g6 20. Rc1 (but not 20. Rf6 Kg7 21. Raf1 Bd7 22. e6?! Bxe6 23. Nxg6 Rfe8!) 20. ... b6 21. b4! Be6 (21. ... cxb?! 22. Nxc8 Raxc8 23. Rxc8 Rxc8 24. Rxf7+, followed by 25. Rxa7) 22. bxc Rfe8 23. Nc6, and a probable draw.

18. ...	Rf8-d8!
19. Nd5-c7	Ra8-b8
20. Ra1-f1	Rd8-d7
21. Nc7-b5	Rd7-e7
22. Nb5xa7	Bc8-d7
23. a2-a4	Rb8-a8

Black would gain nothing by playing either 23. ... Rd8, because of 24. b4! Bxa4 25. bxc Be8 26. Rb1; or 23. ... b6, because of 24. Nb5 Bxb5 25. axb Rd8 26. e6 fxe 27. b4 (A. Mikhalchishin).

24. Na7-b5	Bd7xb5

Not so clear is 24. ... g5! ? 25. Re4.

25. a4xb5	Ra8-a5

The continuation 25. ... Ra2 26. b4 cxb 27. Rxb4 Rxe5 28. h4 Ree2 29. Rg4 Rab2 30. Rg5 Kf8 31. h5 f6 32. h6! would also lead to a draw.

26. b5-b6	Ra5-b5

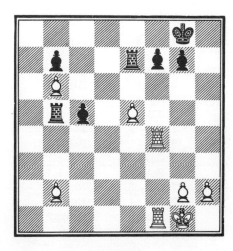

No. 135

27. b2-b4!	c5xb4
28. Rf1-b1	b4-b3
29. Rf4-f3	b3-b2
30. Rf3-f2	Re7xe5

Or 30. ... Rxb6 31. Rfxb2 Rxb2 32. Rxb2 Kf8 33. Kf2! etc.

31. Rf2xb2

Game drawn. After either 31. ... Re1+ 32. Rxe1 Rxb2 33. Re8+ Kh7 34. Re7 Rxb6 35. Rxf7, or 31. ... Rxb2 32. Rxb2 Re6 33. Kf2 Kf8 34. h4 Ke7 35. Kf3 Kd7 36. g4 Kc6 37. h5 f6 38. Kf4, there is no doubt that the game would end in a draw.

Time: 1.56-1.38

GAME TWENTY-TWO

Catalan Opening

G. Kasparov	A. Karpov
1. d2-d4	Ng8-f6
2. c2-c4	e7-e6
3. g2-g3	d7-d5
4. Bf1-g2	Bf8-e7
5. Ng1-f3	0-0
6. 0-0	d5xc4
7. Qd1-c2	a7-a6
8. a2-a4	Bc8-d7
9. Qc2xc4	Bd7-c6
10. Bc1-g5	a6-a5
11. Nb1-c3	Nb8-a6
12. Ra1-c1	Qd8-d6
13. Nf3-e5	Bc6xg2
14. Kg1xg2	c7-c6

14. ... Qb4 is also worth considering.

15. Bg5xf6	g7xf6
16. Ne5-f3	Rf8-d8

No. 136

17. Rf1-d1 ...

The continuation 17. e4! Qb4 18. Qe2 would be more vigorous.

17. ...	Qd6-b4
18. Qc4-a2	Rd8-d7
19. e2-e3	Ra8-d8
20. Rc1-c2	

Game drawn.
Time: 1.38-1.24

GAME TWENTY-THREE

Queen's Gambit Declined

A. Karpov	G. Kasparov
1. Ng1-f3	d7-d5
2. d2-d4	Ng8-f6

3. c2-c4	e7-e6
4. Nb1-c3	Bf8-e7
5. Bc1-g5	h7-h6
6. Bg5-h4	0-0
7. Ra1-c1	d5xc4
8. e2-e3	...

On 8. e4, 8. ... Nc6! would be a good move (Tukmakov-Belyavsky, Tilburg, 1984).

8. ...	c7-c5
9. Bf1xc4	c5xd4
10. Nf3xd4	Bc8-d7
11. 0-0	Nb8-c6
12. Nd4-b3	Ra8-c8
13. Bc4-e2	...

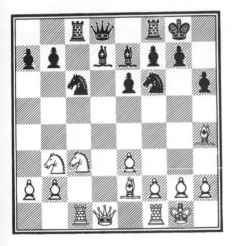

No. 137

13. ...   Nf6-d5!

The manoeuvre which leads to equality. If 14. Bg3, then 14. ... Ncb4.

14. Bh4xe7	Nc6xe7
15. Nc3xd5	Ne7xd5
16. Rc1xc8	Qd8xc8

17. Qd1-d4	Qc8-b8
18. Be2-f3	Nd5-f6
19. Nb3-c5	Bd7-b5
20. Rf1-d1	b7-b6
21. Nc5-e4	Nf6xe4
22. Bf3xe4	Rf8-c8

Game drawn.
Time: 1.43-1.22

16 November 1984

GAME TWENTY-FOUR

English Opening

G. Kasparov   A. Karpov

1. Ng1-f3	Ng8-f6
2. c2-c4	c7-c5
3. Nb1-c3	Nb8-c6
4. d2-d4	c5xd4
5. Nf3xd4	e7-e6
6. g2-g3	Qd8-b6
7. Nd4-b3	...

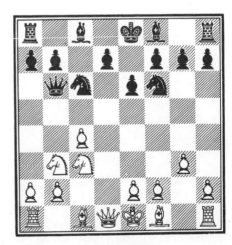

No. 138

201

7. ...	d7-d5! ?

A currently popular variation introduced by Yugoslav players.

8. c4xd5	Nf6xd5
9. Bf1-g2	Nd5xc3
10. b2xc3	Bf8-e7
11. 0-0	0-0
12. Bc1-e3	Qb6-c7
13. Nb3-d4	Rf8-d8
14. Qd1-a4	Rc8-d7
15. Nd4xc6	Bd7xc6
16. Bg2xc6	b7xc6
17. c3-c4	

White could have retained some pressure on the Queen's side by playing 17. Rab1.

Game drawn.

Time: 1.56-1.38

19 November 1984

GAME TWENTY-FIVE

Queen's Gambit Declined

A. Karpov	G. Kasparov
1. Ng1-f3	d7-d5
2. d2-d4	Ng8-f6
3. c2-c4	e7-e6
4. Nb1-c3	Bf8-e7
5. Bc1-g5	h7-h6
6. Bg5-h4	0-0
7. e2-e3	b7-b6
8. Ra1-c1	Bc8-b7
9. Bf1-e2	Nb8-d7
10. c4xd5	...

In the seventeenth game, Karpov played 10. 0-0 c5 11. Bg3, but gained no advantage.

10. ...	e6xd5
11. 0-0	c7-c5
12. d4xc5	b6xc5

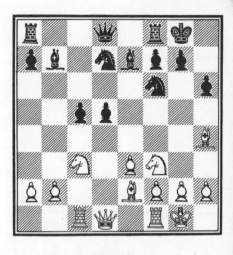

No. 139

13. Rc1-c2!	...

An improvement over the move in this position during the first game of the 1981 World Title Match in Merano, where after 13. Qc2 Rc8 14. Rfd1 Qb6 15. Qb1? (15. Qb3 is correct) 15. ... Rfd8 16. Rc2 Qe6 17. Bg3 Nh5 18. Rcd2 Nxg3 19. hxg3 Nf6, Karpov, playing Black, conveniently regrouped his forces, and the breakthrough d5-d4 soon brought him victory.

13. ...	Ra8-c8
14. Rc2-d2	Qd8-b6
15. Qd1-b3!	...

White's plan involves the exchange of the Queens, followed by pressure on the opponent's centre. The defence Kasparov has found is probably the best one.

15. ...	Rf8-d8
16. Rf1-d1	Qb6xb3
17. a2xb3	Nd7-b6
18. Nf3-e5	Kg8-f8
19. h2-h3	a7-a6!
20. Be2-f3	Bb7-a8

Having brought the b5-square under control and having prepared to parry the threat of Ne5-c4, Black intends to answer 21. Ra1?! by 21. ... d4!, and the d-Pawn, previously weak, would become strong.

21. Ne5-g4	...

After 21. Bxf6 Bxf6 22. Ng4, the variation 22. ... Bxc3 23. bxc a5! is sufficient for equality; for instance, 24. Ra2 c4 25. Rxa5 cxb 26. Rb5 Na4 27. Rxb3 Nxc3, followed by Nc3-e4 (E. Geller).

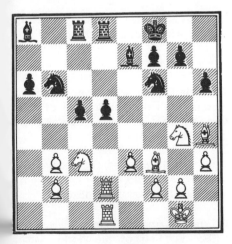

No. 140

21. ...	Nf6-g8!

Now the game is about even, whether 22. Bxe7+ Nxe7, or 22. Bg3 c4 23.

Nxd5 Nxd5 24. Bxd5 Bxd5 25. Rxd5 cxb.

Game drawn.
Time: 2.05-1.34

21 November 1984

GAME TWENTY-SIX

English Opening

G. Kasparov	A. Karpov
1. Ng1-f3	Ng8-f6
2. c2-c4	c7-c5
3. Nb1-c3	Nb8-c6
4. d2-d4	c5xd4
5. Nf3xd4	e7-e6
6. g2-g3	Qd8-b6
7. Nd4-b3	d7-d5
8. c4xd5	Nf6xd5
9. Bf1-g2	Nd5xc3
10. b2xc3	Bf8-e7
11. 0-0	...

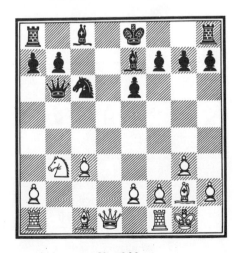

No. 141

11. ...	e6-e5

Avoiding 11. ... 0-0 12. Be3 Qc7 13. Nd4, which occurred in the twenty-fourth game of the match.

12. Bc1-e3	Qb6-c7
13. Nb3-c5	0-0
14. Qd1-a4	Be7xc5!

The introduction to an interesting defensive plan based on a Pawn sacrifice. Another possibility, 14. ... Rd8, would fail because of 15. Na6! (Psakhis-Kramling, Scotland, 1984).

15. Be3xc5	Rf8-d8
16. Rf1-d1	Bc8-e6
17. h2-h3	Rd8xd1+!
18. Ra1xd1	Ra8-d8
19. Rd1xd8+	Qc7xd8
20. Rc5xa7	...

No. 142

20. ...	Qd8-a8
21. Bg2xc6	b7xc6
22. Kg1-h2	h7-h5
23. Qa4-a5	f7-f6

Game drawn.
Time: 1.23-1.10

23 and 24 November 1984

GAME TWENTY-SEVEN

Queen's Gambit Declined

| A. Karpov | G. Kasparov |

1. Ng1-f3	d7-d5
2. d2-d4	Ng8-f6
3. c2-c4	e7-e6
4. Nb1-c3	Bf8-e7
5. Bc1-g5	h7-h6
6. Bg5xf6	Be7xf6
7. e2-e3	...

As the twenty-first game showed, against 7. Qd2 Black has a rather good reply 7. ... dxc.

| 7. ... | 0-0 |
| 8. Qd1-c2 | ... |

Karpov has chosen the line previously adopted with success by ... Kasparov!

| 8. ... | c7-c5 |

The main line. At least it was considered as such until the fourth game of their second match, in which Kasparov came up with 8. ... Na6! ?

9. d4xc5	...
(No. 143)	
9. ...	d5xc4! ?

In the Kasparov-Timman encounter (USSR vs. Rest of the World Match, London, 1984). Black responded with 9. ... Qa5 10. cxd exd 11. 0-0-0! Be6 12. Nxd5 Rc8 13. Kb1! , and Timman failed to solve his defensive problems. Instead of 11. ... Be6, Black should perhaps have played 11. ... Bxc3 12. Qxc3 Qxc3+

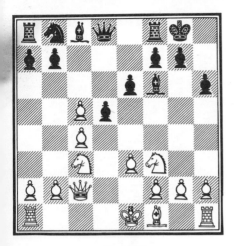

No. 143

(12. ... Qxa2 would be dangerous because of 13. Bd3!) 13. bxc Be6 14. Nd4 Nd7 (if 14. ... Rc8, then 15. e4! , or even 15. Nxe6 fxe 16. c4!) 15. c6 bxc 16. Nxc6 Kh8 17. Nd4 Rfe8 18. Kd2 Rab8, with counterplay for the lost pawn (Novikov-Lputyan, Yerevan, 1984).

The latest preference is the plan beginning 9. ... Nc6.

10. Bf1xc4	Qd8-a5
11. 0-0	Bf6xc3

If 11. ... Qxc5?! 12. Ne4 Qe7 13. Nxf6+ Qxf6 14. Rfd1, White's pressure would be appreciable.

| 12. Qc2xc3 | Qa5xc3 |

At this juncture, 12. ... Qxc5 would give Black more chances for equality than on the previous move; for instance, 13. b4 (otherwise 13. ... Nc6 would follow) 13. ... Qe7 14. Rfd1 (if 14. b5?! , then 14. ... Nd7, and 15. ... Nc5) 14. ... a6, followed by the deployment of Black's Queen-side pieces (Levin-Polovodin, Smolensk, 1984).

| 13. b2xc3 | Nb8-d7 |
| 14. c5-c6 | ... |

A typical move in such a position. The doomed Pawn perishes, but weakens Black's Q-side Pawn structure (A. Suetin).

14. ...	b7xc6
15. Ra1-b1	Nd7-b6
16. Bc4-e2	c6-c5

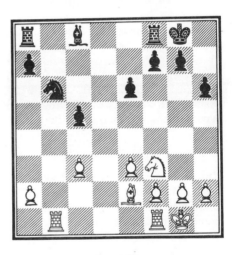

No. 144

In the resulting endgame, White has retained the initiative, because he commands a little more space and his pieces are better developed (E. Geller).

17. Rf1-c1! ...

A subtle move to which all commentators gave an exclamation mark. The seemingly natural 17. Rfd1 would only lead to exchanging the Rooks, while the World

205

Champion wishes to maintain the tension and organize an attack on Black's weak Pawns.

17. ...	Bc8-b7?!

17. ... Bd7! would be safer; for instance, 18. Kf1 Rfd8 19. Rb3! (19. Bb5 Bxb5 20. Rxb5 Rac8 21. Ra5 Rc7 leads to equality) 19. ... Rac8 20. Ra3 Rc7 21. c4 Ba4 22. Rb1 Be8 23. Ra5, giving only a slight advantage to White (Novikov-Sturua, Lvov, 1985).

18. Kg1-f1	Bb7-d5

The more cautious 18. ... Bc6! ?, which would prevent the incursion of White's Rook to b5, deserves consideration. Nevertheless, after 19. Ne5 Ba4 20. Bb5 (or 20. Ba6! ?) 20. ... Bxb5 21. Rxb5 Rfc8 22. Nd3 c4 23. Nb2, White would still have the advantage (E. Geller).

19. Rb1-b5!	Nb6-d7?

This leads to the loss of a Pawn. After 19. ... Rac8 (but not 19. ... Bxa2? 20. c4!) 20. Ra5 Rc7 21. c4 Ba8, Black could still defend himself.

20. Rb5-a5!	Rf8-b8

To counterbalance the activity of the White Rook, Kasparov attempts to gain counterplay along the b-file. Karpov's next moves set out to prevent the invasion of the Black Rook and, as suddenly becomes evident, are also aimed at the Black c5-Pawn (E. Geller).

21. c3-c4	Bd5-c6
22. Nf3-e1!	Rb8-b4
(No. 145)	
23. Be2-d1!	...

No. 145

It is this move that Kasparov possibly underestimated. Black hoped to parry the threat of 23. Nd3 by 23. ... Ra4. Accordingly, White has set up control over the a4-square. Now the manoeuvre Ne1-d3xc5 is inevitable (M. Tal).

23. ...	Rb4-b7
24. f2-f3	Ra8-d8
25. Ne1-d3	g7-g5
26. Bd1-b3!	...

This puts a stop to all attempts at activity by Black. The remaining part of the game can be won by White as a matter of technique.

26. ...	Kg8-f8
27. Nd3xc5	Nd7xc5
28. Ra5xc5	Rd8-d6
29. Kf1-e2	Kf8-e7
30. Rc1-d1	Rd6xd1
31. Ke2xd1	Ke7-d6
32. Rc5-a5	f7-f5

White's plan is to march his King to the centre and to drive away the Black King.

Not wishing to defend himself passively, Kasparov makes an important decision: at the cost of weakening his Pawns he tries to counterplay on the King's side (E. Geller).

| 33. Kd1-e2 | h6-h5 |
| 34. e3-e4 | ... |

Availing himself of the opportunity, White opens up the centre, thus expanding the scope of his Rook. 34. Kd3, intending e3-e4-e5+, would be equally strong.

34. ...	f5xe4
35. f3xe4	Bc6xe4
36. Ra5xg5	Be4-f5
37. Ke2-e3	...

According to N. Popov, 37. h4! ?, pinning down the Black Pawn on h5, is worth considering. For instance, 37. ... Rf7 38. Ke3 Bg4 39. c5+ Kc6 40. Ba4+ Kc7 41. Be8 Rh7 42. Bg6 Rh6 (or 42. ... Rg7 43. Kf4) 43. Be4; or 37. ... Rh7 38. Ke3 Bg4 (38. ... Kc5 39. g3) 39. c5+ Kc6 40. Bc2, and White should win.

37. ...	h5-h4
38. Ke3-d4	e6-e5+
39. Kd4-c3	Bf5-b1
40. a2-a3	Rb7-e7
41. Rg5-g4	...

The sealed move. In the adjournment session, Karpov very neatly exploits his extra Pawn.

| 41. ... | h4-h3 |

If 41. ... Rh7, then White would simply play 42. h3, while after 41. ... e4, White would have won, according to E. Geller,

as follows: 42. Bd1 Rf7 43. Kd4 Rf2 44. c5+ Ke7 45. Bb3 (or 45. Ke3 Ra2 46. Rg7+) 45. ... Rd2+ 46. Kc3 Rd3+ 47. Kb2 e3 48. Ba4 e2 49. Re4+.

| 42. g2-g3 | ... |

White could also have played 42. gxh.

| 42. ... | Re7-e8 |
| 43. Rg4-g7! | ... |

In this way, White wins by force, his c-Pawn deciding the issue.

43. ...	Re8-f8
44. Rg7xa7	Rf8-f2
45. Kc3-b4	...

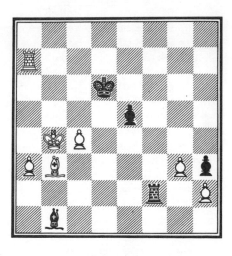

No. 146

| 45. ... | Rf2xh2 |

45. ... Rb2 would also lose because of 46. c5+ Kc6 47. Kc4 Bc2 48. Ra6+ Kc7 49. Rxc2 Rxc2+ 50. Kd5 Rxh2 (or 50. ... Rd2+ 51. Kxe5, and the White King shields itself with the g-Pawn).

51. Ra7+ Kb8 (51. ... Kc8 52. Rh7
Rh1 53. Kd6! h2 54. Rh8+ Kb7 55.
c6+, etc.) 52. Rh7 Rh1 53. Ke4! h2
54. Kf3 Ra1 55. Rxh2 Rxa3+ 56. Kg4
Rc3 57. Re2 Rxc5 58. Kf5; or 54. ...
e4+ 55. Kg2 Rc1 56. Kxh2 Rxc5 57.
Re7 Rc4 58. g4 e3 59. Kg3 (E. Geller).

46. c4-c5+	Kd6-c6
47. Bb3-a4+	Kc6-d5
48. Ra7-d7+	Kd5-e4

Nothing would be changed by 48. ...
Ke6 49. c6 Rb2+ 50. Bb3+ Rxb3+
51. Kxb3 Be4 52. Rd8 Bxc6 53. Rh8
Bg2 54. a4 Kf5 55. Rh4 (N. Popov).

49. c5-c6	Rh2-b2+
50. Kb4-a5!	Rb2-b8
51. c6-c7	Rb8-c8
52. Ka5-b6	Ke4-e3
53. Ba4-c6	h3-h2
54. g3-g4	Rc8-h8
55. Rd7-d1!	Bb1-a2
56. Rd1-e1+	Ke3-f4
57. Re1-e4+	Kf4-g3
58. Re4xe5	Kg3xg4
59. Re5-e2	

Black resigns, the score now 5:0 (with
22 draws) to Karpov.
Time: 3.31-3.33

28 November 1984

GAME TWENTY-EIGHT

Petroff's Defence

| G. Kasparov | A. Karpov |

1. e2-e4	e7-e5
2. Ng1-f3	Ng8-f6
3. Nf3xe5	d7-d6

4. Ne5-f3	Nf6xe4
5. d2-d4	d6-d5
6. Bf1-d3	Nb8-c6
7. 0-0	Bc8-g4
8. Rf1-e1	Bf8-e7
9. c2-c4	Ne4-f6
10. c4xd5	Bg4xf3! ?

This continuation was introduced by
V. Smyslov in his match with R. Huebner
(Felden, 1983). Previously, 10. ... Nxd5
was played here.

| 11. Qd1xf3 | Qd8xd5 |

No. 147

12. Qf3-h3! ?	Nc6xd4
13. Nb1-c3	Qd5-d7
14. Qh3xd7+	Kd8xd7
15. Bc1-e3	Nd4-e6
16. Ra1-d1	Be7-d6
17. Bd3-f5	Kd7-e7
18. Nc3-b5	Rh8-d8
19. Nb5xd6	c7xd6
20. h2-h3	b7-b6
21. g2-g4	h7-h6
22. Be3-d4	Ra8-c8
23. Bd3-c3	g7-g6

| 24. Bf5-c2 | h6-h5 |
| 25. f2-f3 | |

White's powerful Bishops give sufficient compensation for the lost Pawn.

Game drawn.

Time: 1.45-2.09

3 December 1984

GAME TWENTY-NINE

Semi-Slav Defence

A. Karpov	G. Kasparov
1. Ng1-f3	d7-d5
2. d2-d4	Ng8-f6
3. c2-c4	e7-e6
4. Nb1-c3	c7-c6
5. e2-e3	Nb8-d7
6. Bf1-d3	d5xc4
7. Bd3xc4	b7-b5
8. Bc4-e2	Bc8-b7
9. a2-a3	...

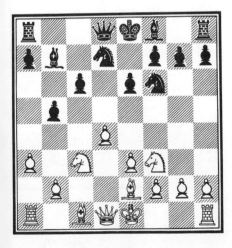

No. 148

| 9. ... | b5-b4 |

A new and good reply to White's unambitious plan initiated by 8. Be2.

10. Nc3-a4	b4xa3
11. b2xa3	Bf8-e7
12. 0-0	0-0
13. Bc1-b2	c6-c5

Black gets rid of his weak Pawn, the resulting position being almost symmetrical.

Game drawn.

Time: 1.39-0.51

5 December 1984

GAME THIRTY

Petroff's Defence

G. Kasparov	A. Karpov
1. e2-e4	e7-e5
2. Ng1-f3	Ng8-f6
3. Nf3xe5	d7-d6
4. Ne5-f3	Nf6xe4
5. d2-d4	d6-d5
6. Bf1-d3	Bf8-e7
7. 0-0	Nb8-c6
8. Rf1-e1	Bc8-g4
9. c2-c4	Ne4-f6

(No. 149)

10. Nb1-c3	d5xc4
11. Bd3xc4	0-0
12. Bc1-e3	Bg4xf3

In this way Black has completely solved his opening problems.

13. Qd1xf3	Nc6xd4
14. Be3xd4	Qd8xd4
15. Re1xe7	Qd4xc4

No. 149

16. Qf3xb7	c7-c6
17. Qb7-b3	Qc4xb3
18. a2xb3	Ra8-b8
19. Ra1-a3	Rf8-e8
20. Re7xe8+	Rb8xe8

Game drawn.
Time: 1.02-1.19

7 December 1984

GAME THIRTY-ONE

Queen's Gambit Declined

A. Karpov	G. Kasparov
1. Ng1-f3	d7-d5
2. d2-d4	Ng8-f6
3. c2-c4	e7-e6
4. Nb1-c3	Bf8-e7
5. Bc1-g5	h7-h6
6. Bg5-h4	0-0
7. e2-e3	b7-b6
8. Ra1-c1	Bc8-b7

9. Bf1-e2	Nb8-d7
10. c4xd5	e6xd5
11. 0-0	c7-c5
12. Qd1-a4	...

In the twenty-fifth game, after 12. dxc bxc 13. Rc2 Rc8 14. Rd2 Qb6 15. Qb3 Rfd8 16. Rfd1 Qxb3 17. axb Nb6, Black succeeded in neutralizing the moderate advantage his opponent had in the endgame.

12. ...	a7-a6

Black could carry out the typical "unloading" operation in the centre by 12. ... Ne4! ?, 13. Bxe7 Qxe7, 14. Ba6 Ndf6, but he prefers to avoid exchanging the light-squared Bishops (E. Geller).

13. d4xc5	b6xc5
14. Rf1-d1	Qd8-b6
15. Qa4-b3!	...

No. 150

15. ...	Qb6-a7?!

210

An important decision. In the event of 15. ... Qxb3 16. axb, White would have a more favourable endgame than in the twenty-fifth game. For instance, 16. ... Rfd8 (16. ,.. Nb6!?) 17. Ne1 Nb6 18. Bf3 Rac8 (but not 18. ... Rd7? 19. Nd3 g5 20. Bg3 Rc8, because of 21. Ne5 Rdd8 22. Nc4!, Lputyan-Dorfman, 52nd USSR Championship Semifinal, 1984) 19. Nd3 Ba8 20. Ra1 d4 21. Bxa8 Rxa8 22. exd cxd 23. Ne2, and Black, according to Lputyan, has not yet reached full equality.

| 16. Bh4-g3 | Ra8-d8 |

Black should have placed his Rooks on c8 and d8, but Kasparov pays attention mainly to the advance d5-d4 (V. Baghirov).

If 16. ... Rfd8 is followed by d5-d4, then the f7-square would be weakened. (E. Geller)

| 17. Nf3-e1! | ... |

Those gathered in the press room mainly considered 17. Ne5!?, but the unexpected retreat of the White Knight poses rather more problems for Black, because he has to advance his d-Pawn without the necessary preparation, in order to defend himself against the unpleasant 18. Bf3!. As a result, this Pawn is a weakness rather than a strength.

17. ...	d5-d4
18. e3xd4	c5xd4
19. Nc3-a4	Rd8-c8

The move 19. ... Bd5 also deserves consideration. After the move actually played, White will win a Pawn almost by force (A. Suetin).

| 20. Rc1xc8 | ... |

Having thought for nearly half an hour, Karpov finds a move to a very difficult game for the Challenger (Ye. Vasyukov).

| 20. ... | Rf8xc8 |
| 21. Be2-c4 | Rc8-f8 |

No. 151

| 22. Qb3-d3! | ... |

The continuation 22. Nd3 (or 22. Nc2 Nc5 23. Nxc5 Bxc5 24. Be5?! d3!, although 24. Ne1 would be stronger) 22. ... Ne4 23. Ne5 Nxe5 24. Bxe5 Bf6 25. Bxf6 Nxf6 26. Nb6 Bc6 would be unclear (E. Geller).

| 22. ... | Bb7-c6 |

After 22. ... Nc5 23. Qxd4, the reply 23. ... Rd8? fails against 24. Qxd8+! Bxd8 25. Rxd8+ Kh7 26. Bb8! Qa8 27. Nb6, and the Black Queen is trapped (A. Lilienthal).

23. Bc4-b3!   ...

"Just in case", the Bishop protects two White pieces at once—a Knight and a Rook. This is important, for example, in the variation 23. ... Nc5 24. Nxc5 Bxc5 25. Be5 Ng4 26. Bxd4 (A. Mikhalchishin).

23. ...   Nf6-e4!

In the event of 23. ... Bxa4 24. Bxa4 Nc5 (if 24. ... Bc5, then 25. Nc2) 25. Qxd4 Rd8 26. Qc4, Black would be left without any compensation for the lost Pawn.

24. Qd3xd4   Qa7-b7
25. Bb3-d5!   ...

A timely simplifying manoeuvre.

25. ...   Nd7-f6
26. Bd5xc6   Qb7xc6
27. b2-b3   Rf8-e8
28. Qd4-d3?!   ...

As all the commentators have noted, after 28. Qc4! Black's counterplay would not compensate him for the lost Pawn.

28. ...   h6-h5!

Creating an outpost on g4 for his Knight.

29. Qd3-c4   Qc6-b7
30. Ne1-f3   Re8-c8
31. Qc4-e2   Nf6-g4
32. Nf3-e5   Ne4xg3

If the move h6-h5 had not been played, this exchange would be ineffective because of Qe2xg4. Now it is the Black Knight on g4 that plays a leading role (A. Suetin).

33. h2xg3   Qb7-b5!

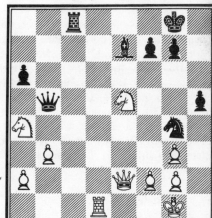

No. 152

34. Ne5-c4   ...

After 34. Qxb5 axb 35. Nxg4 hxg 36. Nb6 Rc2, Black has nothing to fear (V. Baghirov).

34. ...   Be7-f6
35. Na4-b6   Rc8-e8

Kasparov offers a draw which is accepted. With little time to spare, and the insecure position of his King, Karpov could hardly hope to exploit his extra Pawn.
     Time: 2.28-2.22

12 December 1984

GAME THIRTY-TWO

Queen's Indian Defence

G. Kasparov   A. Karpov

1. d2-d4   Ng8-f6
2. c2-c4   e7-e6

```
3. Ng1-f3        b7-b6
4. Nb1-c3        ...
```

The Rubinstein Variation, the subject of dispute in the first half of the match, has disappeared from the scene since the eighteenth game, in which the World Champion demonstrated a clear method of equalizing (I. Dorfman).

```
4. ...           Bc8-b7
5. a2-a3         d7-d5
6. c4xd5         Nf6xd5
7. Qd1-c2        ...
```

The tenth game continued 7. e3 Nd7 8. Bd3 N5f6! ? 9. e4 c5 10. d5 (10. Bf4! ?) 10. ... exd 11. exd Bd6, and Black successfully solved his opening problems.

```
7. ...           Nb8-d7?!
```

Many commentators believe that this is the primary cause of Black's difficulties. The variation 7. ... c5 (7. ... g6! ?) 8. dxc (if 8. e4 Nxc3 9. bxc, then, as is known, 9. ... Nd7 10. Bd3 Qc7! is good for Black) 8. ... Bxc5 9. Bg5 Qc8! 10. Rc1 h6 has recently become fashionable. (**No. 153**)

```
8. Nc3xd5        ...
```

A new and dangerous plan in this position. After 8. ... Bxd5, White can play 9. Bg5 Be7 (9. ... f6 is risky and 9. ... Qc8 10. e4 Bb7 11. 0-0-0 is also in White's favour) 10. Bxe7 Qxe7 11. Qxc7 0-0 12. Rc1, or 12. Ne5, and Black has no compensation for the lost Pawn.

```
8. ...           e6xd5
9. Bc1-g5!       f7-f6
```

No. 153

A risky line. Since the Black c7-Pawn is insufficiently protected, Black would, after 9. ... Be7 10. Bxe7, need to recapture the Bishop with his King, while after 9. ... Nf6 the simple 10. Bxf6 would be unpleasant. Therefore, 9. ... Qc8 comes into consideration, as M. Yudovich suggested.

I. Dorfman, however, is of the opinion that 9. ... Qc8 is rather dubious in view of 10. g3, followed by Bf1-h3.

```
10. Bg5-f4       c7-c5
11. g2-g3!       g7-g6
```

In the event of 11. ... Be7, 12. Bh3 (12. ... 0-0? 13. Bf5!) would be promising.

```
12. h2-h4!       Qd8-e7
13. Bf1-g2       Bf8-g7
14. h4-h5        f6-f5
```

After 14. ... g5 there could follow 15. h6 gxf 16. hxg Qxg7 17. Nh4 with a potent attack.

The main disadvantage of Black's position is that his King has no refuge. Moreover, the Black Pawns on d5 and g6 may become convenient targets for the White pieces (Ye. Vasyukov).

15. Qc2-d2	Bg7-f6

Ye. Vasyukov suggested 15. ... Nf6, with the idea of countering 16. h6 (16. hxg Ne4!) with 16. ... Bf8 17. Bg5 Ne4. But White could play stronger 17. Ng5 Ne4 (17. ... Qd7 18. Qe3+ Be7 19. Ne6) 18. Bxe4 fxe (18. ... dxe 19. d5!) 19. Be5 Rg8 20. Qf4 with an attack.

16. Ra1-c1!	Ra8-c8

The only defence against the threat of Rc1-c3-e3.

17. Rc1-c3	Rc8-c6

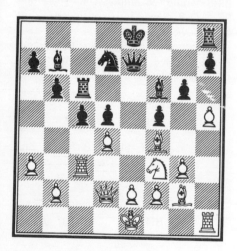

No. 154

18. Rc3-e3	...

18. Bg5! , with the threat of 19. hxg, would be very strong here (L. Polugayevsky). After 18. Bg5! Black could not play 18. ... cxd because of 19. Rxc6 Bxc6 20. hxg (R. Vaganyan).

The thrust 18. Bg5! would have exposed the weakness of the black squares in the enemy camp. For instance, 18. ... Rg8 (or 18. ... 0-0 19. hxg hxg 20. Bxf6 Bxf6 21. Qh6) 19. hxg hxg 20. Re3 Re6 21. Bxf6 Nxf6 22. Rxe6 Qxe6 23. Qf4, and the White Queen is ready for the decisive invasion (I. Dorfman).

18. ...	Rc6-e6
19. Re3xe6	Qe7xe6
20. Nf3-g5	Qe6-e7

Black should not, of course, exchange on g5 because the black squares in his camp would be irreparably weakened (M. Yudovich).

21. d4xc5	...

The line 21. hxg hxg 22. Rxh8+ Bxh8 23. dxc Qxc5 (23. ... Nxc5 24. Bxd5) 24. Ne6 Qa5 25. Nc7+ would also be tempting.

21. ...	Nd7xc5
22. h5xg6	d5-d4!

An ingenious attempt to change the unfavourable course of events. (**No. 155**)

23. g6-g7?!	...

The line 23. Nf7! ? Bxg2 24. Rh2 would lead to great complications. According to I. Dorfman, the correct plan is 23. Bxb7 Qxb7 24. f3 (but not 24. Rxh7?? Rxh7 25. gxh Qh1 mate) 24. ... hxg 25. Rxh8+ Bxh8 26. b4! Nd7 27. Qa2 Nf8 28. Ne6!

No. 155

23. ...	Bf6xg7
24. Bg2xb7	Qe7xb7
25. f2-f3	Qb7-d5! ?

Never at a loss, Karpov offers a Pawn in the hope of gaining sufficient counterplay to enable him to draw. The line 25. ... h6 26. Nh3, followed by Nh3-f2-d3, would lead to a positional advantage for White who would have a good Knight; also, Black's Pawns would be weak (I. Dorfman).

26. Rh1xh7	Rh8xh7
27. Ng5xh7	Qd5-b3?

A time-pressure mistake. As many commentators have noted, after 27. ... d3! White could hardly hope to win. For instance, 28. b4 Ne6 29. Qxd3 Qxd3 30. exd Nxf4 31. gxf Bb2.

28. Bf4-d6!	Nc5-e6
29. Nh7-g5	Bg7-h6
30. Bd6-f4	Bh6xg5
31. Bf4xg5	Nc6xg5

32. Qd2xg5	Qb3xb2
33. Qg5xf5	Qb2-c1+

The resulting Queen and Pawn ending is very difficult for Black, being a Pawn behind and having his King awkwardly placed. But the checks only speed up the denouement, because they drive the White King to a better position. Black should have captured the Pawn on a3 at once to try to promote his b-Pawn sooner (M. Yudovich).

34. Ke1-f2	Qc1-e3+
35. Kf2-f1	Qe3-c1+

Even now, 35. ... Qxa3 would be better.

36. Kf1-g2	Qc1xa3
37. Qf5-h5+	Ke8-d7
38. Qh5-g4+	Kd7-c6
39. Qg4xd4	b6-b5
40. g3-g4	b5-b4

No. 156

41. g4-g5

The sealed move.

Black resigns without resuming play, because after 41. ... b3 42. Qe4+! (but not 42. g6 b2 43. g7 Qa2!) 42. ... Kb6 (if 42. ... Kd6, or 42. ... Kc5, then 43. Qe8! , threatening 44. Qf8+) 43. Qe6+ Ka5 44. Qd5+ Ka6 45. g6 Qe7 46. Qxb3 Qxe2+ 47. Kh3, White would quickly attain his object.

The score is now 5:1 (with 26 draws) in favour of Karpov.

Time: 2.34-2.29

17 December 1984

GAME THIRTY-THREE

Semi-Slav Defence

A. Karpov	G. Kasparov
1. Ng1-f3	d7-d5
2. d2-d4	Ng8-f6
3. c2-c4	e7-e6
4. Nb1-c3	c7-c6
5. e2-e3	Nb8-d7
6. Qd1-c2	...

In the twenty-ninth game White played 6. Bd3.

6. ...	Bf8-d6
7. e3-e4	...
(No. 157)	
7. ...	e6-e5! ?

This is an innovation. Black usually responded here with 7. ... dxe 8. Nxe4 Nxe4 9. Qxe4 e5.

8. c4xd5	c6xd5
9. e4xd5	e5xd4
10. Nf3xd4	0-0
11. Bf1-e2	Nd7-b6
12. 0-0	Nb6xd5

No. 157

13. Nc3xd5	Nf6xd5
14. Rf1-d1	Qd8-e7
15. Be2-f3	Rf8-e8!

By this tactical retort Black has completely equalized the game.

16. g2-g3	Bc8-h3
17. Bc1-d2	Bd6-e5
18. Bf3xd5	Be5xd4
19. Bd2-c3	Bd4xc3
20. Qc2xc3	

Game drawn.
Time: 1.37-1.10

19 December 1984

GAME THIRTY-FOUR

Queen's Gambit Declined

G. Kasparov	A. Karpov
1. d2-d4	Ng8-f6
2. c2-c4	e7-e6

3. Ng1-f3	d7-d5
4. Nb1-c3	Bf8-e7
5. Bc1-g5	h7-h6
6. Bg5-h4	0-0
7. e2-e3	b7-b6
8. Bf1-e2	Bc8-b7
9. Ra1-c1	d5xc4
10. Be2xc4	Nb8-d7
11. 0-0	a7-a6
12. a2-a4	c7-c5
13. Qd1-e2	...

19. Ne4-g3	Qf5-f6
20. Ng3-e4	Qf6-f5

Game drawn.
Time: 1.20-0.59

GAME THIRTY-FIVE

Sicilian Defence
Rauzer's Attack

A. Karpov	G. Kasparov
1. e2-e4	c7-c5
2. Ng1-f3	d7-d6
3. d2-d4	c5xd4
4. Nf3xd4	Ng8-f6
5. Nb1-c3	Nb8-c6
6. Bc1-g5	e7-e6
7. Qd1-d2	Bf8-e7
8. 0-0-0	0-0
9. f2-f4	h7-h6
10. Bg5-h4	...

No. 158

13. ...   c5xd4

An improvement over the move in the
same position during the third game of
the 1981 Merano World Championship
Match, in which White retained some
pressure after 13. ... Ne4 14. Nxe4
Bxe4 15. Bg3.

14. e3xd4	Nf6-h5!
15. Bh4xe7	Qd8xe7
16. d4-d5	Nh5-f4
17. Qe2-e3	Qe7-f6
18. Nc3-e4	Qf6-f5

No. 159

10. ...	e6-e5!?

A comparatively rare line, in which Black succeeds in tapping new resources.

11. Nd4-f5	Bc8xf5
12. e4xf5	e5xf4
13. Kc1-b1	d6-d5!
14. Bh4xf6	Be7xf6
15. Nc3xd5	Bf6-e5
16. g2-g3	...

The move 16. Bc4 (Gufeld-Dorfman, 1975) also deserves consideration.

16. ...	f4xg3
17. h2xg3	Nc6-e7!

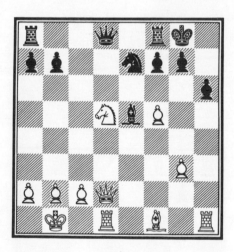

No. 160

Black has solved his opening problems. In the Balashov-Salov game (Lvov, 1984), Black even seized the initiative after 18. Ne3?! (18. Bg2 would be better) 18. ... Qxd2 19. Rxd2 Rfd8 20. Bd3 Bxg3 21. f6 Ng6.
Game drawn.
Time: 1.45-1.22

28 December 1984

GAME THIRTY-SIX

Queen's Gambit Declined

G. Kasparov	A. Karpov
1. d2-d4	Ng8-f6
2. c2-c4	e7-e6
3. Kg1-f3	d7-d5
4. Nb1-c3	Bf8-e7
5. Bc1-g5	h7-h6
6. Bg5-h4	0-0
7. e2-e3	b7-b6
8. Bf1-e2	Bc8-b7
9. Ra1-c1	d5xc4

In games 25 and 31, Kasparov defended his position by 9. ... Nbd7 10. cxd exd 11. 0-0 c5.

10. Be2xc4	Nb8-d7
11. 0-0	c7-c5

In the thirty-fourth game, after 11. ... a6 12. a4 c5 13. Qe2 cxd 14. exd Nh5, Black managed to hold the game balanced.
Perhaps Karpov believed that White's play could be improved (S. Makarychev).

12. d4xc5	Nd7xc5
13. Qd1-e2	a7-a6
14. Rf1-d1	Qd8-e8
(No. 161)	
15. Nf3-e5! ?	...

In the first game of the 1978 Baguio World Championship, White played 15. a3, and Karpov equalized the game by 15. ... Nfe4! The new move played by Kasparov prevents this unloading manoeuvre, but after Black's reply, White's active light-squared Bishop on c4 is in danger of being exchanged.

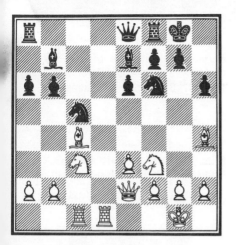

No. 161

| 15. ... | b6-b5! |
| 16. Nc3xb5?! | ... |

Kasparov took thirty-eight minutes over this move. Needless to say, his 15. Ne5 was not intended to seek for equality in 16. Bd3 Nxd3 (16. b4 is no good because of 16. ... Nce4). The sacrifice of the Knight is a natural continuation of Kasparov's plan, although its consequences are far from clear (M. Taimanov).

| 16. ... | a6xb5? |

As all the commentators indicated, Black should have first interposed 16. ... Qb8! In 17. Bg3 axb 18. Nc6 (18. Nxf7 Qe8! , or 18. ... Qa7; neither 18. Ng6 fxg 19. Bxb8 bxc 20. Bg3 Bd5,, nor 20. ... Rxa2 is good for White) 18. ... Bxc6 19. Bxb8 bxc 20. Bd6 Bxd6 21. Rxd6 Bd5, he would have more than sufficient compensation for the lost Queen.

As it is, Kasparov's plan has been fully justified and Black has to defend with no possibility of gaining counterplay A. Gipslis).

| 17. Bc4xb5 | Bb7-a6 |

If 17. ... Qb8, then 18. Rxc5! Bxc5 19. Bxf6 gxf 20. Nd7, posing a very serious threat for Black.

| 18. Rc1xc5 | ... |

The alternative would be 18. Bxa6 Nxa6 (not 18. ... Rxa6? 19. Rxc5) 19. Bxf6 Bxf6 20. Nd7.

| 18. ... | Be7xc5 |
| 19. Bb5xa6! | ... |

Not, of course, 19. Bxf6? Qxb5 20. Qg4, in view of 20. ... g5 21. Bxg5 Qe2! (E. Geller).

| 19. ... | Qe8-a4 |
| 20. Bh4xf6 | g7xf6 |

After 20. ... Qxa6, Black would lose because of 21. Qg4, and 20. ... Rxa6 is refuted by 21. b3! Qxa2 22. Qg4 g6 23. Nxg6.

| 21. Ba6-b5 | Qa4xa2 |
| 22. Ne5-d7 | Bc5-e7 |

After 22. ... Rfc8, the line 23. Qg4+ Kh8 24. Qh4 Bf8 25. Nxf8 and 26. Qxf6+ is good for White (S. Makarychev).

| 23. Qe2-d4+ | Kg8-h8 |

23. ... Kh7 would lose at once after 24. Nxf6+! Bxf6 25. Bd3+ Kh8 26. Qe4 (M. Taimanov).

| 24. Nd7xf8 | Be7xf8 |

The reply 24. ... Rxf8!? is worth considering, because after 25. Rd7 Qxb2 Black still has a chance of defending himself (E. Geller).

| 25. Qg4-f3 | ... |

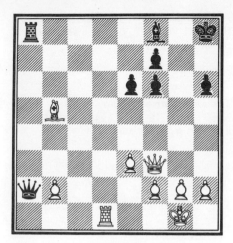

No. 162

25. ...   Bf8-e7?!

As M. Taimanov and S. Makarychev point out, 25. ... f5 would be more resilient.

26. Bb5-c4?! ...

"Kindness for kindness". By playing 26. Rd7! Kasparov could have decided the issue. Neither 26. ... Ra7 27. Rxe7! , nor 26. ... Qb1+ 27. Bf1 Ra1 28. Qe2 (or 27. ... Re8 28. Qb7!) could bring Black relief (M. Taimanov).

26. ...   Qa2-a7
27. Qf3-h5?! ...

27. b4! would be more vigorous here.

27. ...   Kh8-g7
28. Qh5-g4+ Kg7-f8
29. Bc4-f1?! ...

And again 29. b4! would be stronger and if 29. ... Bxb4, then 30. Bxe6! (E. Geller).

29. ...   Ra8-d8
30. Rd1-c1 ...

Several commentators have indicated the possibility of 30. Rxd8+ Dxd8 31. b4! followed by 32. b5

30. ...   Qa7-b8
31. Rc1-c2 ...

White could still have tried to fight for a win by 31. Qh4 Qxb2 (or 31. ... Kg7 32. Rc4!) 32. Qxh6+ (M. Taimanov).

31. ...   f6-f5
32. Qg4-e2 Kf8-g7

According to M. Taimanov, the immediate 32. ... Rc8 would be safer because, as it is, White could sharpen his game with 33. e4.

33. g2-g3 Rd8-c8!

No. 163

This very opportune exchange of Rooks (the b-Pawn is fixed at b4) enables Black to hold the game. Nothing would be changed by 34. Rd2 because Black may reply 34. ... Rd8! 35. Rxd8 Bxd8 (S. Makarychev).

34. h2-h3 Rc8xc2
35. Qe2xc2 Be7-f6
36. b2-b3 Qb8-b4
37. Qc2-d1 Qb4-c3
38. Kg1-g2 Qc3-c6+

39. Kg2-h2	Qc6-c5
40. Bf1-e2	Bf6-e7
41. Kh2-g2	Qc5-c6+

This move was sealed.

Next day the game is agreed drawn without resumption.

Time: 2.32-2.38

2 January 1985

GAME THIRTY-SEVEN

Sicilian Defence
Rauzer's Attack

A. Karpov	G. Kasparov
1. e2-e4	c7-c5
2. Ng1-f3	d7-d6
3. d2-d4	c5xd4
4. Nf3xd4	Ng8-f6
5. Nb1-c3	Nb8-c6
6. Bc1-g5	e7-e6
7. Qd1-d2	Bf8-e7
8. 0-0-0	0-0
(No. 164)	
9. Nd4-b3	...

In the thirty-fifth game, after 9. f4, Kasparov succeeded in levelling the game by 9. ... h6 10. Bh4 e5.

| 9. ... | a7-a5 |
| 10. a2-a4 | ... |

The reply 10. Nd4! ? is also worth considering.

| 10. ... | d6-d5 |
| 11. e4xd5 | ... |

The line 11. Bxf6 Bxf6 12. exd Bxc3 13. Qxc3 exd 14. Nd4 Bd7 15. Bb5 Nxd4 16. Qxd4 Bxb5 17. axb a4 is a good one

No. 164

for Black (Psakhis-Kupreichik, 52nd USSR Championship, 1985), but 11. Bb5! ? seems to be more promising for White (Tal-Sisniega, 1985 Tusco Interzonal Tournament).

11. ...	Nf6xd5
12. Bg5-e7	Nc6xe7
13. Nc3-b5	Bc8-d7
14. Bf1-e2	Ne7-f5
15. Nb3-d4	Nf5xd4

After 16. Qxd4 Rc6, Black's chances are as good as White's.

Game drawn.

Time: 1. 36-0.37

4 January 1985

GAME THIRTY-EIGHT

Queen's Gambit Declined

G. Kasparov	A. Karpov
1. d2-d4	Ng8-f6
2. c2-c4	e7-e6

3. Ng1-f3	d7-d5
4. Nb1-c3	Bf8-e7
5. Bc1-g5	h7-h6
6. Bg5-h4	0-0
7. e2-e3	b7-b6
8. Bf1-e2	Bc8-b7
9. Bh4xf6	Be7xf6
10. c4xd5	e6xd5
11. b2-b4	c7-c5!

The opponents continue their dispute over this opening line which they began in the twelfth game. As is known, the line 11. ... c6 12. 0-0 a5 13. a3 Qd6 14. Qb3 axb 15. axb Nd7 leads to a small advantage for White (Esteves-Karpov, 1973 Leningrad Interzonal Tournament).

12. b4xc5	b6xc5
13. Ra1-b1	Bb7-c6
14. 0-0	Nb8-d7
15. Be2-b5	...

Concerning the problem of bad and good Bishops: "according to all the rules", the White Bishop would seem to be better than his Black antagonist, but it is only by trading the Bishops that White may attempt to put pressure on the weak d5-Pawn (V. Baghirov).

15. ...	Qd8-c7
(No. 165)	
16. Qd1-c2	...

An innovation recommended by V. Baghirov. The twelfth game continued 16. Qd2 Rfd8 17. Rfc1 Rab8 and the players soon agreed to draw.

The previously adopted line of 16. Qd3 Rfd8 17. Qf5 cxd 18. exd g6! leads to equality (Dydyshko-Vladimirov, Moscow, 1983). It is interesting to note that in the eighth game of the second match another attempt was made with

No. 165

this line: after 16. Qd3 Rfd8, White played 17. Rfd1! ?

16. ...	Rf8-d8

In the forty-second game, Karpov will choose 16. ... Rfc8! and the game soon becomes level. The reply 16. ... cxd? is erroneous because of 17. Nxd5.

17. Rf1-c1	Ra8-b8

Black has the Bishop pair; therefore 17. ... c4 would be a grave mistake (E. Gufeld).

18. a2-a4	...

Strengthening his outpost on b5 and threatening 19. dxc (A. Suetin).

18. ...	Qc7-d6

18. ... c4 is again bad in view of 19. Bxc6 Qxc6 20. Rb5.

19. d4xc5	Nd7xc5

After 19. ... Qxc5, 20. Qd2 would be unpleasant for Black.

20. Bb5xc6 ...

The line 20. Bxd5? Bxd5 21. Qxc5 Qxc5 22. Rxc5 Bxf3 23. gxf a6 24. Bd3 Rxb1+ 25. Bxb1 Rd1+ would be wrong, as White would lose a piece. On the other hand, in the variations 20. Nd4 Bxd4 21. exd Ne6, or 20. Ne2 Bxb5 21. axb Ne6, Black's chances are as good as White's (E. Vasyukov).

20. ... Qd6xc6
21. Nc3-b5 Bf6-e7
22. Qc2-f5 ...

No. 166

22. ... Qc6-e8

The colourful variation 22. ... a6 23. Qxf7+! Kxf7 24. Ne5+ Ke8 25. Nxc6 axb 26. axb would lead to a position which is hard to assess (I. Dorfman).

In the case of 22. ...Qe6 23. Qxe6 fxe 24. Nfd4, and 22. ... Qd7 23. Qxd7 Rxd7 24. Ne5 Black's position would be alarming (M. Taimanov).

23. Nf3-e5 ...

White would gain nothing after 23. Nxa7 in view of 23. ... Rxb1 24. Rxb1 Ra8, or 24. ... Nxa4.

23. ... Rb8-b7

23. ... Rb6 would be hardly attractive because of 24. Nc7! (A. Suetin).

24. Nb5-d4 Rb7-c7
25. Nd4-b5 ...

A tacit offer of a draw, although after 25. h3 White could still attempt to seize the initiative, e.g. 25. ... Bf6 26. Ng4, or 25. ... Bf8 26. a5 with a complicated game (E. Gufeld).

25. ... Rc7-b7

Game drawn.
Time: 1.55-1.51

7 and 8 January 1985

GAME THIRTY-NINE

Queen's Gambit Declined

A. Karpov	G. Kasparov
1. Ng1-f3	d7-d5
2. d2-d4	Ng8-f6
3. c2-c4	e7-e6
4. Bc1-g5	Bf8-e7
5. Nb1-c3	h7-h6
6. Bg5-h4	0-0
7. e2-e3	b7-b6
8. Bf1-e2	Bc8-b7

9. Bh4xf6	Be7xf6
10. c4xd5	e6xd5
11. 0-0	Nb8-d7
12. b2-b4	c7-c5
13. b4xc5	b6xc5
14. Ra1-b1	Bb7-c6
15. Be2-b5	Qd8-c7
16. Qd1-c2	Rf8-d8
17. Rf1-c1	Ra8-b8
18. a2-a4	Qc7-d6
19. d4xc5	Nd7xc5
20. Bb5xc6	Qd6xc6
21. Nc3-b5	Bf6-e7

When analysing the thirty-eighth game in the press room, commentators concluded that 22. ... Qxa4? 23. Qxa4 Nxa4 24. Nc6 Rxb1 25. Nxe7+ Kf8 26. Ng6+! fxg 27. Rxb1 leads to a difficult ending for Black.

23. Na7-b5	Qa6xa4
24. Qc2xa4	Nc5xa4
25. Nf3-d4	Rd8-d7
26. Nd4-c6	Rb8-b6

No. 168

27. Nb5-d4 ...

No. 167

A unique event in the history of World Chess Championships: the contestants have repeated the moves of their previous encounter, in which the colour of their pieces was, of course, different, far into the middle-game. The dispute is over the isolated d5-Pawn. In the previous game, Kasparov here played 22. Qf5; Karpov, however, prefers to force the endgame.

22. Nb5xa7   Qc6-a6!

Trading the Knight for the Bishop would simplify Black's task. The diagrammed position would very likely lead to a draw, but it is not level! White has the form of advantage which is highly unpleasant for Black: White cannot lose in such a position, but he can worry his opponent for a long, long time (E. Gufeld).

27. ...	Be7-f6
28. Rb1xb6	Na4xb6

29. Rc1-b1	Nb6-a4
30. g2-g3	Na4-c5
31. Kg1-g2	g7-g6
32. Nd4-f3	Rd7-d6
33. Nc6-d4	Nc5-e6

Several commentators have pointed out the alternative 33. ... Ra6, with the idea of counterplaying against the White f2-Pawn (e.g. 34. Rb5 Ne4 35. Rxd5?! Ra2).

| 34. Rb1-b8+ | Kg8-g7 |

34. ... Rd8 would be a simpler solution of Black's defence problems (E. Geller).

35. Nd4-b3	Rd6-d7
36. Rb8-b5	Bf6-c3
37. Nb3-c1!	...

Maintaining some tension. Now 37. ... d4? is erroneous because of 38. Ne2.

| 37. ... | Ne6-g5 |
| 38. Nc1-e2 | Ng5-e4 |

38. ... Bf6 would be safer (E. Geller). 38. ... Nxf3 is also interesting, but just before the adjournment Kasparov does not want to change the character of his position (E. Gufeld). (**No. 169**)

| 39. Rb5-b3 | ... |

Black would still have had some problems to solve if White had played (now or on move 41) g3-g4! , as indicated by E. Geller.

39. ...	Rd7-c7
40. Rb3-b5	Rc7-d7
41. Ne2-f4	Ne4-f6

The sealed move. Black has prevented

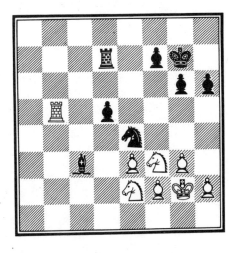

No. 169

the advance g3-g4-g5, White cannot increase his pressure on the d5-Pawn, and the game will be rapidly drawn.

42. h2-h3	h6-h5
43. Rb5-b3	Nf6-e4
44. Rb3-a3	Kg7-g8
45. Ra3-a4	Ne4-f6
46. g3-g4	h5xg4
47. h3xg4	Nf6xg4!
48. Nf4-e2	d5-d4

Repulsing White's last attempt to gain the advantage. Now both 49. Nxc3 dxc 50. Rxg4 Rc7, and 49. exd Bb2 50. Ra2 (or 50. Ne1 Re7) 50. ... Rb7 lead to full equality.

Game drawn.

Time: 3.02-3.02.

GAME FORTY

Queen's Gambit Declined

G. Kasparov	A. Karpov
1. d2-d4	Ng8-f6
2. c2-c4	e7-e6
3. Ng1-f3	d7-d5
4. Nb1-c3	Bf8-e7
5. Bc1-g5	h7-h6
6. Bg5-h4	0-0
7. e2-e3	b7-b6
8. Bf1-e2	Bc8-b7
9. Bh4xf6	Be7xf6
10. c4xd5	e6xd5
11. b2-b4	c7-c5
12. b4xc5	b6xc5
13. Ra1-b1	. . .

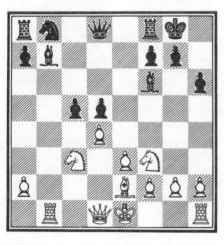

No. 170

13. ... Qd8-a5?!

This possibility was indicated in the press room during the twelfth game, when

Black preferred 13. ... Bc6 (and again in games 38, and 42)

14. Qd1-d2	c5xd4
15. Nf3xd4	Bf6xd4
16. e3xd4	Bb7-c6

After 16. ... Ba6 White would not withhold the incursion of his Queen's Knight.

17. Nc3-b5! Qa5-d8

This retreat is forced. After 17. ... Qxd2+ 18. Kxd2, White would have many positional advantages in the endgame: his forces would be better or, to be more exact, completely deployed; his King would be active; and Black would be left with a bad Bishop doomed to defend the Pawn on d5 (M. Tal).

18. 0-0 a7-a6?!

This pawn advance has further weakened Black's Q-side, but after 18. ... Nd7 19. Rfc1 Qf6 20. Qa5 White's pressure would also be felt (A. Suetin).

In Geller's opinion, after 18. ... Nd7 19. Rfc1 Black could continue 19. ... Bxb5 20. Rxb5 Nf6.

19. Nb5-a3! ...

This is stronger than 19. Nc3, as the c-file should be left open for White's heavy pieces to operate, while the Knight, after going to c2, can be headed for either e3 or b4, where it would be conveniently placed (A. Lilienthal).

19. ... Rf8-e8

19. ... Qd6 20. Nc2 Nd7 is worth considering here.

20. Na3-c2   ...

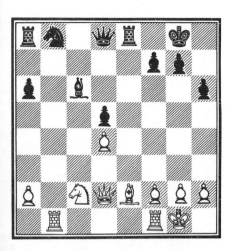

No. 171

20. ...   Re8xe2?!

This exchange only plays into White's hands. After 20. ... Bb5, Black's defence would be easier. According to E. Geller, 20. ... Nd7 is also playable; for instance, 21. Nb4 Qa5 22. Rb2 Bb5 23. Bxb5 Qxb5!

21. Qd2xe2   Bc6-b5
22. Rb1xb5   a6xb5
23. Qe2xb5   ...

In the variation 23. Nb4 Na6 24. Nc6 Qd7 25. Qxb5, Black could defend himself with 25. ... Nb8!

23. ...   Ra8xa2
24. Nc2-e3!   Ra2-a5

24. ... Na6 would hardly be better because of 25. Rc1; and 25. ... Qf6 loses in view of 26. Rc8+ Kh7 27. Qb1+ (I. Dorfman). After 25. ... g6 26. h3 (or

26. Nxd5 Ra5) 26. ... h5 27. Nxd5 Ra5 28. Rc8, Black's life is far from pleasant (M. Taimanov).

25. Qb5-b7   Qd8-e8!

At the cost of a Pawn Karpov wards off the threat of 26. Rc1, to which he will now be able to reply with 26. ... Rb5.

26. Ne3xd5   Ra5-b5
27. Qb7-a8   Qe8-d7
28. Nd5-c3   Rb5-b4

28. ... Rb3 would perhaps be more resilient.

29. d4-d5   ...

29. Rd1 also comes into consideration (A. Suetin).

29. ...   Qd7-c7
30. Nc3-d1   Rb4-b5
31. Nd1-e3   ...

It seems that after 31. Qa2 Qa5 32. Qe2 it would be easier for White to carry the game through with the Queens on the board, because 32. ... Rxd5? would fail against 33. Qe8+ and 34. Qxb8 (I. Dorfman).

31. ...   Qc7-a5

Karpov agrees to exchange Queens, because the variation 31. ... Ra5 32. d6 Qd8 33. Qb7 is unacceptable to him.

32. Qa8xa5   Rb5xa5
    (No. 172)
33. Rf1-d1?!   ...

Those in the press room clearly preferred

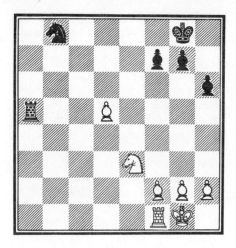

No. 172

33. Rc1! , with the possible continuation 33. ... Nd7 34. Rc8+ Kh7 35. Kf1, and if 35. ... Nb6, then 36. d6! to give White victory.

As it is, White has more difficulty in exploiting his extra Pawn.

33. ...	Nb8-d7
34. g2-g4	g7-g6
35. Kg1-g2	Ra5-a4
36. h2-h3	Kg8-g7
37. d5-d6	Ra4-a6

Black should perhaps have preferred 37. ... Rb4, or 37. ... Re4 (A. Suetin).

In Tal's opinion, White's task would be more complicated after 37. ... Kf6, in order to meet 38. f4 with 38. ... Ke6.

38. f2-f4	Ra6-c6
39. h3-h4	Kg7-f8
40. g4-g5?	...

Now Black will "miraculously" save himself from defeat. This miracle would hardly have happened in the event of 40. h5! (M. Tal).

The simple 40. Kf3 would not be bad, either (A. Suetin).

40. ...	h6xg5
41. h4xg5	...

This move was sealed.

Karpov's task would be far more difficult if White played the move on the board. Then Black would have to find the solution (and the only one!) over the board in a limited time (M. Tal).

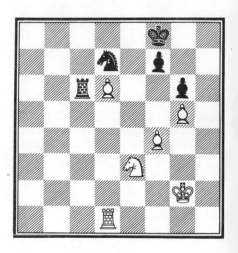

No. 173

41. ...	f7-f5!

But not 41. ... f6?, because of 42. Ng4! fxg 43. Ne5.

42. Rd1-d4	...

228

It becomes clear that 42. gxf would merely result in a draw: 42. ... Kf7 43. Ng4 Ke6 44. Re1+ Kf5! 45. Nh6+ (45. Kg3 Rxd6) 45. ... Kf6 46. Ng8+ Kf7 47. Re7+ Kxg8 48. Rxd7 Rc3! 49. Rc7 (49. Kf2 Kf8) 49. ... Rd3 50. d7 Kf8, etc. Yet the text makes it possible for Black to destroy his opponent's dangerous passed Pawn, by giving up instead the Pawn on g6.

42. ...	Kf8-f7
43. Ne3-c4	Kf7-e6
44. Kg2-f3	Rc6-c5
45. Kf3-e3	Rc5-b5
46. Ke3-d2	Rb5-d5!
47. Rd4xd5	Ke6xd5
48. Nc4-e5	Kd5xd6
49. Ne5xg6	Nd7-c5

No. 174

The resulting Knight and Pawn ending should lead to a draw. Yet, in Geller's opinion, 49. ... Nb6 50. Ke3 Nd5+ 51. Kd4 Nc7 would be a simpler solution of Black's defensive problems.

50. Ng6-h4	Kd6-e6
51. Kd2-e3	Nc5-e4
52. Nh4-f3	Ke6-f7
53. Ke3-d4	Kf7-e6
54. Kd4-c4	Ne4-f2!

The only defence: Black has created counterplay against the White f4-Pawn (Nf2-h3! is the threat). **(No. 174)**

55. Kc4-d4 ...

White could still pose some problems for his opponent by 55. Ng1! ? (E. Geller).

55. ...	Nf2-e4
56. Nf3-e1	Ke6-d6
57. Ne1-c2	Ne4-c5
58. Kd4-e3	Nc5-e6
59. Nc2-d4	Ne6-g7
60. Ke3-d2	Kd6-c5
61. Kd2-d3	Kc5-d5
62. Nd4-e2	Ng7-h5
63. Kd3-e3	Nh5-g7
64. Ne2-g3	Kd5-d6
65. Ke3-f3	Kd6-e7
66. Ng3-e2	Ng7-e6
67. Ne2-g3	Ne6-g7
68. Ng3-f1	Ke7-f7
69. Nf1-e3	Kf7-g6
70. Ne3-d5	Ng7-e6

Game drawn. 71. Ne7+ Kh5 72. Nxf5 can be met with 72. ... Nxg5+.

Time: 3.42-3.57

GAME FORTY-ONE

Petroff's Defence

A. Karpov	G. Kasparov
1. e2-e4	e7-e5
2. Ng1-f3	Ng8-f6

A surprise! For the first time Kasparov adopts the opening against which he played without much success in games 28 and 30.

Kasparov's decision has probably been influenced by his desire to find out which line his opponent considers the best for White (M. Taimanov).

3. Nf3xe5	d7-d6
4. Ne5-f3	Nf6xe4
5. d2-d4	d6-d5
6. Bf1-d3	Bf8-e7
7. 0-0	Nb8-c6

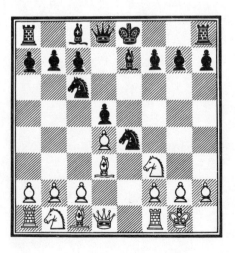

No. 175

8. c2-c4	...

This is more vigorous than 8. Re1, as occurred in games 28 and 30.

8. ...	Nc6-b4

Another possibility is 8. ... Nf6 (see forty-eighth game).

9. Bd3-e2!	...

White should, of course, avoid exchanging the active Bishop, which will soon take an excellent position (A. Suetin).

In the variation 9. cxd Nxd3 10. Qxd3 Qxd5 11. Re1 Bf5 12. Nc3 Nxc3 13. Qxc3 Be6! 14. Qxc7 Bd6 15. Qc2 0-0, Black would have sufficient compensation for the sacrificed Pawn (Huebner-Smyslov, Candidates' Match, Felden, 1983).

9. ...	d5xc4
10. Be2-c4	0-0
11. Nb1-c3	...

11. Ne5 also deserves consideration here (N. Kroghius).

11. ...	Ne4-d6

M. Taimanov indicated the possibility of 11. ... Bf5, and 12. Ne5 would be met with 12. ... Nc6. The line 11. ... Nxc3 12. bxc Nd5 13. Qb3 is in White's favour.

12. Bc4-b3	Be7-f6

After 12. ... Bg4, White could continue 13. h3 and if 13. ... Bh5 14. g4 Bg6 15. Ne5 followed, White would have a dangerous initiative (Ye. Vasyukov).

13. h2-h3	...

The continuation 13. Ne5! Nc6 (if 13. ... c5, then 14. Bf4; even worse would be 13. ... Nf5? 14. Nxf7! , or 13. ... Bxe5? 14. dxe Nf5 15. Bxf7+!) 14. Bf4 Nf5 15. Nxc6 bxc 16. d5 would be more dangerous for Black (Sokolov-Agzamov, 52nd USSR Championship, 1985).

13. ...   Bc8-f5
14. Bc1-e3   Rf8-e8
15. a2-a3   ...

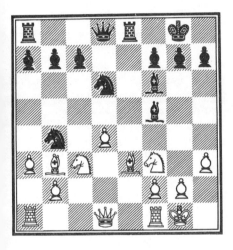

No. 176

15. ...   Nb4-d3! ?

An active continuation, which gives great interest and excitement to the following stages of the game. The more circumspect 15. ... Nc6 would hold the game roughly balanced (A. Suetin).

16. Ra1-b1!   ...

After 16. Qd2 b5! , threatening 17. ... Nc4, White would have run a serious risk of getting into Black's bind.

16. ...   c7-c5
17. d4xc5   Nd6-e4

Not, of course, 17. ... Nxb2 18. Rxb2 Bxc3, in view of 19. cxd! Bxb2 20. Bxf7+! Kxf7 21. Qd5+, which would give White a powerful attack (M. Taimanov).

18. Bb3-c2!   Nd3xb2

In reply to 18. ... Ng3?! 19. fxg Rxe3 20. Qd2 Bd4 21. Nxd4 Qxd4 22. Kh2 Bg6, M. Taimanov recommended 23. Nd5! , whereas A. Suetin preferred 23. b4 Qe5 24. Rf3. The prospects would be better for White in both cases.

19. Qd1xd8   Ra8xd8
20. Rb1xb2   Bf6xc3
21. Rb2xb7   Ne4xc5
22. Be3xc5   Bf5xc2
23. Rb7xa7   ...

As a result, White has won a Pawn, but he should perhaps have done this by 23. Rc1 Rd1+ (or 23. ... Be4 24. Rxa7) 24. Rxd1 Bxd1 25. Rxa7 (M. Taimanov).

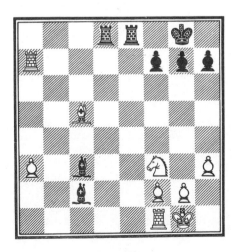

No. 177

23. ...   Bc2-d1!

By locking in the White Rook on f1, Black has significantly counterpoised his opponent's material advantage.

24. Ra7-e7   Re8xe7
25. Bc5xe7   Rd8-d3
26. Nf3-g5   Bc3-b2
27. Be7-b4   ...

Black's threat was 27. ... Bc2, and the Pawn on a3 would be doomed. But now 27. ... Bc2 can be countered with 28. Re1! (A. Suetin).

27. ...   h7-h6

Many commentators were of the opinion that 27. ... f6 would be more expedient, and if 28. Ne4 then 28. ... Bc2 29. Nc5 Rd1 30. Rxd1 Bxd1 31. Kf1 Bd4, maintaining the balance.

28. Ng5-e4   f7-f5

Black should have played 28. ... Bc2 (M. Taimanov).

29. Ne4-c5   Rd3-d5
30. Rf1-e1   f5-f4?

A time-trouble mistake. Black should have replied with 30. ... Kf7, or 30. ... Bc2.

31. a3-a4!   Rd5-d4

Here 31. ... Be5 would be bad in view of 32. a5 Bd6 33. a6 Bxc5 34. Bxc5 Rxc5 35. Re8+ Kf7 36. a7 (M. Taimanov).

32. a4-a5   Rd4xb4
   (No. 178)
33. Re1xd1?   ...

No. 178

In the press room, Grandmaster I. Dorfman pointed out an elegant move 33. a6! Analysis revealed the following:
    1) 33. ... Ba4 34. a7 Bc6 35. Re6 Bd5 36. Rd6;
    2) 33. ... Bb3 34. Nxb3 Ra4 (34. ... Rxb3 35. Re8+, and 36. a7) 35. Nc5 Ra5 36. Re4! Kf7 37. Ra4! Rxa4 38. Nxa4 Rd4 39. Nc3! ;
    3) 33. ... Rb8 34. Rxd1 Ba3 35. Nb7! , White winning in all these variations.

After 33. a6! , the World Champion could bring to a successful end both the game and the whole titanic battle. After his slip, the fight flares up again (M. Taimanov).

33. ...   Bb2-d4
34. Nc5-e6   Bd4-a7
35. Rd1-d7   ...

At this point, 35 Nxg7! ? Rb2 36. Nf5 Bxf2+ 37. Kf1 is worth considering.

35. ...   Rb4-b1+
36. Kg1-h2   Ba7xf2

37. Ne6xf4	Rb1-a1!
38. Nf4-e6	Ra1xa5

After 38. ... g5! , Black's task would have been simpler; for instance, 39. Rg7+ (39. Rd5 Be1) 39. ... Kh8 40. Rg6 Kh7 41. Nf8+ Kh8 42. a6 (or 42. Rxh6+ Kg7 43. Rg6+ Kxf8 44. Rf6+ Kg7 45. Rxf2 Rxa5) 42. ... Bg1+! 43. Kg3 Ra3+ 44. Kg4 Ra4+! , with an inevitable draw (I. Dorfman).

39. Rd7xg7+	Kg8-h8
40. Rg7-f7	Bf2-e3
41. Kh2-g3	...

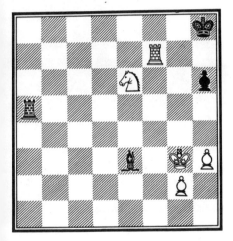

No. 179

Here the game was adjourned. It is very hard (if at all possible) for White to exploit his slight advantage, because the few remaining Pawns are all on the same wing (Ye. Vasyukov).

41. ...	Be3-d2
42. Rf7-d7	Bd2-c3
43. Kg3-f3	Kh8-g8
44. Ne6-f4	Ra5-f5

45. Kf3-e4	Rf5-f7!
46. Rd7-d8+	...

The more dangerous for Black would be 46. Rxf7 Kxf7 47. Kf5.

46. ...	Kg8-h7
47. Rd8-d3	Rf7-e7+
48. Ke4-f3	Bc3-b2
49. Rd3-b3	Bb2-c1
50. Nf4-d5	Re7-e5
51. Nd5-f6+	Kh7-g6
52. Nf6-e4	Re5-f5+
53. Kf3-e2	Rf5-e5
54. Rb3-b4	Re5-e7
55. Rb4-c4	Re7-e8
56. g2-g3	...

56. Rxc1 Rxe4+ would hardly be better.

56. ...	Bc1-b2
57. Ke2-f3	Re8-e6
58. Rc4-c5	Bb2-d4
59. Rc5-d5	Bd4-e5
60. Rd5-b5	Be5-c7
61. Rb5-c5	Bc7-b6
62. Rc5-c8	Bb6-d4
63. Rc8-g8+	Bd4-g7
64. h3-h4	Re6-a6
65. Kf3-f4	...

Or 65. h5+ Kxh5 66. Rxg7 Ra3+ 67. Kf4 Rf3+, and the Black Rook would go berserk.

65. ...	Ra6-a5
66. Rg8-e8	Ra5-f5+
67. Kf4-e3	Rf5-e5
68. Re8-g8	Re5-e7
69. Ke3-f4	Re7-f7+
70. Kf4-g4	h6-h5+!
71. Kg4-h3.	

Game drawn.
Time: 4.01-4.24.

16 January 1985

GAME FORTY-TWO

Queen's Gambit Declined

G. Kasparov	A. Karpov
1. d2-d4	Ng8-f6
2. c2-c4	e7-e6
3. Ng1-f3	d7-d5
4. Nb1-c3	Bf8-e7
5. Bc1-g5	h7-h6
6. Bg5-h4	0-0
7. e2-e3	b7-b6
8. Bf1-e2	Bc8-b7
9. Bh4xf6	Be7xf6
10. c4xd5	e6xd5
11. b2-b4	c7-c5
12. b4xc5	b6xc5
13. Ra1-b1	Bb7-c6
14. 0-0	Nb8-d7
15. Be2-b5	Qd8-c7
16. Qd1-c2	...

No. 180

| 16. ... | Rf8-c8! |

This is a simpler way of solving Black's problems of defence than 16. ... Rfd8, as was played in games 38 and 39.

17. Rf1-c1	Bc6xb5
18. Nc3xb5	Qc7-c6
19. d4xc5	Nd7xc5
20. Qc2-f5	Qc6-e6
21. Nf3-d4	Qe6xf5
22. Nd4xf5	Nc5-e6
23. Rc1xc8+	Ra8xc8
24. Nb5xa7	Rc8-c2
25. Na7-b5	Rc2xa2
26. h2-h3	Ra2-a5

No. 181

Game drawn.
Time: 1.31-1.21

18 January 1985

GAME FORTY-THREE

Sicilian Defence
Scheveningen Variation

A. Karpov	G. Kasparov
1. e2-e4	c7-c5

2. Ng1-f3	d7-d6
3. d2-d4	c5xd4
4. Nf3xd4	Ng8-f6
5. Nb1-c3	a7-a6
6. Bf1-e2	e7-e6
7. 0-0	Bf8-e7
8. f2-f4	0-0
9. Kg1-h1	Qd8-c7

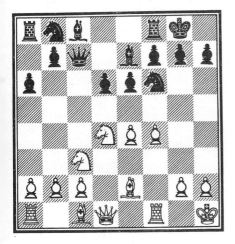

No. 182

In the fifth and forty-fifth games, Karpov preferred to restrict Black's counterplay by a2-a4. This time he chooses a sharp line leading to forced play, but Kasparov successfully handles all the difficulties.

10. Qd1-e1	b7-b5
11. Be2-f3	Bc8-b7
12. e4-e5	Nf6-e8
13. f4-f5	d6xe5
14. f5xe6	Bb7xf3
15. e6xf7+	Rf8xf7
16. Nd4xf3	Nb8-d7
17. Bc1-g5	...
(No. 183)	
17. ...	Be7-f8!
18. a2-a3	Ne8-d6

No. 183

19. Nf3-d2	Rf7xf1+
20. Qe1xf1	Qc7-c6
21. Ra1-e1	Ra8-e8

Game drawn.
Time: 1.43-0.45.

21 January 1985

GAME FORTY-FOUR

Ruy López

G. Kasparov	A. Karpov
1. e2-e4	e7-e5
2. Ng1-f3	Nb8-c6

The opponents have so far preferred Petroff's Defence (2. ... Nf6) in this match.

3. Bf1-b5	a7-a6
4. Bb5-a4	Ng8-f6
5. 0-0	Bf8-e7

6. Rf1-e1	b7-b5
7. Ba4-b3	d7-d6
8. c2-c3	0-0
9. h2-h3	Bc8-b7

In recent years, this dynamic approach, in which Black exerts pressure on the centre, has largely superseded the classical variation 9. ... Na5 10. Bc2 c5 11. d4 Qc7 (M. Taimanov).

10. d2-d4	Rf8-e8

The point of Black's tenth move is that 11. Ng5 Rf8 12. f4 can be repulsed by 12. ... exf 13. Bxf4 Na5; for instance, 14. Bc2 Nd5! (Ljubojević-Gligorić match, 1979), or 14. Nd2 Nxb3 15. axb c5! ? (recommended by E. Gufeld and M. Chiburdanidze) 16. dxc dxc 17. Qc2 h6 18. Ngf3 Qb6 19. c4, giving an unclear game.

An important contribution to the development and elaboration of this system has been made by one of Karpov's seconds, Grandmaster Igor Zaitsev (A. Suetin).

11. a2-a4	...

The more common continuation is 11. Nbd2 (game 46 of the present match).

11. ...	h7-h6

The retreat 11. ... Bf8 is premature, as was demonstrated by Karpov in his game against Miles (London, 1984): 12. d5 Na5 13. Ba2 c6 14. Na3! cxd 15. exd bxa 16. Qxa4 Nxd5 17. Ng5! , which provided White with a crushing attack.

12. Nb1-d2	e5xd4! ?

This is a relatively new idea. The usual line is 12. ... Bf8, to counter 13. Bc2 with 13. ... exd 14. cxd Nb4, or with 13. ... Nb8, as in the ninth game of their second match.

13. c3xd4	Nc6-b4

No. 184

14. Qd1-e2	...

An interesting move. Kasparov deliberately delays clearing the situation in the centre (T. Gheorgadze).

The Tseshkovsky-Ivanov game (1984) went as follows: 14. d5 c5 15. dxc Nxc6 16. Nf1 Bf8 17. Ng3 Ne5 18. Nd4 d5 19. f4 Nc4 20. e5 Ne4 21. Nxe4 (if 21. Bxc4, then 21. ... bxc 22. Qg4 Qc8) 21. ... dxe 22. Bxc4 bxc 23. Be3 and, according to A. Ivanov, the continuation 23. ... f6! ? 24. e6 f5 25. Nxf5 Rxe6 26. Qg4 Qe8, showing sufficient counterplay, deserves consideration.

14. ...	Be7-f8
15. e4-e5	Bb7-c6

In the event of 15. ... dxe (but not 15. ... Qd7? 16. axb! axb 17. Rxa8 Bxa8 18. e6) 16. Nxe5 Bd5 17. axb Bxb3! 18. Nxb3 Qd5, Black would have a good game (R. Kholmov).

A more promising line after 15. ... dxe is 16. dxe, whereupon 16. ... Nd3 17. Rd1 Bc5 would be bad because of 18. Nf1. According to V. Lepeshkin, 16. ... Bc6 is more precise; for instance, 17. e6 fxe 18. Bxe6+ Kh7, with an unclear game.

16. a4xb5	Bc6xb5

Some of the commentators preferred 16. ... axb.

17. Qe2-d1	Nf6-d5
18. Nd2-e4	c7-c6

White has the initiative and Karpov attempts to strengthen his bastions in the centre. In the case of 18. ... c5 19. Bxd5 Nxd5 20. exd c4 (or 20. ... cxd 21. Qxd4 Bxd6 22. Bxh6) 21. Ne5 Bxd6 22. Qh5, Black would have difficulties in defending his King (M. Taimanov).

19. Ne4-c3	...

Also interesting is 19. Ng3, with the idea of transferring the Rook by Re1-e4-g4 to attack the King's side (R. Kholmov).

19. ...	Ra8-b8

The variation 19. ... Nd3 20. Re4 Nxc3 21. bxc Nxc1 22. Qxc1 d5 23. Rg4 would give White a chance to attack (I. Dorfman).

The reply 19. ... Qc7, trying to contest for the a-file, is worth considering (R. Kholmov).

20. Nc3xb5	a6xb5
21. e5xd6	...

White could also play 21. Ra3! ? The point is that after 21. ... c5 White has the strong continuation 22. Bxd5 Nxd5 23. dxc dxc 24. Rd3! (E. Gufeld).

After 21. Bd2 c5! ? 22. dxc dxc 23. e6! , the game would be very complicated; for instance, 23. ... Rxe6 24. Rxe6 fxe 25. Bxb4 Nxb4 (25. ... cxb 26. Ne5!) 26. Bxe6+ Kh8, or 23. ... c4 24. exf+ Kxf7 25. Ne5+ Kg8 (I. Dorfman).

21. ...	Bf8xd6
22. Bc1-d2	...

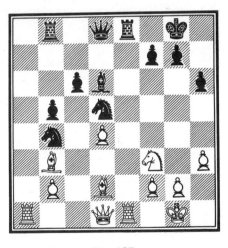

No. 185

22. ...	Qd8-c7

The commentators also suggested 22. ... Qd7, as well as 22. ... Qf6, which could be countered by 23. Ra7.

23. Qd1-b1!	...

Covering the d3-square and preparing for the invasion of the White Queen on f5.

23. ...	Qc7-d7
24. Nf3-e5	Bd6xe5
25. Re1xe5	Re8xe5
26. d4xe5	c6-c5
27. Qb1-e4	c5-c4
28. Bb3-d1	Nb4-d3

Some experts think that 28. ... Re8 is safer.

29. Bd1-g4	Qd7-b7?!

Black should have played 29. ... Nc5! 30. Qf3 (if 30. Qd4, then 30. ... Nb3!) 30. ... Qb7.

No. 186

30. Qe4-d4?!   ...

Analysis has revealed that after the thrust 30. e6! Black would have very serious problems. For instance,

1) 30. ... Nf6, (if 30. ... Nc5, or

30. ... Re8, then 31. Qd4) 31. Qxb7 (or 31. Qd4!?—M. Taimanov) 31. ... Rxb7 32. Ra8+ Kh7 33. Bf5+ g6 34. Bxd3 cxd 35. exf Rxf7 36. Rd8 (36. f3! ?—R. Kholmov) 36. ... Rd7 (36. ... Nd7 37. f4) 37. Rxd7+ Nxd7 38. f4 (or 38. Kf1), and the White King makes his way to the d3-Pawn;

2) 30. ... N5f4 31. exf+ Qxf7 32. Be3, threatening Ra1-a7 (M. Taimanov).

Now Karpov finds an ingenious manoeuvre which enables him to hold the position in balance.

30. ...	Qb7-b6!
31. Qd4xd5	Qb6xf2+
32. Kg1-h2	Qf2xd2
33. Ra1-f1	Qd2-g5!
34. Qd5xf7+	Kg8-h8
35. e5-e6	Nd3-e5
36. Qf7-f5	Ne5xg4+
37. h3xg4	Rb8-e8
38. Qf5xg5	

Or 38. Qe4 Qe7! 39. g3! Qd6 40. Re1 Qd3 41. Qe5 b4 42. e7 c3, maintaining the balance (R. Kholmov).

Game drawn. After 38. ... hxg 39. Rf5 Rxe6 40. Rxb5 Re2, all resources for further struggle are exhausted.

Time: 2.25-2.23.

23 January 1985

GAME FORTY-FIVE

Sicilian Defence
Scheveningen Variation

A. Karpov	G. Kasparov
1. e2-e4	c7-c5
2. Ng1-f3	d7-d6
3. d2-d4	c5xd4

4. Nf3xd4	Ng8-f6
5. Nb1-c3	a7-a6
6. Bf1-e2	e7-e6
7. 0-0	Bf8-e7
8. f2-f4	0-0
9. Kg1-h1	Qd8-c7
10. a2-a4	...

As the forty-third game showed, Black has a good reply to 10. Qe1, namely 10. ... b5.

| 10. ... | Nb8-c6 |
| 11. Bc1-e3 | ... |

It is known that after 11. Nb3 Black can well answer 11. ... b6 12. Bf3 Rd8 13. Qe1 Rb8 14. Be3 Na5! with counterplay.

| 11. ... | Rf8-e8 |

Black is not in a hurry to play Bc8-d7, the delay being dictated not only by tactical considerations (he wants to keep the d7-square unoccupied for the retreat of the Knight on f6, should White play g2-g4-g5) but also by the more profound, strategical ones: Black wishes to carry out a plan associated with Nc6xd4 and e6-e5 to put pressure on the White e4-Pawn (A. Suetin).

| 12. Be2-f3 | ... |

The line 12. Bg1! ?, which occurred in the tenth game of the second match, is also interesting.

12. ...	Ra8-b8
(No. 187)	
13. Qd1-d2	...

In the fifth game, after 13. Re1 Bd7 14. Qd3 Nxd4 15. Bxd4 e5 16.

No. 187

Ba7 Rc8 17. Be3 Qc4, the game soon became level. And 13. Bf2 Bf8 14. Re1 Nd7 15. Qe2 Nxd4 16. Bxd4 b6 17. e5 dxe 18. fxe (Razuvayev-Kasparov, 46th USSR Championship, 1978) can be met with 18. ... Bc5! (Black may also respond with 13. ... Nxd4 and 14. ... e5, or may interpose 13. ... Bd7).

In his preparations for the match, Kasparov had undoubtedly given much primary consideration to the aggressive 13. g4! ? (E. Gufeld).

| 13. ... | Nc6xd4 |

Kasparov takes about forty minutes over this move. The preliminary 13. ... Bd7 (as in the second game of the second match) also deserves consideration.

| 14. Be3xd4 | e6-e5 |
| 15. Bd4-a7 | ... |

As in the fifth game, White takes measures against b7-b5.

239

| 15. ... | Rb8-a8 |
| 16. Ba7-e3 | Bc8-d7 |

The solution 16. ... exf 17. Bxf4 Be6 would be more conventional (M. Taimanov).

| 17. a4-a5 | Ra8-c8 |
| 18. Bf3-e2 | ... |

After 18. f5, the retort 18. ... Qc4 promises good counterplay.

| 18. ... | Bd7-c6 |

No. 188

19. Qd2-d3   ...

In the press room, the more consistent 19. Bd3 was the main consideration. After 19. ... exf?! , Dorfman gives the sequence 20. Bb6 Qb8 21. Rxf4 d5 22. exd Nxd5 23. Nxd5 Bxd5 24. Rf5 Be6 25. Rh5 h6 26. Bd4! Bf8 27. Be5 Qa7 28. Qf4, and it is not easy for Black to defend his position.

19. ...   Qc7-d8! ?

Intending d6-d5. White prevents this and Black then does his best to increase pressure on the White e4-Pawn.

20. Rf1-d1   ...

M. Taimanov prefers 20. Bb6 Qd7 21. Rad1.

20. ...	e5xf4
21. Be3xf4	Be7-f8
22. Be2-f3	Qd8-e7!

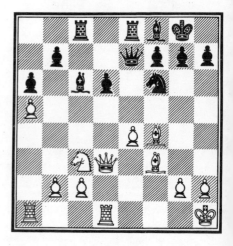

No. 189

Now both sides have weak centre Pawns, and 23. Nd5 promises little in view of 23. ... Bxd5 24. exd Qc7 (E. Gufeld), or 23. ... Nxd5 24. exd Bb5 (M. Taimanov). Accordingly, Karpov tries to simplify the game.

23. Bf4xd6	Qe7xd6
24. Qd3xd6	Bf8xd6
25. Rd1xd6	Nf6xe4

A neat retort, but after 25. ... Re5, followed by Rc8-e8, Black would also avoid the risk of losing (M. Taimanov).

240

26. Rd6xc6	Rc8xc6 .
27. Nc3xe4	...

If 27. Bxe4, then 27. ... Rxc3.

27. ...	Rc6-e6
28. Kh1-g1	...

The White Knight must not retreat, because of 28. ... Re1+, and it cannot be defended either directly (28. Re1 f5 29. Nf6+ Kf7!) or indirectly (28. Rd1 f5!). So White has to give away the material advantage (I. Dorfman).

28. ...	Re6xe4
29. Bf3xe4	Re8xe4
30. Ra1-d1	g7-g5
31. Rd1-d5	h7-h6
32. c2-c3	Re4-e6

The Rook and Pawn ending clearly indicates a draw. With his last move, Black wishes to get rid of the weak Pawn on b7, and he prepares for b7-b6 (A. Suetin).

33. Kg1-f2	Kg8-g7
34. g2-g4	b7-b6
35. h2-h3	Kg7-g6
36. Kf2-f3	h6-h5

Game drawn.
Time: 2.07-2.15

28 January 1985

GAME FORTY-SIX

Ruy López

G. Kasparov	A. Karpov
1. e2-e4	e7-e5

2. Ng1-f3	Nb8-c6
3. Bf1-b5	a7-a6
4. Bb5-a4	Ng8-f6
5. 0-0	Bf8-e7
6. Rf1-e1	b7-b5
7. Ba4-b3	d7-d6
8. c2-c3	0-0
9. h2-h3	Bc8-b7
10. d2-d4	Rf8-e8
11. Nb1-d2	...

Kasparov adopts a different order of moves, thereby excluding the variation 11. a4 h6 12. Nbd2 exd! ? 13. cxd Nb4, which occurred in the forty-fourth game.

11. ...	Be7-f8
12. a2-a4	Qd8-d7

Karpov takes twenty-six minutes over this move and Kasparov—thirty-four minutes over his next move. The line 12. ... h6 is more frequently played.

13. a4xb5!	a6xb5
14. Ra1xa8	Bb7xa8
15. d4-d5	...

No. 190

15. ...	Nc6-d8?!	22. ...	Ba8xc6
		23. Bc2-b3	Na6-c7
		24. Qd1-f3	Nc7-e6
		25. h3-h4	Qd7-d8
		26. Re1-d1!	Qd8-a8

15. ... Ne7 would probably be better, but Black would still have difficulties (S. Makarychev).

In the fifth game of their second match Karpov played 15. ... Na5! 16. Ba2 c6 17. b4 Nb7, which was stronger (but not 17. ... Nc4 18. Nxc4 bxc, because of 19. Bg5!).

16. Nd2-f1	h7-h6

If 16. ... c6, White has the unpleasant retort 17. Bg5.

17. Nf3-h2	...

The fight is for the possession of the d5-square. After 17. ... c6 (or 17. ... c5 18. c4!), White can continue 18. Ng4 Nxg4 19. hxg cxd 20. exd, and the d5-Pawn would be reliably protected (A. Suetin).

17. ...	Nd8-b7
18. Bb3-c2	Nb7-c5

The line 18. ... c6 19. Ne3 cxd 20. exd would be good for White (M. Taimanov).

19. b2-b4	Nc5-a6
20. Nh2-g4	Nf6-h7

The alternative 20. ... Nxg4 21. hxg is bad for Black; for instance, 21. ... c6 22. Ne3 Nc7 23. Bb3.

21. Nf1-g3	c7-c6
22. d5xc6	...

White could avoid exchanging on c6. M. Taimanov, for example, suggested 22. b4! ? cxd 23. exd.

White's threat was 27. Nxe5. Black could not play 26. ... Qxh4, because of 27. Nf5 Qd8 (27. ... Qh5 28. Ngxh6+!) 28. Nxe5 Neg5 (more stubborn would be 28. ... Nhg5 29. Qg4 Bxe4 30. Nxf7!) 29. Bxf7+! (S. Makarychev).

No. 191

27. Bb3-d5?! ...

Now all White's pieces are taking part in the attack, and Kasparov should have attempted to decide the game by the blow 27. Bxh6! In reply to 27. ... gxh, I. Dorfman suggested 28. Rxd6! , while S. Makarychev—28. Nh5! In either case it would be very hard for Black to defend himself.

27. ...	Bc6xd5
28. e4xd5	...

Kasparov frees the e4-square for one of his Knights, while the other will be placed on f5. The Challenger thus sets up a powerful "cavalry" bastion (A. Suetin).

28. ...	Ne6-c7
29. Ng3-e4	Qa8-c8
30. Ng4-e3	Qc8-d7
31. Ne3-f5	Re8-a8

M. Taimanov's recommendation 31. ... Kh8 deserves consideration.

| 32. Qf3-h3 | ... |

White threatens 33. Nxh6+. The possibility 32. Nexd6!? (but not 32. Qg4 Kh8 33. Nexd6? Nf6!) 32. ... g6! 33. Qg4 was variously evaluated. According to S. Makarychev, after 33. ... Rd8 34. h5 Nf6, or 33. ... Kh8, White would have gained nothing by sacrificing his Knight. On the other hand, M. Taimanov assessed the positions arising from either 33. ... Bd8 34. Nb7! h5 35. Qg3 Rb8 36. Nh6+ Bxh6 37. Nc5, or 33. ... Kh8 34. Nxh6 Qxg4 35. Ndxf7+ Kg7 36. Nxg4 Kxf7 37. Nxe5+ as advantageous for White.

| 32. ... | Ra8-d8 |
| 33. Bc1-e3 | ... |

A timely move. From this square the Bishop will get to b6, and the pin on the Black Knight on c7 will be very unpleasant for Karpov (I. Dorfman).

| 33. ... | Qd7-c8 |
| 34. Qh3-f3 | ... |

A. Suetin and M. Taimanov are of the opinion that 34. Bb6!? would pose more problems for Black to solve. For instance,

if 34. ... Qb7 (34. ... g6 35. Nfxd6!), then 35. Bxc7 Qxc7 36. Qg4 (or 36. h5) 36. ... Kh8 37. h5, maintaining pressure on the King's side (the manoeuvre Rd1-d3-g3 being the attacking resource).

34. ...	Nc7-e8
35. Be3-b6	Rd8-d7
36. h4-h5	Qc8-b7
37. Bb6-e3	Kg8-h8
38. g2-g4	Bf8-e7!?

Just in time! The Bishop threatens to go to g5 (or d8). A piece sacrifice would hardly be correct now, e.g. 39. Bxh6 gxh 40. Nxh6 Bf8!, or 39. Nxh6 gxh 40. Qxf7 Qc8! (T. Georgadze).

39. Nf5xe7	Rd7xe7
40. g4-g5	h6xg5
41. Be3xg5	Re7-c7

Game drawn.

According to S. Makarychev, White has to agree to the end game arising from the line 42. Qf5 Qc8 43. Qxc8 Rxc8. There may follow: 44. Be7 Rc7 45. Bxd6 Rc4 46. Bc5! Rxe4 47. d6 Nxd6 48. Rxd6 Nf6 49. h6, and neither side would gain the advantage.

Time: 2.33—2.27

30 January 1985

GAME FORTY-SEVEN

Queen's Gambit Declined
Cambridge Springs Variation

A. Karpov	G. Kasparov
1. Ng1-f3	Ng8-f6
2. c2-c4	e7-e6
3. d2-d4	d7-d5

4. Nb1-c3	c7-c6
5. Bc1-g5	Nb8-d7
6- e2-e3	Qd8-a5

For the first time in his chess career, Kasparov has adopted the Cambridge Springs Variation against which he had to play in the Candidates' Final match with Smyslov (Vilnius, 1984). Of course, having to play the system as White, the Challenger studied it thoroughly during that match (A. Suetin).

| 7. c4xd5 | Nf6xd5 |
| 8. Qd1-d2 | Nd7-b6 |

This old move was introduced by A. Bekker. In the match just mentioned, Smyslov twice adopted 8. ... Bb4, but on both occasions White seized the initiative with 9. Rc1.

9. Nc3xd5 ...

Forcing simplifications. The more ambitious continuation is the sharp theoretical 9. Bd3! ? Nxc3 10. bxc Nd5 11. Rc1 (11. 0-0! ?) 11. ... Nxc3 12. 0-0 Bb4 13. a3 Qxa3 14. Ra1 Qb3, and then 15. Rfc1 Na2 16. Qxa2 Qxd3 17. d5 0-0 18. Rd1, or 15. Ne5! ? (A. Alekhine), with compensation for the sacrificed material.

9. ...	Qa5xd2+
10. Nf3xd2	e6xd5
11. Bf1-d3	a7-a5
(No. 192)	
12. a2-a4?!	...

This move, which has weakened the b4-square, was condemned by all the commentators. It would have been better for White to play 12. 0-0 or 12. f3, with a roughly equal ending.

No. 192

| 12. ... | Bf8-b4 |
| 13. Ke1-e2 | Bc8-g4+ |

Thereby solving the "eternal" problem of developing the light-squared Bishop. Now all the Black pieces are engaged in active operations (R. Kholmov).

| 14. f2-f3 | Bg4-h5 |
| 15. h2-h4 | ... |

R. Kholmov suggests 15. Rhc1! as the stronger alternative, while M. Taimanov prefers 15. b3 0-0 16. Rac1.

15. ...	0-0
16. g2-g4	Bh5-g6
17. b2-b3	...

White should perhaps have continued 17. Bxg6 (I. Dorfman).

This could be answered with either 17. ... hxg 18. b3 Rfe8 19. Rac1 Nd7 20. Nb1 c5 21. Rhd1 Rac8 22. dxc Nxc5, or 17. ... fxg! ? 18. Nf1 (both 18. Rhf1 Rae8 19. Kd3 Bxd2 20. Kxd2

Nc4+ and 18. e4 Rae8 19. e5 c5! are worse) 18. ... Rae8, with some advantage to Black (R. Kholmov).

17. ...	Bg6xd3+
18. Ke2xd3	Rf8-e8
19. Ra1-c1	...

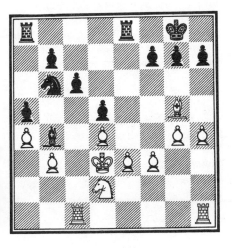

No. 193

19. ...	c6-c5!

With this sudden breakthrough Black seizes the initiative. Now 20. dxc will be met with 20. ... Nd7! (M. Taimanov).

20. Bg5-f4	Ra8-c8
21. d4xc5	...

This Exchange is forced. White could not play 21. e4, because of the simple 21. ... cxd (Ye. Vasyukov).

21. ...	Nb6-d7
22. c5-c6	...

After 22. Bd6 b6! 23. c6 Nc5+, followed by Rc8xc6, Black has an excellent game (A. Suetin).

22. ...	b7xc6
23. Rh1-d1	Nd7-c5+
24. Kd3-c2	...

If 24. Ke2, then 24. ... Ne6 25. Be5 f6! And after 25. Kf2 Nxf4 26. exf c5!, White would still have a very inferior position (R. Kholmov).

24. ...	f7-f6
25. Nd2-f1	Nc5-e6
26. Rf4-g3	Re8-d8
27. Bg3-f2?!	...

The variation 27. Kb2 c5 28. Ka2 would be better than the above move (M. Taimanov).
If 27. Be1, then 27. ... Bxe1 28. Rxe1 d4! is very unpleasant for White (A. Suetin), but after 29. Kb2! White's defence would be easier (R. Kholmov).

27. ...	c6-c5
28. Nf1-d2	...

According to Taimanov, even now 28. Kb2 would be safer, whereas after 28. e4 Black could reply strongly with either 28. ... c4, or 28. ... Ba3 29. Ra1 Nd4+. **(No. 194)**

28. ...	c5-c4!
29. b3xc4	Ne6-c5
30. e3-e4?	...

A more stubborn defence would be 30. Ra1, whereupon Black could choose between 30. ... dxc 31. Nxc4 Rxd1 32. Rxd1 Nxa4 33. Kb3 Nc5+, and 30. ... Nd7! ?, followed by 31. ... Ne5 or 31. ... Nb6.

30. ...	d5-d4
31. Nd2-b1	...

No. 194

If 31. Ra1, then 31. ... d3+ 32. Kb2
Rb8.

| 31. ... | d4-d3+ |
| 32. Kc2-b2 | d3-d2 |

White resigns.

Time: 1.57-2.07

The score is 5:2 (with 40 draws)
in favour of Karpov.

8 and 9 February 1985

GAME FORTY-EIGHT

Petroff's Defence

G. Kasparov	A. Karpov
1. e2-e4	e7-e5
2. Ng1-f3	Ng8-f6
3. Nf3xe5	d7-d6
4. Ne5-f3	Nf6xe4
5. d2-d4	d6-d5
6. Bf1-d3	Nb8-c6

| 7. 0-0 | Bf8-e7 |
| 8. c2-c4 | ... |

The World Champion played this move
in the forty-first game. Now the Challenger decides to follow suit. Previously,
Kasparov first interposed 8. Re1 after
both 7. ... Bg4 (game 28) and 7. ...
Be7 (game 30). It is worth mentioning
that the move 8. c4 will also be employed
in reply to 7. ... Bg4 in the fifteenth
game of their second match.

| 8. ... | Ne4-f6 |

The forty-first game continued: 8. ...
Nb4 9. Be2! dxc 10. Bxc4 0-0 11.
Nc3 Nd6 12. Bb3 Bf6, and here, by
paying 13. Ne5, Karpov could retain the
initiative.

| 9. Nb1-c3 | 0-0 |
| 10. h2-h3 | ... |

An important move, which prevents
the pin on the White King's Knight and
poses Karpov the problem of completing
the development of his pieces (M. Taimanov).

| 10. ... | d5xc4 |

In the Velimirović-Schüssler game
(Smederavska-Palanka, 1979), after
10. ... Nb4 (if 10. ... Be6, then 11. c5
is good) 11. Be2 c5 12. a3 Nc6 13.
dxc dxc 14. Be3, White gained a small
advantage.

11. Bd3xc4	Nc6-a5
12. Bc4-d3	Bc8-e6
13. Rf1-e1	...

An elastic decision. After 13. Be3 Nc4
14. Qc2 Nxe3 15. fxe, White's position

would be active, but Black's Bishop pair could become quite dangerous (M. Tal).

| 13. ... | Na5-c6 |

The reply 13. ... c5!? (but not 13. ... Bc4? 14. Bxc4 Nxc4 15. Qe2) is also interesting, but continuing 14. Be3, or 14. dxc Bxc5 15. Bg5, White would retain the better prospects (M. Taimanov).

| 14. a2-a3 | a7-a6 |
| 15. Bc1-f4 | ... |

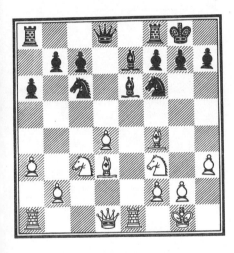

No. 195

| 15. ... | Qd8-d7 |

The continuation 15. ... Nd5, intending to simplify the game, also deserves consideration (A. Yusupov). However, in Taimanov's opinion, this would not save White from difficulties after 16. Bg3.

| 16. Nf3-e5! | Nc6xe5 |
| 17. d4xe5 | Nf6-d5 |

| 18. Nc3xd5 | Be6xd5 |
| 19. Qd1-c2 | g7-g6 |

In the event of 19. ... h6?!, Kasparov could respond with 20. Rac1 c6 21. Re3, and it would be difficult for Black to defend the position of his King (A. Yusupov).

| 20. Ra1-d1 | c7-c6?! |

20. ... Qc6, reconciling himself to a somewhat inferior ending after 21. Qxc6 Bxc6 22. Bc4, would be safer for Black (M. Taimanov).

| 21. Bf4-h6 | Rf8-d8 |

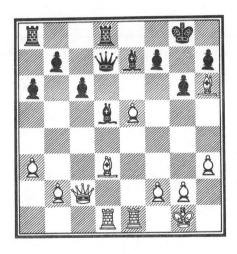

No. 196

| 22. e5-e6! | f7xe6 |

22. ... Bxe6 would be bad, because of 23. Bxg6, while after 22. ... Qe8 White could continue 23. Qc3 f6 24. f4!

| 23. Bd3xg6 | Be7-f8 |

Those in the press room also analysed
23. ... Bf6!?, retaining the Bishop
in order to cover the important diagonal
a1-h8.

24. Bh6xf8	Rd8xf8
25. Bg6-e4	Rf8-f7

According to M. Taimanov, 25. ... Rf4
26. Re3 Kh8 would be better than the
text.

26. Re1-e3	Rf7-g7
27. Rd1-d3!	...

A rather unusual attack in which White's
heavy pieces make use of the third rank
(M. Tal).

27. ...	Ra8-f8
28. Re3-g3!	Kg8-h8

This move is forced, as White is threatening 29. Bxh7+.

29. Qc2-c3	...

The strongest continuation of the attack,
whereas 29. Rg4 Qc7 30. Rdg3 Rxg4
31. Rxg4 Rg8 32. Qc3+ Rg7 33. Qf6
Qf7 would allow Black to retain material
equality (T. Georgadze).

29. ...	Rf8-f7
(No. 197)	
30. Rd3-e3!	...

Taking aim at the main defect in Black's
position, the weak Pawn on e6. Now
30. ... Qd6 is unplayable because of
31. Bxd5, and Black would have to
respond with 31. ... Qxd5, because he
could play neither 31. ... exd, in view of
32. Re8+, nor 31. ... cxd, in view of
32. Qc8+ followed by 33. Qxe6 (M. Tal).

No. 197

30. ...	Kh8-g8

After 30. ... Bxe4 31. Rxe4 Kg8 32.
Rxg7+ Rxg7 33. Qe5, White's initiative
would be decisive (M. Taimanov).

31. Qc3-e5	Qd7-c7

Defencing himself against the threat of
32. Rxg7+ Rxg7 33. Qb8+, Karpov
sacrifices a Pawn.

32. Rg3xg7+	Rf7xg7
33. Be4xd5	Qc7xe5
34. Bd5xe6+	Qe5xe6
35. Re3xe6	...

The Rook and Pawn ending is won for
White: he will be able to set up two
connected passed Pawns on the King's
side, while Black has no answer to this
threat.

35. ...	Rg7-d7
36. b2-b4	...

M. Taimanov recommended 36. g4 Kf7

37. Re3, enabling the White King to march to the centre; 38. Re2 would also suffice.

36. ...	Kg8-f7
37. Re6-e3	Rd7-d1+
38. Kg1-h2	Rd1-c1
39. g2-g4	b7-b5
40. f2-f4	...

Another posibility worthy of consideration is 40. Re5 Rc3 41. Kg2 Rxa3 42. Rc5 (M. Taimanov).

40. ...	c6-c5
41. b4xc5	...

The sealed move.

41. ...	Rc1xc5
42. Re3-d3!	...

This finesse is essential for White's plan. The threat of 43. Rd7+ compels the Black King to stay away from the K-side, where its presence is so important.

42. ...	Kf7-e7
43. Kh2-g3	a6-a5
44. Kg3-f3	b5-b4
45. a3xb4	a5xb4
46. Kf3-e4	Rc5-b5
47. Rd3-b3	Rb5-b8
48. Ke4-d5	Ke7-f6

In the event of 48. ... h5 49. Kc5 hxg 50. hxg Rg8 51. g5 Ke6 52. Rxb4, Black would be lost anyway.

49. Kd5-c5	Rb8-e8
50. Rb3xb4	Re8-e3
51. h3-h4	Re3-h3
52. h4-h5	Rh3-h4
(No. 198)	
53. f4-f5?!	...

No. 198

Had he played 53. g5+! Kf5 54. h6, White would have achieved his object much more rapidly; for instance, 54. ... Rh1 55. Kd6 Re1 56. Rb8! Kxf4 (or 56. ... Rd1+ 57. Kc5) 57. g6 hxg 58. h7 Rh1 59. h8Q Rxh8 60. Rxh8 g5 61. Kd5, and the fight would be over.

53. ...	Rh4-h1
54. Kc5-d5	Rh1-d1+
55. Rb4-d4	Rd1-e1
56. Kd5-d6	Re1-e8?!

By playing 56. ... Rg1! Karpov could make White's task considerably more difficult. But, according to M. Taimanov, White would still have won; for instance, 57. Kd7 Kf7 58. Kd8 Rg2 (or 58. ... Kf8 59. h6) 59. h6 Kf8 (59. ... Kf6 60. Rd6+ Kf7 61. Rd7+ Kg8 62. Ke7!) 60. Kc7! Kf7 61. Rd7+ Kg8 62. Rg7+ Kh8 63. Re7! Kg8 64. Kd7! Rxg4 65. Ke6 Kf8 66. Ra7 Re4+ 67. Kf6 Re8 68. Rxh7 Kg8 69. Re7.

57. Kd6-d7	Re8-g8

Or 57. ... Re1 58. Rd6+ Kg5 59. f6

58. h5-h6	Kf6-f7
59. Rd4-c4	Kf7-f6
60. Rc4-e4	Kf6-f7
61. Kd7-d6	Kf7-f6
62. Re4-e6+	Kf6-f7
63. Re6-e7+	Kf7-f6

64. Re7-g7	Rg8-d8+
65. Kd6-c5	Rd8-d5+
66. Kc5-c4	Rd5-c4+
67. Kc4-c3	

Black resigns.

Time: 3.53-3.23

The score is 5:3 (with 40 draws) in favour of Karpov.

Yuri Averbakh

CHESS TODAY
(Thoughts on the Karpov-Kasparov Match)

And so, the first match is now history. It contained nearly fifty games, giving a wealth of extremely interesting material. The match, of course, was played between two chess masters in a class of their own, between two players who stand out above the rest of the chess élite. Their success in matches and tournaments is ample evidence of this. The Karpov-Kasparov match reflects the spirit of the age, the condition of modern chess and the paths along which it is developing.

First and foremost, we have again seen that matches at the highest level are not distinguished by a high number of wins by either player, as opposed to games drawn. We have been aware of this for a long time. In the Capablanca-Lasker match in 1921 the wins made up only 28.5 per cent of the games played. And in the historic Alekhine-Capablanca match in 1927 the wins were even lower—only 26 per cent. The 1927 match, incidentally, was played under the same rules as the present match, the winner being the first to win six games, drawn games not counting.

It may seem that this is connected with the way in which the competition is arranged, and that with a limited number of games the situation would be different. But the Botvinnik-Petrosyan match in 1963 and the first encounter between Petrosyan and Spasski (in 1966), played as the best of twenty-four games, showed results little higher—31 per cent and 29 per cent respectively.

Of course, the number of wins in a contest is dependent on many factors, on the temperaments and styles of the opponents, on their will to win and on the degree of admissible risk for each of them. No less important, however, is the way in which the game progresses, how it develops.

The Karpov-Kasparov match set up its own record—the wins made up only 14.5 per cent of the games played. In previous world-title matches they have never been so few.

So why is this? We know that Karpov and Kasparov are attacking players, they are both capable of winning, and of taking the necessary risks to do so, when they wish.

It seems to me that the low level of wins in the match as a whole was determined to a great extent by the way in which the match itself developed.

At the beginning Kasparov was in totally aggressive mood, took many—possibly too many—risks and, as a result, in the first nine encounters he suffered four defeats. Then he changed his tactics completely: he began to play with the utmost caution, avoiding even the smallest risk.

Karpov, so firmly in the lead, was apparently quite satisfied with this development. And as a result another record was set up: seventeen consecutive games drawn. In the Alekhine-Capablanca match the number was only eight. This series of draws seriously delayed the end of the match and yet another factor—endurance—entered the contest. The simplest thing, of course, is to blame the two players for their excessive caution at this stage, but in world-title matches the goal—the champion's crown—is so momentous that each player has the right to take his own path to the finish line.

The match highlighted yet another feature of modern chess at the highest level—the fact that the "shield" is now mightier than the "sword". And this despite the fact that Kasparov is famous for his aggressive, attacking play, and that Karpov, as a master of an active, positional style, has long since shown how capable he is of winning against even the most powerful opponents. In this match both players demonstrated models of defence, although each defended in his own manner. Karpov several times balanced on the edge of an abyss, defending á la Lasker, throwing one obstacle after another at his opponent to hamper his advance as much as possible, and most inventively taking advantage of the least opportunity to counter-attack. And Kasparov, skilfully building up his piece play, showed that he is capable of neutralising an opponent's material advantage.

But there is no reason to wonder that the "armour" of modern chess is stronger than its "bullet". The techniques of defence in the modern game have been developed far better than those of attack. The most diverse methods have been devised, for example, of neutralising an opponent's advantage, particularly a dynamic, temporary advantage.

It is worth noting here that the preponderance of defensive means over the means of attack is partly due to the nature of the game itself. There is only one way of winning—checkmating the opposing king. But if we add up the number of ways of reaching a draw, we find: firstly, coming to a position where the material advantage is insufficient to reach mate; secondly, stalemate; thirdly, perpetual pursuit, the most common occurrence being perpetual check; fourthly, the construction of an unassailable fortress; and lastly, the blockade, whereby at least one of the opponent's pieces is excluded from the game, thus neutralising his material advantage. All these five ways of reaching safety, widely developed by the theorists of the game, have become part and parcel of the theory of the end game.

The end game itself, too, is far better developed than in the past, and developed—like the rest of the modern game—towards means of defence. Let us take as an example the common ending of a Rook and a Pawn against a Rook. Comparatively recently, only some fifty years ago, this end game was a stumbling block even for chess masters, but now you can find it in the most elementary text-books.

A purely numerical comparison will show how our knowledge of the end game has increased. In Rabinovich's popular reference book of the 1930s, *The End Game*, the author described approximately 400 situations, while the five-volume Chess Endings, contains 3,500 situations!

Despite the development of modern end game theory, this match gave us much that is new and interesting in this respect. A number of endings (particularly those of the 6th, 9th and 27th games) will go into text-books as models of the masterly technique shown by Karpov.

But if we talk of chess theory as a whole, then we have to say that it is now developing first and foremost in the area of openings. Along with the ever-increasing flow of chess literature—the "information boom"—the theory of openings has grown in recent years far faster than that of other phases of play. The study of openings is advancing on all fronts, and the theorists develop their ideas not only into the middle game but even as far as the end game.

The fact that the theory of openings has been developed into the heart of the game has led to a situation where the real game, the real contest, begins somewhere between the twentieth and thirtieth moves, all earlier moves being well-known in advance. In situations like these it is often not the ability of a player which decides the outcome of a game, but rather his store of knowledge. The one who knows and remembers more will win, somewhat like in a general knowledge quiz.

Delving into the theory of the game as deeply as this, incidentally, makes for yet another unfortunate feature of modern chess: theorists have devised ever more means of side-tracking the game into a cul-de-sac, into a position where all tension and sense of struggle is lost. For those who do not wish to take risks and plunge themselves into wanton carnage there is always the temptation to reduce the tension by simplifying everything and reaching the safety of a draw. This, then, is another reason for the proliferation of draws in the modern game.

I would also like to point out that great players of the past, such as Lasker and Capablanca, paid little attention to openings, relying on their feeling for the game and on their understanding of positions; the whole weight of the battle was thus carried into the middle and end game. Nowadays, such an approach would be quite disastrous.

Fully in the spirit of our age, both Karpov and Kasparov devote considerable attention to the first phase of a game, continually working to perfect their repertoire of openings, and striving to open up new routes into a game. And it is for this reason that the openings used in the match are particularly significant. Never before in world-title matches have we seen the use of such a wide range of systems and variations. The match has already set a trend towards a further development of the theory of openings. It would be enough simply to list the interesting innovations which the two players have introduced into the Ruy López game and Petroff's defence, and into the Semi-Slav and Sicilian defences. The match also was a detailed practical test of the current variations of the Queen's Gambit (the Tartakover-Makagonov-Bondarevski system) the Queen's Indian Defence, and the Catalon and English openings. Further, the Tarrasch Defence was dealt a severe blow.

We might also take note of the distinctive tactical and psychological moves widely used by both Karpov and Kasparov: if one of them realised the merits of a system played by his opponent, then he would waste no time in adding the system to his own armoury and using it himself. I cannot remember such a stratagem having been used in any world-title match in the past. It is also a feature of modern chess as a whole.

And, finally, what has the match given us in the middle game? There is no doubt that both Grandmasters have shown us something new in this phase of the game also. Karpov, for example, played the twenty-seventh game magnificently: he used a minimal positional advantage with exceptional finesse, won a pawn and realised the advantage with impeccable technique. This game was by far the best of the match. Kasparov built up his attack in the forty-eighth game with great precision and élan.

And many of the other games were filled with interesting strategic and tactical struggle.

We have already mentioned the fact that the defensive tactics in the match as a whole were stronger than the attacking manoeuvres; therefore the examples of fine and effective combinations are relatively few. And there is an explanation for this. I shall risk expressing an heretical opinion and say that the intensity of the struggle—and in world-title matches it reaches extraordinary heights—has a detrimental effect on the players' combinational awareness. How else can we explain the blunder which Kasparov made in the sixteenth game when he failed to complete a winning combination? On the other hand, it is notable that Karpov did not realise that the combination was being set up. As we know, however, both players do have a sharp combinational awareness, as they have shown on many occasions in the past. Simple errors imcompatible with the level of competition, incidentally, are clearly a result of the intensity and tension of the contest, and we have seen them in practically all the world-title matches. And it is perhaps to be wondered at that they are really so few.

The middle game, it must be said, is the most "backward" in its theoretical development. The many reference works on the subject, however classified, are little help in developing a real theory of the middle game, a qualitative and generalised theory which would actually help chess players to find their way through the endless expanse of the middle-game ocean.

. It is now time to draw our conclusions. The Karpov-Kasparov match has clearly demonstrated the complexity and variety of modern chess, as well as the gaps in the develpment of chess theory. Perhaps the theorists should now consider how to redress the balance between the theory of openings and the middle game.

Index of Openings
A. Karpov — G. Kasparov

Nos. Openings	Number of Games	Score (Won, Lost, Drawn)	1984-85 Match	1985 Match
			Game Numbers	
A. Karpov–G. Kasparov				
1. Queen's Gambit Declined	16	+5−1=10	(7),(9),17,19,21,23,25,(27),31,39,[47]	(4),6,8,20,(22)
2. Sicilian Defence	14	+1−2=11	1,(3),5,35,37,43,45	2,10,12,14,[16],18,[24]
3. English Opening	2	=2	11,13	−
4. Semi-Slav Defence	2	=2	29,33	−
5. Queen's Indian Defence	1	=1	15	−
6. Petroff's Defence	1	=1	41	−
Total	36	+6−3=27	+4−1=19	+2−2=8
G. Kasparov–A. Karpov				
1. Queen's Gambit Declined	9	=9	12,34,36,38,40,42	3,21,23
2. Queen's Indian Defence	8	+1−1=6	2,4,[6],10,14,16,18,(32)	−
3. Nimzo-Indian Defence	6	+3−0=3	−	(1),7,(11),13,17,(19)
4. Ruy López	4	+0−1=3	44,46	[5],9
5. Petroff's Defence	4	+1−0=3	28,30,(48)	15
6. English Opening	3	=3	20,24,26	−
7. Catalan Opening	2	=2	8,22	−
Total	36	+5−2=29	+2−1=21	+3−1=8

O − White won
□ − Black won